Warman's
Duck Decoys

By Russell E. Lewis

Published by

kp **krause publications**

An Imprint of F+W Publications

700 East State Street • Iola, WI 54990-0001
715-445-2214 • 888-457-2873

Our toll-free number to place an order or obtain
a free catalog is (800) 258-0929.

Library of Congress Catalog Number: 2006922402

ISBN 13-digit: 978-0-89689-404-4
ISBN 10-digit: 0-89689-404-5

Designed by Sharon Laufenberg
Edited by Dennis Thornton

Printed in China

Dedication

As with all of my previous works on sporting collectibles, this would not have been completed without a wife who both loves me and understands my passion for inanimate objects of fishing and hunting memorabilia. Thus, to you Wendy, I dedicate this work on duck decoys and game calls. Thank you for your constant support, one of life's true pleasures.

It is with great sadness that I must report the passing of one of the kindest gentlemen I ever knew, Harvey Pitt. Mr. Pitt passed away July 28, 2005, and it is to his memory and the kindness afforded to an endless number of collectors, visitors and school children examining his wonderful collection that this new edition is dedicated.

Acknowledgments

This book would not have been possible without the cooperation and assistance of many friends and fellow collectors, including:

Harvey and Mickey Pitt, collectors extraordinaire of decoys.

McKendree College, benefactors of the Pitt decoy collection.

Joe and Janice Jaroski for their assistance on game calls.

Gary Campbell for sharing photos of his personal collection and for arranging for Griff Evans to contribute photos to this work.

Hank and Judy Norman for sharing photos of their collection.

I would like to thank one of the leading duck decoy auction houses in America for contributing approximately 150 photos and prices realized for this work. Guyette & Schmidt holds auctions of duck decoys and related memorabilia at various sites on the East Coast and is known for its leadership in decoy collecting, appraising and sales. Thanks again for your assistance in this project.

I would also like to thank Decoys Unlimited, Inc., and Ted and Judy Harmon for providing me with prices realized on their Spring Decoy Auction held March 17, 2006, featuring some of the Pitt Collection. They will be selling the entire Pitt Collection and readers can keep abreast with other future sales by checking www.decoysunlimitedinc.com.

Please write or e-mail me with any new data that will help future volumes be even more useful to the collector. I may be contacted at findingo@netonecom.net or lewisr@ferris.edu or via mail at 9268 Balsam Road, Evart, MI 49631-9606.

Contents

Dedication	**3**
Acknowledgments	**3**
Introduction	**6**

Chapter One:
A Foundation of Knowledge	**9**
Decoy Value Trends	12
Using the Internet in Collecting	13
Major Factors That Determine Decoy Values	14
Finding Items	16
Using Decoys and Calls	17
Beginning the Search	21
Dictionary of Terminology	22
Identification of Antique Decoys	26
Brands	27
User Brands	28
Maker Brands	29
Decorative and Reproduction Decoys	29
Misrepresentations, Forgeries and Fakes	31
Restoration and Repairs	32
Care of Your Collection	34

Chapter Two:
Traditional Carvers and Their Schools	**35**
Maritime Provinces	36
Maine	38
Massachusetts	41
Connecticut (Stratford)	48
New York State	50
Long Island	53
Barnegat Bay (New Jersey)	56
Delaware River	58
Susquehanna Flats	60
Maryland Eastern Shore (Dorchester County)	69
Crisfield (Maryland)	72
Virginia Eastern Shore	78
Cobb Island	82
North Carolina	83
South Carolina	85
Louisiana	86
Illinois River	89
Missouri	95
Indiana and Ohio	96

Michigan 97
St. Clair Flats 107
Wisconsin 112
Pacific Coast 123

Chapter Three:
Factory Decoys from the Vintage Period 125
J.N. Dodge 127
Evans Duck Decoy Company 128
Hays Decoys 131
Mason's Decoy Factory 131
Peterson Decoy Factory 144
William E. Pratt Manufacturing Co. 144
Sperry Decoy Factory 145
H.A. Stevens 146

Chapter Four:
Modern Factory Decoys 147
Dating Techniques of Modern
  Sporting Collectibles 148
The Modern Era 151
The Modern Decoy Companies 151
Animal Trap Company of America (Victor) 152
Armstrong Decoys 158
B&J Mfg. Co. 159
Benz Decoys 160
Carry-Lite Decoys 161
Dunster Sporting Goods Company
  (Dupe-A-Goose) 168
General Fiber Company (Ariduk) 168
Fairfax Decoys (McGuire, Featherlite) 171
Herter's, Inc. 175
William R. Johnson Company 179
K. and D. Decoys 182
L.L. Bean 183
J.S. McGuire Decoys 184
Neumann & Bennets, Inc. (Plasti-Duk) 185
A.W. Randall Co. 188
Real-Lite Decoy Co. 189
J.W. Reynolds Decoy Factory 190
Tuveson Decoys 192
Wildfowler Decoys, Inc. 192

Chapter Five:
Duck Calls and Other Game Calls 199
Identification and Evaluation of Calls 200
Identification of Calls 201
Construction and Nomenclature of Calls 201
A History of Duck and Game Calls 203

Chapter Six:
Modern Duck, Goose, and Game Calls 209
Black Duck Calls 210
Burnham Brothers Calls 211
Duk-Em Duck Calls 211
Dye-Call Company 212
Faulk's 212
Fetch-It 216
Herter's, Inc. 216
Hoosier Crow Call 217
Joe Jaroski Jr. Calls 217
KumDuck Calls 221
Lohman Calls 221
Mallardtone Game Calls 225
Ken Martin Calls 227
Natural Duck Call Manufacturing Company 228
Perfectone Calls 228
P.S. Olt 229
Scotch Game Calls 236
Thompson Calls 238
Trutone Calls 239
Unknown Calls and Newer Calls 239
Weems Wild Call 242

Chapter Seven:
Hunting Collectibles 243
Shot Shell Boxes 244
Magazines, Catalogs, Etc. 249
Shot Shell Crates 252
Reloading Equipment and Practice Equipment 252
Duck Stamps, Licenses and Artwork 253
Oilers, Oil Cans and Cleaning Tools 253

A Short History of
The Bird Decoy in North America

From humble beginnings more than 1,000 years ago, decoys have evolved into beautiful creations such as this Ward Brothers Mallard pair. They were made in 1948 of balsa and are in original paint.

Value is $6,000-$7,000 for the pair.

Griff Evans Collection

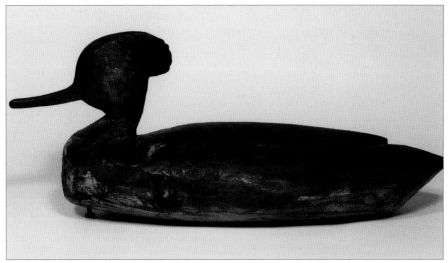

Early decoys were crude but effective. A very rare Ira Hudson Hooded Merganser hen, circa 1900, is one of the earliest of all documented Ira Hudson decoys.

Value is $10,000-$15,000.

Gary Campbell Collection

The origin of the decoy in America as we know it today lies in early American history, but not with the early settlers as might be reasonably assumed. Rather it pre-dates the American pioneer by at least 1,000, perhaps 2,000 years. In 1924, at an archeological site in Nevada, the Lovelock Cave excavations yielded a group of 11 decoys beautifully preserved in protective containers. Among this group of decoys were some stuffed skins, but there were 11 totally artificial decoys fashioned of twisted and bundled tulle rushes or bulrushes (reeds) and feathers in a startlingly realistic form that is unmistakably that of a Canvasback duck. The careful manner of their storage preserved them for us to enjoy an estimated 1,000 to 2,000 years later. More importantly, the extreme care the early natives took in the preservation of their duck decoys suggests the critical importance to them of duck hunting. The obtaining of the meat of wildfowl must have been an important factor in their survival.

When the first settlers came to North America their survival was just as dependent upon hunting wild game for food as it was for the Indians. It did not take them long to notice the various methods the Indians used to lure wildfowl within bow and arrow range. They used a little of everything, from piles of rocks to clumps of mud and dead birds to make likenesses of their prey. Quick to seize upon the idea, those early settlers just as quickly improved it. They began to fashion likenesses of their prey out of different materials, ultimately finding that wood was an ideal raw material. Thus the carving of wildfowl decoys was born out of necessity for food.

It is not likely that those early Americans carved a bird likeness and then said, "Aha, a decoy." The lures were called many things, but the word "decoy" was not yet in their vocabulary. Just when the word did come into common use is not precisely known, but its etymology or origin is known. Its roots are European, in particular Dutch. Decoy is derived from the Dutch word used to describe a cage-like affair into which hunters in boats drove the birds. Later, domesticated ducks were placed inside to lure unsuspecting wildfowl into it. The name given to this cage was ende-kooi. This method was used before the advent of guns in wildfowl hunting.

Among the first writings of North American hunting to mention decoys was a letter from an official of the government of the then French colony of Newfoundland dated 1687. In describing a hunting expedition, he detailed a blind he called a "Hutt" and went on to say: "For a decoy they have the skins of geese, Bustards and ducks, dry'd and stuff'd with Hay. The two feet being made fast with two Nails to a small piece of a light plank, which floats around the Hutt." Historical records indicate wooden decoys were in general use as early as the 1770s, but it seems likely based upon the 1687 letter that they would have been widely used before then. Up to the middle of the 1800s, there was not sufficient commercial demand for decoys to enable the carvers to make a living at selling them, so most decoys were made for themselves and friends.

The middle of the 19th century saw the

birth of the market gunners. These men were in the business of providing markets with the hundreds of thousands of birds necessary to feed the increasing North American population. These hunters, using huge guns and much of the time deploying rigs of hundreds of decoys, killed hundreds of birds of any sort in one outing. There were no game laws at the time and the seemingly inexhaustible supply of wildfowl provided them with a living and the population of the larger Eastern Seaboard cities with relatively cheap meat. The market hunters and other hunters killed anything that flew, from Red Breasted Robins and Passenger Pigeons to the majestic Heron and Whistling Swan. Their activities are usually associated with the Chesapeake Bay area, but this slaughter was taking place in all the major flyways.

The sad result of this indiscriminate destruction of wildfowl is that the coup de grace was administered to many bird species, rendering them extinct. Some others are on the endangered list as a result. A few examples are Passenger Pigeon, Labrador Duck, and the Heath Hen. The United States Congress, with the passage of the Migratory Bird Treaty Act in 1918, outlawed the killing of waterfowl for sale.

During the market-gunning period, many carvers began making a living with their decoys and the first factory-made decoys came into existence. The huge numbers of decoys needed to supply the market hunters (who often utilized up to 500-600 decoys at a time) and the rising numbers of hunters for sport or sustenance made commercial decoy carving possible.

Following the passage of the 1918 act came the demise of the factory decoys of the day. The large numbers of decoys needed declined because of the act and many of the smaller commercial carvers had ceased to ply their trade by the 1920s. There were a few of these small, one- or two-man or family operations that continued to carve birds, and with the great increase in the popularity of sport hunting, the commercial carvers soon found the demand for their production rising. Some of these craftsmen continued to work right on up into the 1950s.

Today a few truly great contemporary carvers carry on their tradition. They produce incredibly intricate, lifelike birds. The serious contemporary carvers' products have to meet strenuous requirements, making the decoy such that it could be hunted over. The prices these carvings command make it unlikely that they will float anywhere but in a competition water tank. What these contemporary carvings represent is that decoy carving is one of the few early American folk arts that has survived into our modern fast-paced times and is still being pursued.

Chapter One:

Current Trends in Collecting

The reasons for the growing interest in many types of collectibles are several, but they boil down to three things:

1. A large population of "baby boomers" who grew up with these items.

2. The availability of items manufactured since 1940.

3. The affordability of items manufactured since 1940.

Collectors once laughed at papier-mâché duck decoys and Faulk game calls. Now, those same people are ready and willing to buy any and all high quality (e.g. good condition) papier-mâché duck decoys and company game calls they can find. They are paying about three to five times the prices of 1995. When I offered a mint condition Carry-Lite papier-mâché drake Mallard for $25 in 1995, it was too much. Now that

A Victor D-9 was sold by the author for $60 online in September 2002.

decoy is worth three to five times that amount. If it is one of those made for Sears or Montgomery Ward, it could be worth six times as much as it was in 1995. The $10 calls are now at least $30-$40 calls.

As the high-end Masons can no longer be found, or not afforded if found, the beginning and intermediate collectors have searched elsewhere to satisfy a collecting desire and niche. Some collectors argue that there is no place in a duck decoy collection for plastics and I would have to vehemently disagree. I would love to add a mint D-11 Victor Pintail to my collection. Or how about the plastic Victor D-9 Mallard I sold for $60 on an online auction? Not bad for a plastic decoy.

There is indeed a place for plastic duck decoys, fiber decoys, rubber decoys, cardboard decoys and mass-produced calls. Many of our finest antiques were mass-produced and are now rare 100-plus years later. The same may become true of certain items made in the 1940s and '50s, and even later, if most collectors have bypassed them for something else. Would we all like a pair of pristine, never rigged, Charles Perdew Mallards? Of course. But, not many of us will ever even handle a pair, let alone find some for sale at a price we can afford. Yet many of us will still find a string of Herter's Model 50s still in a

gunnysack from their last use in 1959.

They are not pricey or particularly rare, but they are getting harder and harder to find. I would be tickled to run into any of the Victors, Herter's, Carry-Lites, Ariduks or related decoys at a price that is affordable.

The main thing is that only you, the collector, can decide what to collect. Do not let others tell you what to collect. Do not be taken in by the snobbery of those more fortunate than you financially to detract from the fun of the find, regardless of whether it is a Herter's or a Mason. We all want to find the best birds possible. But enjoy the fun of the hunt, whether for rare and pricey decoys or ones that fit into your collection.

One of the toughest decisions in any collecting venture is to decide on what to concentrate. I personally love Canvasbacks and Bluebills. I hardly ever see a Canvasback in the wild and Bluebills are very common in my Great Lakes region. But what I really like is the shape, the symmetry of the decoys. Plain as they are, Bluebills are beautiful to me. Canvasbacks are beautiful to most, with their distinctive heads and frontal features.

I also concentrate on Michigan, Wisconsin and Great Lakes bird decoys, with a small influence

A Mason tack-eyed Bluebill is in the author's collection.

A Wisconsin hollow decoy is from a string of a dozen.

from the Illinois River region. I live in Michigan, have lived in Wisconsin, Illinois and Indiana; and I can find those decoys in my back yard. Sure, in this mobile society one will find a Perdew in Arizona and an Eastern Seaboard decoy in Wisconsin. But a Michigan decoy is more likely to be found in Michigan than in Maine. Also, I have hunted waterfowl and I am more familiar with these types of decoys.

You must decide on the best way to build your collection. I would start with well-known, easily identified factory decoys or those of prominent carvers that you can spot. I would add to a factory decoy collection, decoys from your own region or flyway. These should be most familiar to you and hopefully will be available at antique shops and shows. But only you can decide. All of our collecting interests are still ultimately controlled by economics. Unless, like Bill Gates, you have earned a fortune by inventing a better mousetrap, you should consider your financial limitations.

Finally, you should always only buy what you want and can afford to keep. I have had three instances where I bought beautiful strings of decoys and then found that I was taken by the greed monster and sold most of them for a profit. Well, here I am years later wishing I had the opportunity to find the same strings. They were once in a lifetime deals. Hopefully you will learn from my mistakes:

1. A string of one dozen (all drakes) Mason Standard grade tack eye Bluebills, all in moderate to very good plus condition. This was a hunting rig I broke up and only kept the poorest of the bunch.

2. A string of one dozen (nine drakes, three hens) Mason Standard grade painted eye Bluebills, all in above average to very good-plus condition, a second hunting rig I broke up with none left.

3. A string of one dozen working decoys by an individual carver from Wisconsin. These were glass-eyed hollow decoys that were exceptional in quality but of a nondescript brown wood color, not painted, just natural wood with painted wing details. Gorgeous and profitable, but now I wish I would have left them intact as a group.

Obviously, sometimes we sell items to make a profit, sometimes to upgrade a collection, sometimes because our collecting interests change and grow. But do not sell without knowing the fact that decoys are difficult to replace, if not impossible. I collect and deal in both fishing and hunting collectibles, meaning primarily lures and decoys. However, I can assure you that there are far more Heddon Punkinseeds out there than there are strings of one dozen Masons. So learn from one collector's experience. Keep the really great items or you will likely miss them in the future. As Harvey Pitt, who collected for 42 years, told me, "Every bird that lands in this nest stays here for life." That is good advice if you can afford to do it.

Decoy Value Trends

Values in antiques and collectibles are driven primarily by age, rarity, condition and desirability of a particular brand or maker. Usually, the older the item, the greater the rarity, but not always. Also, the older the item, the less important its condition compared to a newer item. With decoys, some collectors will only desire wooden ones, others cork, others anything. Overall the field supports the values of wooden decoys the most, with fairly light interest in even the better quality carved cork decoys.

In the past 30 years, we have seen a revolution in decoy pricing. The breakout year when decoys started hitting five-figure amounts was 1971. Now we have unique, desirable, rare decoys approaching $700,000. This is double what the record-setting decoy brought just a few years back. Does that mean that all decoys are worth thousands of dollars? No. Most decoys are worth $50-$500, with the range being toward the lower end. However, many decoys are now worth $1,000 to $5,000, a few are worth $5,000 to $50,000, and even fewer are worth more than $50,000. Most Mason collectors could build a decent collection with $300 birds five years ago. Now beginning prices would be close to the $500 mark and an average of $1,500-$2,000 would not be hard to believe for the better birds. Wildfowlers were fairly inexpensive five years ago, bringing less than $100 each, and now they have taken the place of the Masons in both pricing and collecting circles. Most collectors scoffed at papier-mâché and plastic ducks five years ago. Now they bring $25-$150 each in pristine condition.

For specific values, see the sections on different decoys. In general, decoys have been going up on a 10 percent to 15 percent per year basis the last few years. Of course this cannot be guaranteed to continue, but will likely keep rising slowly. They simply do not make any more of the rare and collectible birds. So the market will likely continue to grow in the future for these beautiful pieces of "floating sculpture."

Regarding advice on valuation, I would suggest keeping up with the sales data from auction houses, reviewing the Year in Review issue of *Decoys Magazine*, going to local auction houses and farm auctions, visiting antique stores, and reading as much as you can find on decoys. Also, prudent following of online auctions is an excellent test of what people are actually willing to pay for a particular item. As to deciding the best place for an investment, again, only you can decide. However, I think it important to note that better birds retain and increase value more rapidly than mediocre birds. This is true in all antique and collectible areas. In other words, if you can afford to buy a Premier Grade Mason instead of a Standard Grade, you will more likely see a quicker increase in value on your investment. Or if you buy wooden factory birds you are going to see more value increase than if you buy a lot of plastic, rubber or cork decoys. But it is your choice to make, not mine or anyone else's.

A collection of Mason decoys lines the shelves. See the individual listings in chapter three for details and values.
Pitt Collection

Using the Internet in Collecting

The Internet became a viable tool for selling and buying collectibles and antiques, beginning in 1995 with the birth of many online auction houses. Only a few remain today and most of the market is consumed and controlled by eBay. eBay is a registered trademark of the largest online auction house. PayPal is also owned by eBay. An entire decoy collection could be purchased without leaving the seat of my chair at my computer desk.

I make a substantial number of sales per year on eBay and frequently use it as a tool. However, for many, this is a bewildering area still not trusted or understood. Even if you do not buy even one decoy over the Internet, it is still a great tool to learn about decoys and related items. More and more dealers, auction houses and publishers are making online sites available for all of us to visit and expand our knowledge about decoys. Many collectors are sharing their collections and knowledge online by adding technically accurate listings of items for online sales with references given to major research works.

One can buy and sell on the Internet with confidence if only a few simple rules are followed. The first and most important rule is to deal only with those dealers with a positive reputation. This is the same for online dealers or those with storefronts. Just as one usually selects a mechanic or an attorney based upon reputation, one should also select a dealer the same way. With online dealers, there is usually a mechanism known as "feedback" that can easily be checked to determine how others have fared in their dealings with the dealer. If all others are happy with the service, the timeliness of delivery, the quality of the items, the proper description of the items sold, etc., then it is likely you are dealing with a reputable individual or company. If the individual or company lacks feedback, positive or negative, I would not spend a large amount of money in my purchases from them.

Make sure you know and can live with the seller's return policies. Also, for a $3,000 item, will the seller accept funds being escrowed to a third party until the transaction is completed? If not, that is not a guarantee of problems, but escrow does give one more option for very valuable items. Also, most auction services and electronic payment services (such as PayPal) are now offering guarantees that may be purchased at the time of electronic payment.

Finally, the best guarantee is in past dealings with the seller personally by the buyer. That way, one knows first hand if he/she is satisfied with the past performance of a seller and with the product(s) supplied.

My advice to all with access to a computer and the Internet is to get on the "Net" and learn to use it as a tool. It is a great way to find items that trips to the local antique store would take years to accomplish. Any item on the Internet is available to anyone for the looking and buying. It allows us to fill in our collections far more easily and more rapidly than any other technique, albeit at a more costly price in many cases. Sometimes there can be bargains had when a seller lists an item with which he/she is not familiar or during times of a soft economy. I have found some real buys on the Internet for both reasons. The most important advice is to learn by experience and have fun along the way.

Some Major Factors That Determine the Value of Old Decoys (By Hal Sorenson)

(Reprinted by permission)

Unlike the rather precise determinants of value assigned to individual stamps, coins, and other collectible items, one must contend with many variables when assessing old decoys. Five collectors could look at one decoy and easily come up with five different appraisals. In judging the general value of one decoy over another, the following major factors must be taken into consideration.

RARITY: The number of examples in existence of a particular species by a particular maker. How many or few examples constitute "rare" is difficult to discern. Usually the price assigned to a decoy by a knowledgeable seller is a good indicator of how unique the example is.

A Pratt Mallard drake, well worn, is from a Henry, Ill., hunt club. Its condition limits its value as a collectible.

MAKER: The relative importance of a carver's name, whether an individual or a factory, will have considerable bearing on the value of a decoy. For instance, with two different but equally handsome old Redhead drakes in similar condition, one by a "named" maker and the other by "maker unknown," the "named maker" decoy will undoubtedly command the higher price. The work of a "named maker" will also be worth more to a collector who specializes in that maker's decoys or who specializes in decoys from that region. However, many "known" carvers are not "named" carvers regardless of how many birds they may have produced. Collectors and publicity determine who is and who is not recognized as a "named" carver.

CONDITION: In the case of an old decoy, the word condition applies both to the physical appearance of the decoy and the painting. A Shourd's Merganser in fine original paint, but with the bill broken off and a large gouge in one side, would be comparable in condition to the same style decoy in near perfect physical state but with 90 percent of the original paint worn off, or the same decoy having been repainted.

Collectors vary in their interpretation of words such as excellent, very good, fair, etc. The breakdown between categories should be considered a general guideline.

Mint: 100 percent perfect, original condition. A decoy in mint condition would generally be unused.

Excellent: Near mint, with minor wear.

Very Good: At least 90 percent of the original paint is still intact; probably has a few nicks and bruises. A repaired bill is acceptable if not noticeable.

Good: Shows quite a bit of wear but still has 60 percent to 90 percent of the original paint left. Minor restoration such as bill repair and breast retouching are acceptable.

Fair: In pretty rough shape and probably needs restoration to make it worthy of a spot on the collector's shelf.

Poor: Both body and paint in bad condition; perhaps major body cracks. A decoy in this condition is hardly worth picking up unless it is exceedingly rare.

Repainted: Whether an old or new paint job, it was probably done by someone other than the

A Mallard drake "minnow chaser" is a very rare pose, made by an unknown carver from the southern Gulf coast, likely Alabama or Louisiana. This was hunted over on Mobile Bay in the 1920s. It is made of one piece of cypress, hollowed from below with an inset bottom board.
$5,000
Hank and Judy Norman Collection

carver. Certain of today's decoy artists specialize in restoring old named decoys with a sincere effort to capture the appearance of the originals. Others will take any old block, good or bad, and repaint it in whatever pattern or colors they happen to feel like at the moment.

PHONIES, FAKES, COPIES, ETC.: A newly made decoy that appears to be an old original by a known maker; or a recently made decoy that looks old, but is unsigned or undated by the maker. Some fakes are so good they fool the experts. Study your proposed purchase carefully. Any honest dealer or collector will be glad to let you do so and most will give you a money-back guarantee. When in doubt, however, try to consult a knowledgeable third party.

SPECIES AND SEX: These two factors affect price because certain species are much rarer than others and some species are more highly prized than others. In addition, both the old hand carvers and the factories produced far more drakes than hens. Drake Wood Duck decoys are very rare compared to most species; hen Wood Duck decoys are almost non-existent. Species such as Merganser and Teal have wide appeal. While both were produced in pretty fair quantity, collectors tend to snap them up and hang onto them, resulting in a relative shortage in the marketplace.

GRADE: Most factories and some individual carvers produced their decoys in two or more grades. The fancier the painting and the most detailed the

carving, the higher the original selling price. In most cases, the same holds true when a collector goes to make a purchase today.

STYLE: Carving and painting patterns constitute "style." The Ward Brothers and the factory decoys made by Mason are two examples of those who produced a number of different styles especially in carving pattern over their many decoy-producing years. A collector who studies enough examples by a particular maker will be able to determine which of the styles he likes best.

AESTHETIC AND ARTISTIC PREFERENCES: Both of these factors are personal in nature except for certain classics agreed upon by the majority of decoy enthusiasts. Strip away a name, disregard rarity, species, etc., and one gets down to aesthetic consideration: do you like the decoy or not? Disagreements in preference will most likely arise over the primitives—those decoys with no pedigree, which border on crude workmanship and yet have appeal from aesthetic and artistic viewpoints.

HISTORICAL ASSOCIATIONS: Some people put considerable value on who-shot-over-what-decoy. Unless the association is a personal one, I consider it immaterial whose hands previously held one of my pride-and-joys.

REGIONAL PREFERENCES: Because decoy styles vary from region to region, many collectors prefer to specialize in decoys from a specific area, i.e., Delaware River, Cape Cod, Barnegat Bay,

Chesapeake Bay, Illinois River, etc. As mentioned earlier, a person who specializes in a certain area is likely to place a higher value on decoys that originate from there.

AGE: All other factors considered, the actual age of a particular decoy is not very important. Take two similar decoys by the same maker: it matters not whether one is 10 or even 20 years older that the other. From a collector's standpoint, it also makes little difference if a clunker was made in 1970 or 1900…it is still a clunker.

DECOYS IN UNUSUAL POSES: Sleeper, swimmers, feeders, preeners, callers, and the like are rare in the overall decoy picture. As a result, this factor probably belongs under the rarity category. Such poses add interest to the decoy shelves and dollars to the value.

Finding Items

It is tougher and tougher to find items "on the street," so to speak. However it can still happen. I use every available technique known to find items for my collections. Every once in a while I get lucky and find a good item for a low price. But it takes work and diligence to be successful. Collectors finding items with the most regularity are not just "lucky," they are also "industrious." I know one picker who is always finding great things, but he is out of bed early, at estate sales to get No. 1 and works at least four days a week finding items. Also, he is willing to pay for an item. Many people think that items are out there at ridiculously low prices just waiting to be discovered. Trust me, this is the exception and not the norm. The norm is that an estate dealer prices items fairly, with enough profit margin left for the dealer to also make a dollar or two. Thus, decoys at estate sales are not "cheap," but are fairly priced in most instances.

The point is that I have a real issue with those who do not want to pay a fair price for an item. Sure, we all like bargains if found, but please do not always try to beat down prices when someone has an item for sale.

In the same fashion, if one is asked the actual value of an item, I believe it is our ethical duty as collectors and dealers to tell them the truth the best we know it. If I go to a garage sale and see a string of Masons, not priced but hanging on the wall, and ask them if they would sell the decoys, I should also be prepared to tell them the value of them when asked. This is not to say that we have to tell people the value of an item that is already priced. This I do not think is necessary.

But if one is relying upon our knowledge and experience and we are after something of theirs that is not already priced, we have a duty to be honest about the value. Of course, I am not suggesting it is only fair to pay full retail for an item, only that the seller has a right to know the full retail if asking. Each of us will make our own decisions on how much to pay, but we should be duty-bound to be fair and ethical in all of our dealings. I know that in my own experiences this has only resulted in positive repeat dealings with people and me having access to collections denied others desiring the same access.

How does one find items? Well, a list could be quite long, but I will attempt to summarize in the following list:

1. Dealers
2. Antique shops and malls
3. Farm and household auctions
4. Sporting shops
5. Advertising in local papers
6. Advertising in regional magazines
7. Advertising in retirement homes
8. Telling each and every friend of your interests

9. Buying advertising space on a billboard
10. Visiting shows dedicated to sporting collectibles/decoys
11. Visiting areas rich in waterfowl hunting history
12. Visiting Internet sites where one can buy/sell/learn about decoys
13. Visiting museums with decoys and related items
14. Going to auctions dedicated to decoys and sporting collectibles
15. Joining every organization related to decoys and sporting collectibles
16. Joining a local organization dedicated to carving decoys
17. Giving lectures on the topic to community service groups
18. Giving lectures on the topic to local school groups
19. Developing a network of collector-to-collector exchanges
20. Lots of footwork, phone calling, e-mailing, and other contacts
21. Training and using a quality picker or pickers to assist you

Using Decoys and Calls

Not all who hunt decoys and calls have also hunted real birds using decoys and calls. I happen to be one who does both, as do many collectors. Others just like the beauty of the sculpted bird and/or the nostalgia of a more peaceful period gone by.

Regardless of one's relationship to waterfowl, it is helpful for the collector to know a bit about hunting and the use of decoys and calls to better explain the chance of finding certain items within certain regions. It is also important to have at least a limited sense of technological history and waterfowl hunting history as they relate to decoys and related items. This knowledge simply better prepares the collector for hunting decoys and calls in the field.

There are basically two ways in which one can hunt waterfowl: over decoys or without decoys. Some hunters use dogs, but not all hunters have the luxury of a great retriever. Calls are normally used with decoys for those with the skill to do so, but not often used without decoys. At one time, one could also use "live decoys" to decoy wild waterfowl and use bait to bring the birds into land. Now, we have more collectibles to discover, as these practices were made illegal at the federal level in 1935. Now we can look for items such as leg holds and bait decoys (ears

of corn, etc.). Keep in mind that the market hunters of the 1800s and early 1900s indeed did use dozens, if not hundreds, of decoys for their hunting purposes.

Decoy collectors who hunt ducks and geese frequently get interested in other hunting collectibles. An early Nitro Club Remington/UMC two-piece 20-gauge box with Mallard drake, full, shows a little edge wear. But all the shells are perfect and the graphics are in great shape.
$400+
Lewis Collection

Hunters place the decoy spread on "Pitt Lake" in Southern Illinois.

When one hunts over decoys for sport, usually somewhere between 50-100 decoys would be used if hunting the diver ducks, depending on the size of the water, the species sought and the time of year. Historically, most people could likely only afford one to three dozen working decoys when they were made from wood or cork. Then, after World War II, when decoys were a dollar each and made from the new miracle materials developed during the war, hunters expanded their rigs to 50-100 decoys in most instances.

If one was hunting the puddle ducks such as Mallards, it was more common to use between a half-dozen and two dozen decoys. The puddle ducks respond to decoys well, travel in smaller numbers and are not so leery to land on water with just a few other birds (fake or real). The diver ducks travel in large groups and they decoy better to large spreads.

An individual would normally use a boat to put out the decoy spread. However, the other night I noticed a neighbor with about 30 decoys out at the edge of the lake and he was simply standing in the cattails. He put them out from shore without a boat. The

Calling ducks is an art form and these calls are works of art. Fancy inlay work on one call is displayed, along with Joe Jaroski's two new duck/goose calls, including one miniature call. See chapters five and six for details.

point for our decoy hunting lesson is that it would be uncommon to find more than one or two dozen of any given species in the possession of most sport hunters prior to the advent of modern materials. And even then, only the hunters of diving ducks needed to amass large decoy spreads for their prey.

When one hunts with decoys and a dog, the same rules would normally apply regarding the number of birds set out in a spread. But, again, a boat may not be needed as even a bird brought down at some distance could be retrieved without a boat by using a good retrieving dog. This is how a friend and I hunted ducks in northern Wisconsin. We spread decoys (usually not more than 24-30), but never used a boat on many smaller bodies of water. On a large lake, we used a boat and a dog.

A call is used as an enticement to get birds to land over one's spread of decoys. Sometimes the decoys alone will not bring the ducks down, but the right sounds along with the "silent ducks" may be enough to entice the real ducks down to the water. I have seldom been successful with just a call, but a call with the right spread will bring in birds nearly every time. A call is also used as an attention getter and as a method to at least turn a flock of waterfowl in the direction of your spread. Calling is a real art form and something that takes practice and patience. But a good caller will have success over one without the skill or the tool (the call). Calls, of course, can be used with a boat, without a boat, with decoys, with a dog, without a dog, or even without decoys (but with far more limited success). However, it needs to be stressed that a person who does not know how to call properly will likely scare away more birds than one with just decoys or even without decoys.

A third form of waterfowl hunting is to "jump shoot" birds. This is a form that can be used successfully on small water holdings such as farm ponds and small lakes. There is also a Chesapeake Bay variation on this theme wherein the decoys are spread and then one goes away from the decoys and sneaks back silently in a boat or punt in the hopes of getting shots.

In the process of jump shooting, the hunter prowls like a tiger up to a small body of water ready to shoot when the pond explodes with ducks or geese propelling themselves through the air. This works especially well on Ring-bills on small ponds in the north. Another fun form of jump shooting is to use a canoe and canoe down a small to intermediate size stream and use the element of surprise to advantage, against the waterfowl on the stream. The Chesapeake Bay version mentioned is similar except one has spread the decoys in the water, paddled away, and only returned once the ducks settle into the spread. This type of jump shooting did contribute some decoys for collecting.

A fourth type of duck hunting, similar to jump shooting, is called "pass shooting." It also can be used even on big water if you want to hole up in a blind on shore prior to shooting hours. It is then referred to as "pass shooting" as one waits in the spot over which birds traditionally pass. The hunter uses the natural cover of the body of water and hides in wait for birds to arrive or even constructs a blind in a "bird thoroughfare." Some ammunition and guns were designed specifically for "pass shooting." The birds were usually at 40 to 45 yards and not 25 to 35 yards as with most shooting over decoys.

Decoys in history are fairly simple to understand. Market hunting was big business in the late 1800s and early 1900s. In other words, harvesters would harvest Mallards, Canvasbacks, Pintails, geese and other waterfowl, including shore birds, for sale to restaurants and grocery stores. This supported a large "factory decoy" business and was the heyday of such companies as Dodge, Peterson, Mason and others. Once market hunting was outlawed in 1918, most decoy companies had seen the last of their large orders for production of wooden decoys and they were closing their doors forever by the mid-1920s. Clearly, we all owe a great deal of thanks to the government for banning market gunning for a variety of reasons, one of the most important being the surplus of Mason decoys that became available to potential collectors decades later.

The next development of historical note is the banning of the use of live decoys and baiting by federal law in 1935. This ended many businesses that furnished live ducks and geese to hunters, ended the need for the production of leg holds, live traps, cages, etc., associated with the use of live birds. It created an entire industry of making fake corn and other wildfowl foodstuffs to replace the now illegal baits. In other words, more collectibles were created with the stoppage of techniques while a new form of collectible, "decoy baits," was created by replacing live baits with a fake. For example, corn was first carved from wood and later produced as papier-mâché. The first Federal Waterfowl Stamp arrived in 1934, spawning yet another important decoy-related collectible and leading to the preservation of millions of acres of wetlands for waterfowl breeding grounds. Thank goodness President Franklin D. Roosevelt was an avid stamp collector.

One of the most important historical developments was the introduction of modern construction techniques and raw materials developed prior to, during, and just after World War II. Though Carry-Lite began the use of pulp in making papier-mâché decoys as early as 1939, the most important change occurred with the development and use of Tenite and other plastic molding techniques in the production of decoys. Tenite was a new construction material that was developed by Eastman Kodak as a possible material for gunstocks during the war effort. Early Tenite 1 items from the mid to late 1930s are unstable. They can, and will, deteriorate. However, the later Tenite 2 materials are very stable and were used to make great fishing lures and duck decoys, most notably the Herter's Model 50s.

Plastic molding techniques and the plastics themselves became state of the art by the early 1950s, leading to the decline of production of wooden, cork, and even papier-mâché birds. Of course, there had been early (1930s) mass produced cork-body birds by Herter's with the printed fabric over cork bodies. But there was nothing on the scale of papier-mâché as a byproduct of pulp mills and

plastic bodied decoys, both hollow and solid. The 1950s definitely ushered in the "dollar a duck" days for hunters buying decoys and again freed up an entire family of decoys for collectors: most wooden ones, early cork ones, eventually papier-mâché ones, and then even early plastic ones.

Today we see high quality decoys being produced with graphics and colors better than most anything that had gone before. Many are now manufactured overseas and imported for our hunting use. Most of these are not collectible as they are easily available and new. However, their predecessors from the 1950s have gained some collecting interest and many of the early models, small companies, short production runs, and others, have become of interest to collectors. Also, there has been a nostalgic revival of interest in wooden decoys and many makers still are producing the wooden ducks for use. Some of these decoys will likely find permanent homes on mantelpieces and bookshelves, too. It is impossible to determine a "collectible" during the time of production in most instances. However, it is safe to say that some collector 40 years from now will be looking for decoys produced in the early years of this century for his/her collection.

But for now, look for those old factory decoys by Mason, Dodge, Peterson, and others that were made up until the end of market gunning. Look for the factory birds that were made in the 1920s and later by Pratt, Herter's, Evans, and others. Look for the mass produced decoys that survived until much later, such as Herter's. Look for the more recently semi-mass produced decoys such as the Ward Brothers and Waterfowlers. Look for the early papier-mâché birds in pristine shape. Look for unusual, early or rare plastic decoys from the 1950s. Look for anything else that you enjoy for your own collection. Hopefully, after reviewing this entire text you will be able to better identify decoys, makers of decoys, and your own desires in building a collection. Good hunting!

Beginning the Search

There are many ways to approach the idea of collecting decoys. There are hundreds of known carvers and numerous factories, even more of each being discovered every year we avidly collect. There are also dozens of species of birds represented, as well as many different hunting areas and major waterfowl flyways. With this in mind, the collector may choose to specialize in one of the areas. For instance, one might wish to concentrate on decoys that are indigenous to the area in which one lives, a particular species of bird, factory made decoys, decoys of only one factory, etc. Another satisfying way of collecting is to obtain any decoy within your means that pleases you and build a collection around those acquisitions.

There are three major groupings of decoys defined as to maker:

1. Commercially produced decoys carved and painted by hand for purposes of sale to others for use.

2. Non-commercially produced decoys are those produced by a hunter for his/her own use or a friend's use and not sold, as a rule. The C.C. Roberts birds shown in the first chapter on decoys are an example of this.

3. Factory produced decoys are those made in a commercial facility, usually turned out in great numbers by machine lathes or other mass production techniques such as injection molding. Not all factories were large. It is the machine carving or molding that makes it a factory.

In this book the first two categories are discussed together as hand-carved decoys in the first chapter on decoys. Then in the second and third chapters on decoys, the factory-made decoys are discussed in detail. Examples of all decoys are shown with illustrations to assist the collector in identifying decoys by region and maker. Again, the decoys shown are only the tip of the iceberg and a collector must invest great amounts of time and study to learn even the nuances of one small region of a flyway.

Most decoy collectors refer to certain geographic areas where decoys were carved and hunted over as "schools" of decoy makers. There are probably 30 or more identifiable schools of carvers in the various flyways. But for the purpose of simplification, this book will present only about 20 of the major areas or schools wherein the carvers lived and worked. The information and photographs attempt to give you some basic tools that should enable you to look at a particular decoy and at least identify what part of the country it is from. The discussion and the photographs within each school are chosen to give you construction techniques and painting styles that are typical of that school.

The general information section presented in the book should provide valuable identification data and prepare one for the more technical data included in the discussion of each major school of carvers. Information given in the text related to valuation of the decoys and other collectibles will be presented as actual valuation when known, related to sales and will also be presented in ranges and, in many cases, widely varying ranges. The value ranges are given merely as a guide and most of them have been derived from auction catalogs and dealers' sales lists.

When using the value ranges in this book, the collector should bear in mind several factors. If, for instance, there is a particularly rare and hard-to-find decoy known to exist only in four or five collections and suddenly, however unlikely, a group of 20 to 25 is found in an old barn loft and offered for sale at auction, the resulting prices realized might be considerably less than the heretofore-accepted value.

Marks on the decoy can also affect value, and condition can have a heavy influence. The values presented with the listings here are for decoys in good to excellent condition. There is a tendency for collectors to take a book such as this one and use it as the final authority. This would be unwise as it is only one source in many needed to make value determinations. The collector must use this book in conjunction with his own experience, the word of a trusted dealer, and all the other sources of value information he can get his hands on: dealer lists, periodical articles, sales ads, auction lists, etc.

Dictionary of Terminology

Here is some terminology you will encounter in the remainder of this book and in dealing with other collectors and sellers. A working knowledge of the terminology will make it easier to read sales and auction lists, and to describe your pieces to other collectors.

ANCHOR LINE TIE—These are as varied as the men who carved decoys. There were screw eyes, leather loops, or simply nails. The makers used whatever was available but some used the same type most of the time, giving the collector another clue as to the origin of a decoy. It should be pointed out that over the years of use, a hunter may have altered or changed the line tie to suit himself.

A Raymond Lead Co. of Chicago lead keel weight was used on Illinois River decoys. This is an Animal Trap or Padco wooden decoy found in Henry, Ill.

BALLAST—Some decoy makers used ballast to make the decoy more stable in the water. In some cases the ballast is incorporated into a keel, but most are simply weights attached to the bottom in some manner. A few makers had a distinctive method for attaching them, helping in identifying the decoy. The weights vary from anything heavy lying around, such as pieces of horseshoes or any chunk of metal, to a well-made lead or iron casting. Some were attached before painting, some after, and some consisted of molten lead poured into a cavity hollowed out for the purpose by the maker. There was one school in the Mississippi Flyway that used decoys with a swing keel with the ballast at the end, much like some small sailboats use today. Do not forget that many hunters applied their own ballast or weights, or they may have been removed, so it is not always a reliable indicator of maker or school.

BANJO TAIL—A style of carving usually associated with the Virginia Eastern Shore School of carvers and in particular with Ira Hudson.

BATTERY [Boat]—See SINK BOX.

BATTERY GUN—See PUNT GUN.

BLOCK—A term sometimes used to mean decoy. Apparently this usage is derived from the block of wood a carver begins with to create a decoy.

BOTTOM BOARD—Many decoys are found with a hollowed-out body and a flat board fitted to the bottom to seal it off and provide a base. The use and sometimes the thickness of a board can be a clue to maker or school in some cases. Also, many cork decoy carvers used a bottom board as a base. An example is seen later in the book under Herter's.

BRANDS—A word used to describe a broad spectrum of marks found on decoys. They can range from simple carved initials all the way to complicated company logos. For a detailed description of brands, see the section immediately following the dictionary.

CHECKING—This is the cracking of wood due to the natural oils and moisture drying or evaporating over the years.

COMB FEATHER PAINTING—This is a method of painting a decoy wherein the maker will paint the final coat and set the decoy aside to partially dry. When the paint reaches the proper consistency, the maker then uses a comb or comb-like instrument to scratch feather patterns into the paint. This gives a very realistic texture to the finished product.

CONFIDENCE DECOY—The confidence decoy is a decoy of any species of bird that can instill confidence in another bird. Its presence indicates to a game bird that food is below and that the area is safe for feeding. Swans, gulls, crows, and herons are good examples of confidence decoys. Some duck species are also used as confidence decoys as they are more wary than others. Their use on or near a duck blind conveys a sense that nothing is amiss below.

CRAZING—This is a term applied to paint that has cracked in a manner that looks somewhat like a mosaic. Very characteristic of old paint.

DOVE TAIL— See **INLET**.

EYES—The method a maker used to represent eyes on the decoys varied considerably and, in some cases, can be indicative of the maker or the school from which the decoys came. They used glass eyes that were either imported taxidermy eyes or simply the hatpins so popular with the ladies of those days. Sometimes they merely painted the eye on or carved it right into the head. Upholstery tacks, screws, and even .22 caliber shell cases sometimes were used.

FLAT BOTTOM—Exactly as the name implies, this term refers to the bottom of a decoy that has a uniformly flat bottom. See **V-BOTTOM** and **ROUND BOTTOM**.

GUNNING SCOW—This was a special sailboat rigged out with hoists and other necessary equipment

for deploying the sink box or battery boats. There were three rather famous ones plying the Chesapeake Bay: the Susquehanna, the North Carolina, and the Reckless. See section on **BRANDS** following, **PUNT GUN** and **SINK BOX**.

HAWK WATCHING—A term describing the head and neck position of a decoy: up and wary.

HOLLOW BODY—Describes the fact that the decoy body is hollowed out. Generally the hollow-bodied decoys are of two-piece construction, but can be three or more.

IN-USE REPAINT—See **REPAINT**.

INLET—This usually refers to a specific method of attaching a head to a decoy body through the process of inlaying. The carver fashions a hole or cavity in the appropriate area of the body, and carving the base of the head or neck portion to fit the receptacle precisely accomplishes it. This renders the decoy much stronger and makes it more resistant to breakage by the natural tendency of many users to pick up the decoy by the head. Although used to a much lesser extent, the method is also occasionally found used to attach wings, bills, and sometimes other parts of a decoy. Use of this construction technique can help to determine the carver or school from which the decoy came. This inlaying is usually a modification of a carpenter's mortise and tenon or dovetail joint. Frank Lewis' decoys of Western New York are classic examples.

KEEL—Just as in a boat, a keel gave the decoy both upright and lateral stability. They were placed on decoys mainly in areas where the waters tended to be rougher than usual, but not limited to those areas by any means. Keels come in all shapes and materials. Most were fashioned as you would expect, of a strip of wood of varying depths placed longitudinally along the bottom of the decoy. The material and style can vary widely, however. There are fixed keels, swinging keels, folding keels, etc., and they can also be a combination of keel and ballast made of metal and/or wood. See **BALLAST**.

LOW HEAD—A self-descriptive term describing decoys with little or no neck. The head is either very low or even almost tucked down into the top of the breast.

MARKET GUNNER—The market gunner was a hunter who made his living killing wildfowl for sale at market. See **SINK BOX** and **PUNT GUN**.

MORTISED—See **INLET**.

NAIL—A small protrusion situated at the front and top of the tip of the upper mandible or bill of some species of birds and carved by some decoy carvers.

NARES or NOSTRILS—These are holes, one on either side of the upper mandibles. Some makers represented them with carving, others with paint or not at all. Occasionally the way a maker carves or paints these feathers is an identifying characteristic.

NECK NOTCH—A term describing a carved depression in the body of a decoy just behind the neck.

ORIGINAL PAINT sometimes abbreviated O.P.—This refers to a decoy that has the first or original paint that was applied by the maker. The term does not, however, appropriately describe a decoy that has been repainted by its original maker, see **REPAINT**.

OVERSIZE—Refers to a decoy made in a scale larger than the normal size associated with the species of bird being carved or molded. See the decoys used in the Great Lakes for common examples of oversized birds due to such big water.

PADDLE TAIL—A tail carved in a paddle shape, usually protruding from about the center of the rear end of the body.

PUNT GUN—Also called Battery Guns, these were the guns used by the market hunters. These formidable guns could kill many, many birds with one shot. A typical punt gun would be 12 feet in overall length with an eight-foot barrel with a 1 1/2- to 2-inch bore and weighing 100 to 125 pounds. They were capable of firing a whole pound of shot at once. Some were even bigger, being double-barreled.

RAISED WING CARVING—Some decoy makers took pains to carve the body with the wings clearly raised slightly from the body. This is typical of pre-1915 decoys by Elmer Crowell. Sometimes called simply wing carving.

A beautiful Charles/Edna Perdew sleeping Mallard was repainted by Carla Steele.

RECENT REPAINT—See **REPAINT**.

RE-HEAD—Because the head is the most vulnerable part of a decoy, it is the part most usually damaged. There can be many decoy bodies with heads from another decoy. These are called Re-heads.

REPAINT—There are three different types of repainted decoys: (1) a repaint done by the original maker, (2) a repaint done by the owner and (3) a repaint done by a professional restorer. Although the most desirable repainted decoy, by far, is one that has been repainted by the original maker, even it is less desirable than a decoy with the original or first painting by its maker. The user or owner repaint (other than the maker/user) is called a Working Repaint or In-use Repaint and is the most common condition for an old decoy. The third type, the restorer's work, is strictly a matter of owner or potential buyer preference.

RIG—A word used to describe a group of working decoys. The decoys you hunt with are your rig of decoys.

RIGGING—This is used to describe everything from the line tie and anchor line down to the anchor.

ROOTHEAD—This is appropriately used to describe decoys with heads made out of a root. Most of the roots were embellished by carving and/or painting, but some were used as is because of natural resemblance to the bird's head.

ROUND BOTTOM—A decoy with a rounded bottom as opposed to a V-bottom or flat bottom, etc., is described as round-bottomed.

SCHOOL—This is a broad term describing a group of decoy makers whose products share some common characteristics. Almost always a school of makers is also a certain geographical area in which they lived and worked. Their decoys were certainly influenced by the condition under which they were used, materials readily available, and last but not least individual makers' influence on each other's products. A strict boundary delineating each school of makers is not possible to define. The schools overlap, for the waters they hunted and the birds hunted tended to blend slowly from one type to another within the flyways.

SCRATCH FEATHER PAINTING—This is a method of feather painting where the maker lets the paint dry somewhat, then comes back and scratches a feather pattern into the partially dry paint. This gives a very realistic texture to the finish.

SCULL BOAT—The scull boat was used all along the Eastern Seaboard from Maine all the way down through the Virginia Eastern Shore. The boat was used to hunt in the following manner: The hunter would deploy his rig of decoys in a likely spot and back off as much as a quarter of a mile and wait for the quarry to spot the rig and land. The boat made a slow, silent approach by sculling with a single oar over the stern of the boat and then the hunters fired on their quarry.

SHADOW DECOY—This is a two-dimensional decoy such as a silhouette cut from a plank. Some of them have a bit of three-dimensional carving. The latter appears mostly in head carving. Shadow decoys usually come in one of two forms. One is used as a stick-up; another, sometimes called Double Shadows, usually consists of two silhouettes fastened on either end of a couple of strips of wood with six more in various positions nesting in between.

SHELF or SHELF CARVING—This term refers to a style or characteristic construction wherein the body is carved with a definite rise, making a portion of the bird's neck to receive the head, or head and neck, portion.

SILHOUETTE DECOY—See **SHADOW DECOY**.

SINK BOX—Also known sometimes as batteries or Battery Boats. These were used extensively by market gunners in the Atlantic Flyway, particularly in, but not limited to, the Chesapeake Bay area. They were usually one-man, narrow wooden boats with very narrow decks and wings of wood or canvas stretched on frames that extended the decks all around. On these wings were placed Wing Ducks fastened to the deck for both ballast and decoy. The hunter would frequently spread out 500 to 600 decoys. The sink box along with the hunter and his gear was deployed by sailboats rigged for this specific purpose. They were called gunning scows.

SLAT BODY—A type of decoy construction that utilizes wood slats bent over a frame. This lightweight construction was usually employed in the making of large decoys. Some decoys are commonly found with one-slat bodies.

SLEEPER—A decoy carved in such a way as to represent a sleeping bird. Sometimes inaccurately called a confidence decoy. See **CONFIDENCE DECOY**.

SNEAK BOX—Usually associated with the Barnegat Bay area of New Jersey. This long, fairly narrow boat was completely decked over with only a small cockpit for the hunter. It was used extensively in the area. Lightweight in construction with a very shallow draft, it did not have much weight capacity. This latter factor is said to have influenced the high development of hollow body decoys from that area; ostensibly developed to allow the hunter to carry many more in the sneak box than if they had been made with solid bodies. When the market gunner returned from his hunt he would often have bagged more than a hundred ducks.

SOLID BODY—Refers to construction of a decoy

body from solid wood as opposed to a hollow body. Generally the solid body will consist of one piece of wood, but they have been found also made of two, three or more laminated layers of wood.

SPLIT TAIL—Some decoy makers carved their decoys more realistically than others. This term refers to the differentiated carving of the tail feathers, showing as definite upper and lower sections. Generally associated with the Delaware River School.

A typical stick-up shore bird is this root head Yellowlegs carved by Mark McNair.

STICK-UP—Frequently a decoy was made and mounted to one or more sticks or dowels representing legs (sometimes) that allowed the hunter to stick them into the ground or the bottom of a shallow or marshy area. There have been stick-ups of many species found, but the greatest majority is of shore birds.

STOOL—Once commonly used to describe a single decoy or a rig of decoys. The theory is that the word is derived from the European practice of fastening a live bird, usually a pigeon, to a movable pole or perch called a stool. One can readily surmise

that this also probably gave rise to the phrase stool pigeon.

STOOLIES—Used to describe dead birds used as decoys.

THUMBPRINT CARVING—See **NECK NOTCH**.

V-BOTTOM—Refers to the bottom of a decoy being in a V shape, when viewed from front or rear. See **FLAT BOTTOM** and **ROUND BOTTOM**.

WATERLINE—A term utilized in describing where the joining of the upper and lower portions of a two-piece construction decoy is located; i.e., above the waterline or below the waterline. The waterline itself is the level at which the decoy floats.

WING CARVING—See **RAISED WING CARVING**.

WING DECOY—Usually made of cast iron or lead, these birds were made to serve a special purpose. They were made for use with the Sink Box or Battery Boats utilized by the market gunners as a means of balancing the boat and helping to camouflage the boat by lowering it in the water so that it presented a lower profile. They weighed anywhere from eight to 40 pounds each, but there have been some found weighing much more. Some were made of wood but they are rarely found. The wooden wing decoy was the upper one-half of a decoy. Some were easily convertible to a regular working decoy by adding an appropriate lower body piece. It can be assumed that this conversion accounts for their short supply. These conversions can be difficult to detect for there were many decoys made with two- or three-piece body construction. See SINK BOX.

WORKING REPAINT—See **REPAINT**.

Identification of Antique Decoys

There are many characteristics of decoys that make identification fairly easy in some cases. A considerable number of decoys, for instance, can be identified as to maker by such simple things as the brands, logo, name or initials on a bird. Many makers can be determined because of a certain style

or shape. Many of these early craftsmen had styles of carving, construction technique or painting that were unique. Those make a decoy unmistakably his, even in the absence of other identifying marks. This is also true of some of the factory-produced birds.

For instance, some maker's decoys are all of the

same distinctive body shape, only painted differently to represent different species of wildfowl. Others had a distinctive style of carving details such as carved delineation of the mandibles and/or carving separating them from the head of the bird. Others used the two-piece hollow construction exclusively, or all with heads inlaid, or all with the upper and lower hollowed-out pieces joined, always above or always below the waterline. The same type of characteristics can be used to at least allow the collector to determine the school or area of the maker, most of the time. The list goes on: paint styles, painting techniques, method of attaching head to body, position of head, species of bird carved, type of wood used, body shape, size of the decoy, eye types, and shaping of the tail and face carving, etc.

Certain designs are meant to be used in shallow marshes while others are obviously made to be used in deep waters subject to weather. Knowledge of changing migratory patterns can be helpful also. For instance, if you know that there were few or no Canada geese migrating through the Chesapeake Bay area prior to the 1930s, then you know any Canada Goose decoy represented as being from there and dated by the seller as being made by a carver earlier than that, is a case of mistaken identification.

This general discussion may lead you to believe it is easy to date and identify the maker of any decoy. Not so. True, there are some that are easy to spot and, with time and experience gained from the easier identifications, you can develop your ability to include identification of other, less obvious examples. The problem is that there are as many types of decoy construction as there are opinions of just what constitutes an effective decoy. For the most part, luckily, carvers within a particular school were influenced by the species of bird hunted in his region and by the local conditions under which they had to be hunted. Therefore, there are common characteristics.

If you are a beginning collector you should not be afraid of what you will find. There seems to be a tendency among novice collectors to pick up what is truly a fine decoy that has no documentation or provenance, in a shop or flea market, and then let it go. This reluctance is understandable, but if it has the look and feel of a good piece, by all means buy it. Many have an inherent ability to recognize good form and design. If you do not have it, you can develop it simply by handling and examining a few that are known entities. Again, this is one of the advantages of attending some decoy shows. You can sometimes be fooled, but not often, by today's decorative reproductions.

Brands

The term brand as used in this book, and by most collectors, encompasses just about any markings placed on a decoy (usually on the bottom) by a user, maker or collector. If a collector places his mark on a decoy, it is usually a paper label or a rubber stamp type. This practice is not particularly widespread as its own distinctive nicks or wear pattern can usually identify each decoy.

User and maker brands can vary significantly in dating a decoy, documenting its maker, and influencing its value. Unfortunately the majority of decoys do not have brands or, at the least, the brand does not mean anything. The latter is particularly true in the case of user brands unless the user can be identified and is of historical importance to collectors.

In the case of a decoy on which both user and maker brand appear, each being known and important, you have a real prize. The importance of either or both brands can have a very positive influence on the value of the decoy. The value can be increased by two to five times, depending on the brand.

What follows are descriptions of some of the most famous and significant maker and user brands that you might find. There are, of course, more than those listed here, but the two lists are of many of those considered most important.

A user or owner brand can be that of the individual owner or of a hunting club or lodge. It usually appears in the form of a genuine brand such as those used in the cattle business. It was not a particularly expensive proposition in those days to have a local blacksmith fashion a branding iron for the impression of initials or name into a wooden decoy by heated iron or by striking with a hammer. Many owners and makers did not go to the trouble but simply carved or painted their marks.

There may be more than one user brand found on a decoy. For instance, there is a Harry Shourds' Black Duck decoy with three brands on the bottom: H.W. Cain, B C P, A C. The C common to all three brands suggests that H.W. might be gramps, A C might be his son, and B C P could be his grandson. Conjecture, yes, but if so, think how exciting it might be for his family to possess this particular bird. Incidentally, this particular decoy was spotted by a collector in someone's front yard being used as a decoration with a heavy coat of chartreuse green.

ACCOMAC was the name of a hunting club in the heart of the Virginia Eastern Shore about 65 miles north of Norfolk. This brand is found mostly on shore birds. However, it is also on a lot of good duck decoys. A decoy would increase in value about four times if the Accomac brand were present.

BARRON is a relatively scarce brand to be found. It is the name of an Eastern Shore Virginia hunting club. The Barron hunters believed faithfully in the Mason factory-made decoys. So far the brand has shown up mostly on Mason decoys, but there have been a few very fine, unidentified decoys found bearing the brand as well. The Barron brand on a Mason decoy increases its value by about 50 percent. When it is present it is usually found in two places, on the back and on the side.

CHATEAU. Fred Chateau was a game warden who lived in Accord, Mass. His brand has shown up on Joe Lincoln's and some Martha's Vineyard decoys, as well as a good many other New England decoys.

GOOSEVILLE G. C. The Gooseville Gunning Club was another Eastern Shore Virginia club. It went out of existence prior to World War I, so any bird found with this brand can be dated no later than 1917. Most decoys found bearing this brand will bring about twice the normal price.

HARD. The Hard Gun Club brand is found on many good factory decoys such as Masons, Dodge and Petersons.

NORTH CAROLINA. The North Carolina was one of three well-known gunning scows. Each of the sailboat's rigs of decoys was branded with the boat's name. As in the case of the other two gunning scows, just about any decoy with the brand would be worth at least $500. The North Carolina sank in 1888 in the Chesapeake Bay.

N P W. The initials in this brand are those of Nelson Price Whittaker. He was one of those who cast the heavy iron wing decoys for use with sink boxes.

ED PARSONS. Parsons was a legendary market gunner who hunted only over decoys made by Ben Dye and Captain John Daddy Holly; therefore, if you find a Parsons brand on a bird it is most likely to be one or the other. The brand was a P within a circle.

RECKLESS. The Reckless was one of the earliest gunning scows. The brand could make an otherwise insignificant upper Chesapeake Bay Canvasback duck decoy in the $100-$200 range worth $500 easily.

SUSQUEHANNA. The Susquehanna was another of the old gunning scows whose brand makes the decoy worth much more than the norm. The Susquehanna sank just before the Civil War so, obviously, a decoy branded with its name pre-dates 1860-65.

SUYDAM. This brand belonged to a wealthy Long Island family that did much sport hunting in Long Island Sound. The brand shows up frequently on good Long Island decoys.

Maker Brands

Few of the thousands of individuals who carved decoys for personal or commercial purposes identified them with a brand, but most of the factory-made decoys did carry brands. The factory brands will be covered in that section of the book. The listing presented here is of several of the more important makers who sometimes, often, or always identified their decoys with a brand. The descriptions below are of brands only.

Joel Barber. He is one of the big names in decoy collecting. After Barber wrote his book, *Wild Fowl Decoys*, he decided he would try his hand at carving decoys himself. His brand, when present, is very distinctive and readily recognizable.

Thomas B. Chambers was a carver from the St. Clair Flats area of Michigan. He did not always place his brand but when he did it was easy to identify. It simply stated Thomas B. Chambers, Maker and was stenciled onto the bottom.

Nathan Cobb Family. The Cobb families were originally New Englanders who migrated south to Virginia. Their products are best identified by construction techniques and style, but they sometimes carved their initials into the bird. Since they did not brand, but carved an initial into their decoys, it is more a matter of interest than anything else. Most of the time you will find only an N for Nathan Cobb, an E or an A carved into their

products, if you find any at all.

Elmer Crowell. Crowell, starting around 1915, customarily used the oval brand and the rectangular version is usually associated with his later work and/or his son Cleon's work. Unfortunately the decoys carved by Crowell prior to 1915, before he adopted a brand, are considered to be his finest work. Collectors should be aware that a few decoys have shown up with an apparently authentic Crowell brand that is known not to be his work.

Lee and Lem Dudley were twins who lived, hunted, and carved decoys in the far northern Currituck Sound area of the outer banks of North Carolina. The brand L. D. found on their decoys could be either brother, although the late Bill Mackey stated in his *American Bird Decoys* that probably it was Lem Dudley who carved most of the decoys. Simplest of the brands to forge, it has been known to happen. So it behooves any collector interested in Dudley decoys to get to know their characteristics intimately.

Mitchell Fulcher was also a North Carolina maker. He, like the Dudleys, also identified his decoys with his initials, M. F.

Laing. Albert Laing's decoys are almost always found with his last name branded large and clear on the bottom.

Decorative and Reproduction Decoys

A discussion of decorative decoys is absolutely necessary in a book devoted to guiding the collector in this hobby. Experienced and seasoned collectors are quite cognizant of these products, but some could very well mislead those who are new to the hobby or contemplating beginning a collection of decoys.

Collectively, decorative decoys comprise several types. These are:

1. Decoys carved and painted by craftsmen/artists

of great talent. They could be called Modern Folk Artists.

2. Reproductions of classic antique decoys. These are almost always offered in a reduced scale from the originals. Some are offered in a limited edition and all are (or should be) well identified as to exactly what they are.

3. Those decoys factory-made or hand-made that are offered to the public strictly as a decorator item.

They have no claim, nor do their makers make any claim, to anything other than that.

4. Those decoys offered by various companies in kit form for finishing by individual hobbyists or those that are made by individuals for their own use or enjoyment.

The first category is the most important of the four. The carvers of these fine bird sculptures, for that is truly what they are, find their progenitors among the early master makers of the working wildfowl decoy. Many of those early makers just were not satisfied with their product unless it reflected their own high knowledge of the anatomy and habit of the living bird. They were truly artists who could not help expressing their talents in the working decoy.

The contemporary carvers are carrying on the active pursuit of this acknowledged original early American Folk Art. It could be said that the competition of today finds its roots in the first organized competition of decoy makers that was held in Bell Port, Long Island, in 1913. Charles E. "Shang" Wheeler, one of the old master decoy makers, entered his work in this competition and walked away the Grand Champion. Most of these contemporary sculptures in wood are easily recognized by their extreme detail and excellent workmanship. In addition to this attention to anatomical and feather detail, the decoy must also pass a set of strict requirements of floating attitude, etc., taken from both the real birds' habits and those that would be necessary for a working decoy. A few contemporary carvers do work in the old style.

The second group, that of reproductions, is probably the most controversial among collectors. Many seasoned serious collectors look upon these products with disdain. But the fact remains that they exist and satisfy the appetites of many individuals. They are usually done in a smaller scale than the original and are well marked as reproductions. Some are machine made and some entirely hand-made. Like the originals, however, even the machine-made likeness has to have finishing, carving, and painting applied by hand.

Third is a group of decoys that is factory-made or hand-made for decorative purposes only. The legitimate makers of these decorator items clearly mark their products so that the new collector should have no problem identifying them. Some are strikingly beautiful and can make wonderful additions for those who decorate their houses with early American style furnishings. There are many carvers in this category that approach the quality of those decoys found in the first category.

The last category is that of the various individual woodworking hobbyists who either create their own designs or finish factory-made kits that are available in various stages of completion. The finished products in this category can vary from crude to wonderfully detailed decorations depending on the abilities of the hobbyist.

Value Range FOR DECORATIVE DECOYS

Do not underestimate the value of these decoys. At the July 2002 Guyette/Schmidt auction, 21 decorative decoys averaged $1,000 each with a range of $100 to $15,000. It is not uncommon for the miniatures and the decorative decoys of known carvers such as Crowell, Perdew and Schmidt to exceed the value of their working decoys.

A number of duck hunters still make and use their own blocks for hunting and some also sell their decoys to others for use. Some of these decoys may indeed become very collectible in the future but should not be confused with the older decoys with values already established based upon collector demand.

All have a particular market, from the active collector of the beautiful decoys created by contemporary artisans to the kits and individually made decorative decoys. They were not originally, however, looked upon as a part of decoy collecting. But, as time passes, many of the artist-carved birds representing ducks have gained in popularity and value. They should likely be considered part of the mainstream of decoy collecting. It is only important for the beginning and intermediate collector to keep in mind that the information is presented more for interest. It is especially important for the neophyte collector so that he may not become confused in the early phases of building a collection and learning about antique decoys. The vast majority of current collectors are interested in decoys made and used prior to the 1960s, and many collectors limit their collections to birds made and used in the 1800s or early 1900s. However, again, only the collector has the right to determine his/her own interests in decoy collecting. The future may see even more people adding contemporary carvers to their collections.

Misrepresentations, Forgeries and Fakes

Fortunately there are very few nefarious dealers in antique decoys and most antique shop owners and flea-marketers are honest. The latter two, however, seldom know decoys in any detail. These shops and flea markets can be good hunting grounds if you know your stuff. You might find a real treasure for just a few bucks.

However, one may also find plastic heads on beautiful old wooden bodies. And we come to the problem of re-heads. Do not misunderstand re-heads as misrepresentations, fakes or forgeries because the discussion appears here. The majority of old bodies fitted with old heads that are not the originals are legitimate decoys. Remember that bills and heads are usually the parts of a decoy most susceptible to damage in handling, so many hunters had to replace heads from time to time. The ability to recognize a re-head most of the time will come with increased familiarity with individual, recognizable characteristics of various makers. Re-heads represent an altered form of a decoy, hence its inclusion here.

So far not too many outright fakes or forgeries have reared their ugly heads, but it has happened. A few obviously inferior decoys have been found with the easily recognizable oval brand of Elmer Crowell. The most popular forged brand is that of Lee and Lem Dudley, for they simply carved L. D. into their products. Fakes of Mason decoys have shown up. By far the most popular subjects of forgers are the decoys made by the Ward brothers, Lem and Steve. In other words, the more expensive the bird, the more likely someone will attempt to recreate it.

So far, so good. Not many of these bogus offerings have turned up. But, as in any area of collecting where some of the items have reached values as high as decoys have, we have to be ready for anything. There are many, many exceptionally talented craftsmen in the United States today and it would be safe to say that among them are a few bad apples. In addition, with the spate of well-formed decorator decoy bodies and kits for the hobbyist, a dishonest individual would not have to be necessarily endowed with great carving talent, only a degree of ingenuity. Also, more than one dealer has realized that paint may duplicate the aging process by leaving a new decoy out in the weather for an extended time. Most of these, fortunately, are blends of several styles or just simply a talented designer's own creation and are marked in such a way as to identify them as modern. The problem is some of them are not so marked and others are actual copies not marked as such. Most experienced collectors and sellers can readily identify these as bogus, but those of us a little less punctilious might be fooled.

There is yet another potential area of fraud that one must know about. With the modern CAD/CAM techniques of a small factory, a person can reproduce any such product identical to the original form. Thus, by using a Dodge as a model, he could reproduce a Dodge in form. Of course, this would still have to be painted correctly. However, one can see how it pays to only purchase rare items when the provenance and authenticity of the items can be verified.

All of this comes down to one cardinal rule of collecting: Establish a good working relationship with one or more knowledgeable and trustworthy dealers. Any reliable dealer would back up his/her sale to you with a guarantee of reimbursement if what you were sold turns out to be other than what was represented.

Restoration and Repairs

There are always two schools of thought among collectors when the subject of restoration comes up. One is labeled the purist approach; that is the strong belief that the decoy should be left "as is," that no restoration effort should be made. Some collectors of this persuasion will, however, approve of taking the years of working repaints down to what is left of the first or original coat.

In the other group are those who advocate complete or partial restoration. This could run the spectrum from a simple paint touch-up to replacing broken or rotten wood parts and faithfully reproducing the style of painting of the original maker.

What you do or think about restoration is strictly a personal decision made under the circumstances. You should know, however, that probably the majority of serious collectors prefer the decoy to be left as it is. Further, if you do elect to have a decoy restored, it is incumbent upon you to be certain that you say it has been done before selling or swapping the bird. My own opinion goes a step further. Each restored decoy should be clearly and permanently marked as such in an inconspicuous place, preferably on the bottom. Then subsequent owners will know exactly what has been done to it. The condition of a decoy can be an extremely important consideration when placing a value on it. A restoration of any sort can have a tremendous influence on its value in either direction. So you must think carefully before having any restoration done and be careful in selecting the person to do the work.

There is presently some controversy brewing about restoring and repairing decoys. While it is easy to be a purist and collect only those examples that are in mint condition, one would find such a collection rather limited by the rarity of such examples, not to

Fine Mason examples are part of the Pitt Collection.

mention expensive. Such examples could command rather daunting prices.

The controversy revolves around the value of restored or repaired decoys. Some collectors feel that a beautifully restored decoy should be worth nearly, if not as much as, a pristine example. Others argue that they should be considerably devalued. This is not a problem with any real solution that would cover all cases. It must, of necessity, be a subjective decision and one which must be made personally by each collector. How could you possibly make a sweeping statement covering all cases? How could you, for example, say that an Ira Hudson decoy restored to perfect condition be worth as much as one that is just as nice that had never been damaged at all? Hudson produced a prodigious number of decoys in his career and there are plenty of nice examples out there. There are other makers, such as Shang Wheeler, who made fine decoys, but in limited numbers. In that case, the restored one could conceivably be valued at near or the same as an undamaged one.

Care of Your Collection

You might think that just because many of your decoys survived the ravages of water and rough treatment by hunters, you do not have to give them any special consideration in display or transport. If you give it just a little thought, millions of decoys were made and used over the years. There can be no realistic estimate made as to how many have survived. But suffice it to say that they are becoming more and more difficult to find in any condition, much less good to excellent condition.

Any wooden object is subject to a number of different hazards. Checking, the splitting or cracking of decoys is not an uncommon problem. Some of it is due to the maker not using sufficiently seasoned wood. Due to subsequent drying out of unseasoned wood, checking can and does happen. Consider also that a decoy may have lain untouched for years in a boathouse, shed or barn with more or less constant moisture conditions. You find it, add it to your collection in your modern climate-controlled home, which is very dry as a rule, and after some months a crack appears. It could be dismaying, but you can do little about the problem unless you have the wherewithal to install expensive systems like the better museums have. This is a problem most of us will have to accept as inevitable. It does not happen often but does happen. There are some precautions you can take to at least retard this problem, and others you can take easily to alleviate the likelihood of damage.

For one thing, make sure that your display is not subjected to direct blasts of heat or cold from a floor or wall register. They look great on a mantel, but if you use your fireplace even just occasionally, do not leave them up there. That is one of the worst places to display them. Heat and smoke will do harm to your decoys. Never let them be exposed to direct sunlight even for a few minutes each day. The cumulative damaging effect of ultraviolet light from the sun can fade the already fragile paint. A little known fact is that continuous exposure to fluorescent light can do the same thing. Try to avoid exposure to either one.

There is also some controversy concerning applying oil or wax to a decoy. Once again a purist might not like this because it alters the original state of the decoy. This must be an individual decision, but it is known that proper application of these materials to any wood acts as a preservative by feeding the wood. You would not hesitate to care for a piece of fine antique furniture in this manner, so why not your decoys? Obviously, rigorous rubbing of an already old and fragile paint job may do it irreversible harm. Judgment enters into the picture.

Not too much has been written about termites, powder-post beetles or lyctid beetles and other wood boring insects, but this problem presents a very real and present danger. If they are in the wood, they can damage or destroy your decoy and also can literally eat your house from around you if they spread to the wood surrounding the infested object.

If you find small piles of fine dust around a decoy, do not panic. Just remove it from your collection and isolate it. Recent research has indicated that freezing the piece of infested wood will usually kill the live lyctid beetles, but not much is yet known about the effect of the larvae of the beetle. My advice would be to freeze for several days and isolate it for about a month, preferably in a sealed plastic bag or tightly lidded metal box. Inspect it periodically for new evidence of the dust-like, powdery spills from the tiny holes made by the beetle. If no new ones are

A wooden boat has been set on end and outfitted with shelves to display additional fine Masons and others. At the top are duck calls by James Korando, Jacobs, Ill., (center calls) and Fred A. Allen from Monmouth, Ill.
Pitt Collection

found, you are probably safe.

A most important consideration in the care of your collection is insurance and theft protection. This can be of paramount importance if your collection has grown for some years and represents a sizable sum of money in appreciated value. Additionally, much of it may be irreplaceable. There are some safeguards against these threats, including insurance. I would bet that a great many collectors are sublimely comforted by the mistaken belief that their homeowners' insurance covers their collection. They are suffering from a common but risky supposition. Most of these policies specifically exclude such collections. A trusted insurance expert should examine the situation. Also, some collecting clubs now offer insurance programs for specialty collections and this may be an

avenue for some to insure their collection.

A careful record of your collection is almost obligatory in its protection. If you have a good record of the items in your collection, it can be of immeasurable aid in documenting in the case of loss due to fire, theft, etc. Law enforcement authorities often turn up stolen goods that cannot be claimed by the true owner because of lack of ownership documentation. As we have already noted, many decoys are documented through auction sales catalog photography and collector familiarity with certain of the better-known examples. Collector Dr. George Ross Star Jr., in the *Wildfowl Decoys* chapter in *The American Sporting Collector's Handbook* (Edited by Allan J. Liu, 1976 by Winchester Press), states, "Personally, I am always pleased with publication of photos of the better birds in my collection on the premise that the more people who can recognize them the harder it would be to sell any illegally and the more apt they are to be recognized and reported if offered for sale." I strongly agree with Dr. Star. However caution should be exercised in your choice of publication. Some collectors I know refuse to be identified when their birds are photographed for publication, for fear of burglary. This is sensible if the collector does not have a sophisticated and reliable security system.

It is strongly recommended that you accomplish a detailed listing of each decoy in your collection. A very effective method is to photograph each of them and record any distinguishing characteristics on the reverse of the photo, such as species, maker, marks or brands, size, and any readily recognizable wear patterns, nicks, etc. You should keep this in a safe place away from your home such as a bank safe deposit box. If you wish to have such a record in your home for the convenience of making changes and additions, make sure it is a second set and be certain that you make the same additions and corrections to the other set in your safe deposit box. With this kind of record, in the event of theft and recovery, you should have no problem reclaiming your decoys. It will also go a long way establishing the amount of your loss to insurance companies.

Chapter Two:

Traditional Carvers
& Their Schools

The schools of carvers are more or less regional
within the various flyways. They are placed in
geographical order beginning with the northernmost
school in the Atlantic Flyway and proceeding southerly
to South Carolina. From there we jump over to the
Mississippi Flyway, starting with the Louisiana School
and going north all the way to Michigan, where the
Atlantic Flyway also affects the eastern side of the state.
Then we go to Wisconsin and then over to the Pacific
Flyway on the West Coast.

Within each of the regional schools, there are many
divisions representing specific areas that are treated
as separate schools by the serious collector. These
smaller, more specific schools are treated in
detail in the various books that specialize in a

study of the makers within them.

These schools of individual carvers are followed by two chapters on many of the more important or popularly collected decoys made by factories. The factory chapters now include many of the more collectible decoys dating from post-1935 made out of newer materials, e.g. papier-mâché, rubber, cork, Tenite, etc. Many of these more recent decoys have become very collectible and will continue to grow in popularity.

A word of caution is in order regarding the typical characteristics presented in the text discussions and photo captions within each of the schools. Few, if any, hard and fast rules govern these typical characteristics. Nor do any definite line boundaries exist separating one school of carvers from another. Rather, each school blends into the next, creating overlapping transitional areas where carvers of each school were influenced by those of the other school or by the changing areas and types of hunting conditions. Consequently you cannot treat a statement such as "Decoys from this school have glass eyes" as true 100 percent of the time. It is a statement of what is usually found.

There are no absolutes. This is true even of some of the well-known and carefully documented makers. It is reasonable to assume that any maker might have experimented with construction or painting techniques. It is known that some of those who almost always used the same techniques or styles accomplished something quite different on special order. Some were free with their carved heads for those carvers who could make a good body but lacked the ability to produce a decent head. There is also the case of a maker being a master at carving his decoys, but lacking in painting ability and having another maker paint them for him.

Finally, a word is in order about values given in the book. The value ranges have been updated with current data. Obviously, there are not specific sales accounting for each and every carver covered in this book. However, most of the major carvers could be documented through the major auction houses in America. Also, the values given to me by major dealers and collectors for specific carvers have been integrated into the ranges. Specific values for specific birds are given whenever possible. For your own research, the two best sources of data are the Year in Review issues of *Decoy Magazine* and the "Prices Realized" lists of the various auction houses. Some auction houses also now include actual sales data on their Web sites.

The sales data from the recent sales likely indicate the values we will see for some time. The bottom line is decoy values will ebb and flow with the economy. One must always keep this fact in mind to fairly evaluate the value of even the rare pieces, but especially when considering the more common items and decoys from the more prolific carvers. So the prices given are only meant as a guide to the general value of decoys for a particular carver and/or region and numerous factors will go into the precise value of any given bird.

Maritime Provinces

There are at least three different sorts of decoys in the Canadian Maritime Provinces school–two are with respect to construction and the other is in paint style. The painting of most of the decoys was not very elaborate because, in the main, they hunted sea ducks not considered particularly wary. Hence there were rather crude and simple paint patterns. The exception to this rule is found in the carving and finishing of Merganser decoys in the south coastal area. They are generally much more sophisticated in appearance. The other two carving types are differentiated in the manner of attaching the heads. In most of Nova Scotia, carvers simply attached the head directly to the body surface. In the extreme southern area, however, they seem to have been influenced by the Maine carvers in using the inlaid method of attaching the heads. A collector from Nova Scotia reports that about 80 percent of the decoys he has observed in the region have inlaid heads.

Bodies of typical Nova Scotia decoys are usually solid and carved from one block of pine, although many are found made of two blocks. Carvers also frequently used spruce and fir. Decoys are characterized by flat bottoms and rounded backs, for the most part. When you examine the bottom of these decoys you will often find evidence of their having been rigged on a line both fore and aft. There may even be remnants of leather thongs present at the front and the rear of the decoy bottom. Use of leather thongs was the common method of providing linc ties in this school of carvers.

Goose decoys are almost always found made of two, three or more pieces because of their size and the relative scarcity of big timber in Nova Scotia. Some carvers of Nova Scotia include: Edwin Backman, Lunenberg; Orran Hiltz, Indian Point; Lindsey Levy, Villagedale, and Stan Sawler from Western Shore.

Value Range FOR MARITIME PROVINCES DECOYS

There is not a lot of sales data on Nova Scotia decoys but one can fairly extrapolate values from the values of Maine decoys, which have gone up to some serious five-figure amounts for known carvers. It would be reasonable to place the common decoys within a range of **$300** to **$1,000**. Some significant carvers or special poses will command premium prices over this range and may even reach five figures as some of the documented Maine sales have done.

From John Ramsay, Summerside, Prince Edward Island, a Canada Hollow Canada Goose has paint on back, sides, tail and breast that appears to be original. It has some old working repaint elsewhere, cracks and a tiny tail chip. *Decoys of Maritime Canada* by Dale and Gary Guyette shows the rig-mate to this bird.
$3,250
Guyette & Schmidt, Inc.

An unknown Maine or Nova Scotia pair of Goldeneye has inlet heads, original paint with average wear and nice patina. The drake has a small chip out of its tail; both are sound otherwise.
$500
Guyette & Schmidt, Inc.

Bufflehead Drakes are by an unknown maker;
Nova Scotia is the likely origin. Excellent paint and
structurally sound decoys.

$500

Guyette & Schmidt, Inc.

Lindsey Levy, Little Tancook Island, Nova Scotia,
may have carved this decoy. It dates from the
second quarter of the 20th century. The work is
similar to that of Levy's, with original paint, split
on underside. Information is from *Decoys of
Maritime Canada* by Dale and Gary Guyette.

$300

Guyette & Schmidt, Inc.

A "Turtle Back" Eider drake from Drumhead,
Nova Scotia, is circa 1920s. Original paint is
worn to primer in places. There is a hairline
crack in the tail.

$250

Guyette & Schmidt, Inc.

Maine

A drake Red-breasted Merganser is representative
of a decoy from the Maine School. It is somewhat
oversize, constructed of solid wood with a flat
bottom. It has very slight, faintly visible raised
wing carving. The head is inlaid in a manner that
is common to Maine decoys, along with the carved
oval eye representation. The overall look of Maine
decoys is sleek and somewhat streamlined. Although
most of the paint patterns the makers used were not

quite so polished as that of the Merganser, they are
in the same stylized type pattern for the most part.
These same characteristics are clearly seen in the
decoys carved by "Os" Bibber, circa 1920.

Augustus Aaron "Gus" Wilson (1864-1950) is one
of the best-known makers from the Maine School.
Common to all of his birds, save products of his
later years, was the unusual carving of details on the
underside of the lower mandible. That is an area of

the head that few carvers paid much attention to, as it would never be seen by a live bird being decoyed. Other common characteristics of Wilson's decoys are the carved oval eyes, raised wing carving, and carved details on both upper and lower mandibles.

Although Wilson was not the only one to carve decoys whose heads were ingeniously fashioned so that they would rock back and forth with wave action, if you were to find one of his rocking head Black Ducks you would have a real prize. From time to time he also carved decoys with mussels or fish in their bills, or with slots for insertion of a piece of leather or other material simulating seaweed or fish. An Eider with a mussel in its bill sold at the Sotheby's Guyette & Schmidt auction in 2000 for $82,250!

Decoys from this school were generally made heavy and oversized to better fit the hunting conditions of the region. Some other Maine carvers are: Orlando Sylvester "Os" Bibber, South Harpswell; George Boyd, Seabrook, N.H.; George Huey, Friendship; Willie Ross, Chebeague Island; Amos Wallace, West Point, and James Whitney, Falmouth.

Value Range FOR MAINE DECOYS

"Os" Bibber: **$1,000-$20,000.**
George Huey: **$500-$2,500.**
Gus Wilson: I would place his current average range at **$1,500 to $6,000** with exceptional birds going for **$10,000 plus.**
Other makers from Maine: **$250-$1,500.**

A Red-breasted Merganser hen is by "Os" Bibber, circa 1920.
$15,000
Hank and Judy Norman Collection

This Old Squaw drake is attributed to "Os" Bibber, circa 1920.
$20,000
Hank and Judy Norman Collection

A preening Eider hen is by "Gus" Wilson, circa early 1900s.
$10,000
Hank and Judy Norman Collection

Gus Wilson, South Portland, Maine, carved a Black Duck pair, with wonderful head positioning and a rare swimming pose. They have original paint, small cracks and chips.
$1,850
Guyette & Schmidt, Inc.

Willie Ross, Cheabeague Island, Maine, carved this Red-breasted Merganser pair, circa second quarter of the 20th century. They have inlet heads and glass eyes, original paint with some repaint to white areas, peacock plumes normally inserted into back of head are missing, dowel protruding, the hen has a crack in the neck.
$1,950
Guyette & Schmidt, Inc.

A Friendship, Maine, area Eider Duck, circa 1900, has an inlet head and original paint.
$6,000
Guyette & Schmidt, Inc.

A Small's Point, Maine, area oversized Eider Duck, circa 1900, has an inlet head and original paint.
$1,250
Guyette & Schmidt, Inc.

Gus Wilson, South Portland, Maine, carved a very rare Red-breasted Merganser Drake in rocking head model.
$8,250
Guyette & Schmidt, Inc.

Gus Wilson, South Portland, Maine, carved this rare White Wing Scoter with extended head position, old working repaint and inlet head.
$2,500
Guyette & Schmidt, Inc.

This is a Gus Wilson, South Portland, Maine, Monhegan Island Style Surf Scoter. Circa first quarter of the 20th century, it has an inlet head, carved eyes and relief carving, old repaint and chips and cracks.
$1,600
Guyette & Schmidt, Inc.

The Massa...chool is where there is the first evidence of a widespread movement toward more refined decoys. They are made in overall shape much more like a live bird. As a general rule however, they lack fine detailing such as wing carving or very intricate paint patterns. But they were well finished with fine sanding and the paint patterns more accurately reflect that of live birds than most early decoys.

Extraordinary exceptions are the decoys of a maker from the Cape Cod area. Elmer Crowell (1862-1951) of East Harwich, Mass., is acknowledged to be a master among makers from any school. The decoys he made from about 1900 to 1920 are those most sought by collectors. After that period his production of working decoys began to decline while his interest in the art of the decoy increased. He concentrated more and more on producing decorative or ornamental decoys. Crowell used a distinctive oval brand, but he did not initiate its use until about 1915. Some collectors consider his 1900-1915 unbranded decoys as the most desirable. The brand measures 3 1/8" by 1 7/8".

Later on, (c.1930) Crowell adopted a smaller rectangular shaped brand that was also used by his son Cleon.

Elmer Crowell's decoys were made with solid white cedar bodies with heads carved from white pine, as were all the typical Massachusetts School decoys. He was an exceptional carver and painter. A common characteristic of his decoy is carved wings with the tips crossed. Additionally he used a rasp to simulate feathers on the breasts and the back of the heads. Almost all of his birds had glass eyes and the bottoms were wide and flat.

There are some decoys by Crowell that are atypical in style, although his painting talent is obvious. These are from a rig he carved for the Monomoy Branting Club. They differ in construction in that they are so narrow-bodied and high that they had to be mounted on a triangular frame, usually in groups of three, to make them float upright.

As Crowell progressed, his working decoys became less and less detailed in carving details but, with one exception, his painting pattern remained as good as ever. This is illustrated by the fact that even when his birds lacked any wing carving at all, he still painted the wings beautifully and detailed to the point of his characteristic crossed wing tips. The exception is a group of Black Ducks he made for a sporting goods store. They are very plain with no carving detail on the body at all. The heads are characteristically rasped and the wing tips painted crossed. These decoys were stenciled on the bottom with the name of the store: Iver Johnson.

A Brant by Joe Lincoln (1859-1938) from Accord, Mass., is a typical Lincoln decoy that was made sometime before 1920. It has a carved separation between the bill and face, glass eyes, and one-piece solid cedar body.

A Lincoln-carved Canada Goose decoy is constructed similarly to Canada Goose decoys of the Massachusetts school. The slat-body is formed by bending lath-like narrow cedar slats over a frame. The earlier examples had canvas or similar material stretched over the body and then the finished product was painted. Later they dispensed with the practice of covering the wood with fabric and merely painted directly on the wood. The heads were normally carved from cedar. He also made very nice hollow body Canada Goose decoys that were hollowed out from the bottom, mounted on a bottom board and open at the rear, making them self-bailing.

Another carver who is representative of this school is Henry Keyes Chadwick (1865-1958) of Martha's Vineyard. It is estimated that he carved upwards of 2,000 decoys during his decoy making years. His birds were also the typical one-piece solid cedar bodies with pine heads. They were flat-bottomed, beautifully carved decoys usually sporting glass eyes, although he sometimes used both tack and painted eye representation. Usually there will be a hole evident on the bottom, beneath the head, through which he inserted a brass screw to hold it in position. His ballast weight was flush with the bottom or inlaid. He would carve out a rounded hole in the bottom and pour in molten lead to accomplish this.

Earlier decoys (pre-1920) made by Chadwick have more slender necks, painted and carved detailed heads with metal or painted eyes, and longer undercut tails than do his later ones. They could be characterized as much more delicately rendered than the later more rugged, thicker necked blocks. One interesting thing is that the later ones will more than likely sport glass eyes in countersunk sockets.

Although Chadwick's paint patterns are fairly good, it is generally accepted that he was a much better carver than painter. It is known that sometimes when Crowell ran short of decoys to sell, he would purchase stock from Chadwick to paint and sell.

Benjamin D. Smith (18   ) was a contemporary of Crowell and Chadwick, and a neighbor of the latter on Martha's Vineyard. Chadwick emulated both Crowell and Smith, but Smith had the greatest influence on his work. This was so much so, that sometimes it can be difficult for the less knowledgeable to tell their pre-1900 decoys apart. Subsequent to that, all of Chadwick's decoys were flat-bottomed, solid bodied with his distinctive flush, circular bottom lead weight. Ben Smith's decoys would sometimes be fashioned with a hollow body and rounded bottoms.

A few other early carvers from Massachusetts are: the Folger family, Nantucket; Bert Hunt, Duxbury; T. Lindberg, Cape Cod; David Goodspeed, Duxbury; Arthur B. Rich, Duxbury; F. P. Smith, Duxbury; William Swift, Sagamore Beach; Charles Thomas, Assinippi; Franklin Wright, Cape Cod; and William J. Wyre, Nantucket.

Value Range FOR MASSACHUSETTS DECOYS

A recent unknown Massachusetts Wood Duck hit $45,100 at auction and an unknown Dowitcher brought $48,875. Thus, makers do not always need to be known. A fine decoy is a fine decoy, regardless of maker.

Joe Lincoln: **$1,000-$10,000.**

Elmer Crowell holds the current world record in pricing. A fair "average" range would be **$2,000** to **$7,000** for decoys.

Henry Keyes Chadwick: **$300-$10,000 plus.**

Benjamin Smith: **$500-$5,000.**

James Whitney: **$250-$1,000.**

Elmer Crowell's Preening Pintail drake, carved in 1915, is the reigning world champion as the priciest decoy, selling for $801,500 at a 2003 auction co-hosted by Guyette & Schmidt and Christie's. The decoy had set the previous record in 2000 at $684,000. The decoy is known as Crowell's finest and is the only known example. It was made for Crowell's friend, Dr. John C. Phillips of Beverly, Mass., for whom Crowell ran a gunning stand at the turn of the century.

$801,500
Guyette & Schmidt, Inc.

An unknown circa 1890 Golden Plover has its original paint.
$4,000-$5,000
Griff Evans Collection

Joseph Lincoln, Accord, Mass., carved these two Widgeons, branded "C. N. SMITH." They date to the first quarter of the 20th century. They have original paint, worn, shot scars, one eye missing and minor wood damage.

$6,500

Guyette & Schmidt, Inc.

Elmer Crowell, East Harwich, Mass., carved this rare pair of cork-bodied Pintails early in the 20th century. Crowell's oval brand is on the underside of each, with slightly turned heads with wooden bottom board on each. They are also branded "F. WINTHROP." The drake has an inlet tail and both have raised "V" wing carving. Original paint with very minor wear and small chips in cork.

$11,000

Guyette & Schmidt, Inc.

Elmer Crowell carved this Goldeneye hen. It has an oval brand, fluted tail, original paint and a few small dents.

$7,500

Guyette & Schmidt, Inc.

Elmer Crowell's Canada Goose, made using the slat body technique common to this area, is a very large goose measuring approximately 42" from bill to tail. It has an oval stamp under the tail, original paint and is strong structurally.

$5,500-$6,000

Guyette & Schmidt, Inc.

Elmer Crowell carved a Black Duck, circa first quarter of the 20th century. It has an oval brand and near mint original paint. Provenance: Chatham Family.

$4,750

Guyette & Schmidt, Inc.

Elmer Crowell carved this Black Duck in the early part of the 20th century. It has an oval brand, slightly turned head with glass eyes, original paint with nice feathering, small touchup on tail, cracks and shot marks.

$750

Guyette & Schmidt, Inc.

A Black-bellied Plover by Elmer Crowell is dated about 1915 and branded "P.W.W." for Parker W. Wittemore of Marblehead, Mass.

$12,500

Hank and Judy Norman Collection

A Golden Plover is from the Morton rig, Nantucket, Mass., circa 1860s, and branded "W.S. Morton."

$9,500

Hank and Judy Norman Collection

An oversized (27" long) great Black-backed Gull is by an unknown Cape Cod carver, circa 1900.

$3,500

Hank and Judy Norman Collection

A Golden Plover is by the Folger family of Nantucket, Mass., circa 1870.

$12,500

Hank and Judy Norman Collection

Yellowlegs is by David Goodspeed, Duxbury, Mass., circa 1890s.

$6,500

Hank and Judy Norman Collection

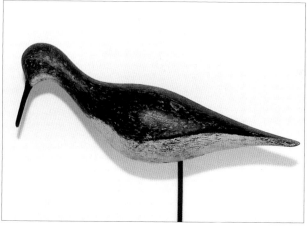

This Willet is attributed to F. P. Smith of Duxbury, Mass., circa 1890s. It features an unusual original aluminum bill. Other birds by this carver have been found on Cape Cod.

$4,250

Hank and Judy Norman Collection

A Golden Plover by Capt. William J. Wyre, Nantucket, Mass., is dated about 1885.

$3,750

Hank and Judy Norman Collection

A miniature (7" long) Least Tern is by Rick Innis of South Dennis, Mass., signed and dated 1968.

$400

Hank and Judy Norman Collection

This pair of Golden Plover is by an unknown Massachusetts carver, circa late 1800s. They feature laminated bodies.

$3,750 for the pair

Hank and Judy Norman Collection

A miniature (4" long) Mallard drake on a wood base is stamped "Fieldcraft, Inc., Boston, Mass." It was carved by Raymond Stanley for Fieldcraft, circa 1940s.

$450

Hank and Judy Norman Collection

A Canada Goose paperweight (9.5" long) is by E. Frank Adams of West Tisbury, Martha's Vineyard, Mass. Adams also carved decoys and marine vanes. The second photo shows Adams' label on the bottom.

$1,000

Hank and Judy Norman Collection.

The bottom of the Canada Goose paperweight by E. Frank Adams shows the carver's label.

Connecticut (Stratford)

The Stratford area was home for three masters of decoy making: Albert Laing (1811-1886), Benjamin Holmes (1843-1912), and Charles E. "Shang" Wheeler (1872-1949). These three represent the best of the makers in the area and their work is very representative of the typical styles and construction type normally used there. That these three men are the best of the school is a bit unusual because not one of them was a commercial maker. It is known that Shang Wheeler never sold any of his decoys and if either of the others did so, it was probably a rare occurrence. They made their decoys for themselves and friends. It is not very likely that any one of them carved more than a few hundred in his lifetime. This fairly low production probably accounts for the superb workmanship exhibited in their respective decoys.

Common to all three of them are the exaggerated upswept breasts carved to enable the decoys to float in and over ice and slush, frequently encountered in the waters of the area. In addition, each of them used a two-piece hollow body with a depression carved in the body top just behind the head. The latter is sometimes referred to as a neck notch or V groove.

Even with these common characteristics, they are fairly easily distinguished from each other. When Laing carved his birds he almost invariably carved his last name quite clearly in large letters on the bottom. Even if this brand is not present, you can tell his from Holmes' birds because Laing always made his two-piece bodies in more or less equal upper and lower halves with the joint being above the waterline. Holmes used a half-inch bottom board to close up the bottom of the hollowed out body. The best way to distinguish Wheeler decoys from the others is by being familiar with his highly sophisticated painting style. It is thought that Wheeler only produced about 500 decoys.

The majority of decoys from the Stratford area are hollow constructed with glass eyes, the exaggerated breasts, and beautiful paint jobs often using the comb-feather technique. When bottom boards were used they will generally be of 1/2" to 5/8" thickness. When the original weight is present it will usually be what is referred to as the Connecticut Pear-shaped Weight. This weight, really more like a teardrop cut in half, was attached with a brass screw so the hunter could loosen the screw allowing him to adjust the weight for balancing the floating decoy. The species most often found is the Black Duck, as it was the species hunted most often.

A Pintail was made by Shang Wheeler about 1925. This decoy has its original paint and is a superb example of Wheeler's talent as a maker. Wheeler took the extra trouble to apply his painting talent even to the bottom of the decoy. This is common to all of his decoys of puddle duck species.

Ben Holmes decoys, like most decoys of the school, were made with bottom boards. As a general rule, decoys of the school are of the two-piece hollow body variety. Early makers used glass eyes later evolving to painted eyes. They did not often use tack eyes, apparently.

Value Range FOR STRATFORD DECOYS

Benjamin Holmes: **$500-$2,000.**

Charles "Shang" Wheeler: **$1,000-$7,000**, with many sales greatly topping this range.

Roswell Bliss: **$500-$2,000** with numerous sales over **$5,000** per bird.

Albert Laing: **$1,000-$5,000** with many examples exceeding this range.

A decorative full-size standing Old Squaw hen is by Homer Lawrence of Norwalk, Conn., circa 1950s, and painted by Sally Riffe.

$3,500

Hank and Judy Norman Collection

Lou Rathmell, of Stratford, Conn., carved a Black Duck, with original paint and minor wear. Provenance: Formerly of the George Ross Starr collection and so stamped. Decoys of the Atlantic Flyway by George Ross Star pictures the exact decoy.

$6,500

Guyette & Schmidt, Inc.

Albert Laing, Stratford, Conn. (1811-1886), carved this Black Duck in the mid- to late- 19th century. This exceptional hollow-carved bird began life as a Canvasback by Albert Laing and it was then later converted to a Black Duck by Shang Wheeler also of Stratford, Conn. It is an old working repaint by Wheeler that comes from the Shelburne Museum collection and is so stamped.

$35,000-$40,000

Guyette & Schmidt, Inc.

Shang Wheeler, Stratford, Conn., carved this sleeping Black Duck, rare position, circa 1920. It has original paint on the head and neck, old repaint on body, small cracks and dents. Provenance: Formerly in the collections of Somers G. Headly and Joel Barber. *American Decorative Bird Carvings* by Ken Basile and Cynthia Doerzbach shows this exact decoy. It is also pictured in *Decoys: A North American Survey* by Gene and Linda Kangas.
$10,000
Guyette & Schmidt, Inc.

Joel Barber's Black Duck, has its original paint, but the head was reglued by Ken DeLong. Provenance: George Ross Star collection, lot 625 in Star collection sale.
$2,750
Guyette & Schmidt, Inc.

A carved Gull from Connecticut dates to the second quarter of the 20th century. It has carved extended wing tips. The inscription on the bottom reads: "FROM JOEL BARBER RIG 1948." Original paint with slight wear and tiny dents.
$5,000
Guyette & Schmidt, Inc.

A rare Shang Wheeler balsa Redhead is circa 1920s. It has original paint with comb details.
$2,000
Guyette & Schmidt, Inc.

New York State

The New York State School is more accurately the Western New York School. Although there was certainly decoy making going on throughout the state, the two areas of most note are on the western side of the state and Long Island. More specifically, this area of the western side of the state is where the St. Lawrence River flows into Lake Ontario,

called Alexandria Bay, and the St. Lawrence Islands, more commonly known as Thousand Islands, and up the river to around Ogdensburg and down the western coast toward Buffalo.

The western New York School boasted very few commercial carvers. Two who did make their living as decoy makers were Frank Lewis (born c. 1880, d.?) of Ogdensburg, and Samuel J. Denny (1874-1953). Their birds are good examples of decoys from this school.

Generally speaking, the typical characteristics of decoys from this school are flat-bottomed, solid bodies with gently low curved backs, ending in a long tail that is sometimes found pointed. Almost all are found with glass eyes. Decoys from the area of Alexandria Bay almost always have a carved horizontal V groove in the side of the head where the eyes are placed.

Up the river from Alexandria Bay in Ogdensburg, Frank Lewis carved commercially for about 10 years and his output was literally in the thousands. It is known that he stated, in one year alone, he carved more than a thousand. He started carving about 1906 and began his commercial venture in 1920. He carved Broadbills, Redheads and Whistlers, all using the same body and head, differentiating between the species with paint patterns and colors. They sport rather deeply carved concave eye grooves. The heads are inlaid into the body. The body itself exhibits a pronounced hump on the back. This unique characteristic gave rise to a descriptive term used by collectors: Ogdensburg Humpbacks.

Alexandria Bay carver Sam Denny made decoys commercially for more than 50 years and during that period probably produced more than 6,000. One characteristic of his product you can almost always count on to help in identification is the presence of a half-inch hole (pre-1918) or two half-inch holes (1918-on) in his flat-bottomed, solid body decoys, filled with dowels rather than putty. His blocks typically have exaggerated, protruding breasts similar to those of the Stratford, Conn., school. They do differ somewhat, in that the Denny birds have a sharp curve back under the head where the shelf has been carved to hold the neck. The front of the breast is flattened considerably, and almost pointed at the top. He did not use inlaid heads, but rather attached them to a carved shelf or raised neck seat. All his heads have a horizontal eye groove.

Value Range FOR NEW YORK STATE DECOYS

Sam Denny: **$250-$1,000.**   Frank Lewis: **$250-$500.**
Frank Coombs: **$300-$1,000.**   Chauncy Wheeler: **$500-$3,000** with many exceeding this range.

Carver of this Black Duck was George Stevens, Weedsport, N.Y., circa 1880s. It is in original paint with moderate wear, small cracks and dents.
$3,300
Guyette & Schmidt, Inc.

Bob Dingman, Alexandria, N.Y., created this Goldeneye hen in the first quarter of the 20th century. It has original paint with a minor touchup.
$900
Guyette & Schmidt, Inc.

This upstate New York early Goldeneye drake has a 45-degree turned head, good original paint, some chipping.

$300

Guyette & Schmidt, Inc.

A flying Snow Goose is by an unknown upstate New York carver, circa 1920s.

$12,000

Hank and Judy Norman Collection

Here is a Frank Lewis Bluebill.

$350

Long Island

The greatest number of decoys from the Long Island School are constructed of solid wood, but there are a few hollow body decoys to be found. The latter will generally be flat-bottomed and somewhat undersized. This school is where root heads and cork body birds first gained widespread popularity among makers of the Atlantic Coast. The root heads are most often found on Mergansers, Pheasants, Brants and Black Ducks. The cork body decoys are usually found made in two or more layers atop a pine bottom board.

Some general observations about wooden Long Island birds are that they are usually of solid construction with a carved shelf for the mounting of the head and there is no detail carving on the face or bill. Carved eye representation, however, is very common. They sometimes used tack eyes. It should also be mentioned that Long Island carvers sometimes used holly roots and pine knots for heads. These are more typically found on Sheldrake, Brant, and some goose decoys. The decoys are simply constructed with no wing or feather carving. They are well sanded and simply but nicely finished in paint patterns. Often they were not painted at all, but simply given an even finish by exposing them to fire. Sadly for the collector, they also were often left to lie in piles on the beach between uses. A common ballast weight for Long Island decoys is a lead weight that has been cast in sand or the hollow in a tree limb or piece of driftwood.

Value Range FOR LONG ISLAND DECOYS

Brants and Black Ducks are fairly typical of decoys from this school. Heron, Wood Duck and Old Squaw decoys from the Long Island school are particularly rare, in that order. They range in value from $750 to as high as $3,000. Good Mergansers can be valued up to about $500 and other species of decoys from the school range upwards from around $75 with most topping out at about $200. A Lloyd Johnson preening Yellowlegs sold for $3,000 in 2002.

Thomas Gelston (1851-1924): **$500-$3,000** for ducks, with shorebirds averaging often into five figures.

Frank Kellum (1865-1935): **$500-$3,000.**

Obediah Verity (c1850-c1940): **$1,500-$6,000.** The high point was a Plover selling for **$156,500** in a 2000 auction. His shorebirds are obviously in great demand.

Al Ketchum: **$1,000-$3,000.** One of his ruddy Turnstones sold for **$2,700.**

A late 1800s Long Island Canada Goose is attributed to the Verity family, Seaford area of Long Island. It shows an unusual technique of hollowing by drilling small holes into the decoy and covering with canvas.

$12,000

Guyette & Schmidt, Inc.

A late 1800s Red-breasted Merganser hen, by an unknown carver, is from Long Island or New Jersey. It has original paint.

$6,000

Guyette & Schmidt, Inc.

A late 1800s Root Head Brant is from Long Island, N.Y. It has old in-use repaint with cracks and dents.

$250

Guyette & Schmidt, Inc.

A Dowitcher (summer plumage) is by John Dilley of Quogue, Long Island, N.Y., circa 1880s.

$8,500

Hank and Judy Norman Collection

A Golden Plover is
by William Bowman,
Lawrence, Long Island,
N.Y., circa 1880.
$25,000
*Hank and Judy Norman
Collection*

A Dowitcher (winter
plumage) is by John Dilley
of Quogue, Long Island,
N.Y., circa 1890.
$7,000
*Hank and Judy Norman
Collection*

This Black-bellied Plover is from
the Delancy Nichol rig, Jamaica
Bay, Long Island, N.Y., circa
1890s.
$4,500
Hank and Judy Norman Collection

Barnegat Bay (New Jersey)

Just about all the makers of the Barnegat Bay area in New Jersey fashioned their decoys from white cedar using the two-piece hollow body method. The heads were carved from white cedar as well. It is exceedingly unusual to find a solid body decoy from this school and the makers from the Barnegat Bay School were masters of the two-piece hollow body style. The bodies they made are proportionally smaller than those from most of the other schools on the Atlantic Coast and the heads were slightly out of scale, being somewhat large for the bodies.

The heads were attached to the body on a carved shelf. The two pieces hollowed out to make the body were joined at a seam above the waterline. The decoys were very light, and for ballast the makers used pads cut from sheet lead. Most of the time these lead pad weights were attached to the bottom only after the decoy had been painted. Not all makers adhered to this practice and one notable exception was a maker named Harry V. Shourds. For ballast on his decoys, he would carve out a rectangular hole in the bottom and pour molten lead into it. He painted the decoy after this operation. Perhaps the most famous of the Barnegat Bay carvers, he is known to have been the sole contributor to his blocks from the careful selection of the wood, white pine for bodies and juniper for heads, to the final sale. His price was $6 per dozen. Imagine, 50 cents each! Nowadays it is not particularly unusual to see some of them sell in the low to mid four-figure range.

Value Range FOR BARNEGAT DECOYS

Harry V. Shourds (1871-1920): **$500-$4,000.** In 2000, one of his Gulls brought the significant price of **$200,500.** See the Shourds Yellowlegs from the Evans Collection.

Ellis Parker (circa 1940): **$200-$500.**

Jesse Birdsall (1852-1929): **$200-$500.**

Charles Birdsall: **$200-$1,000.**

Taylor Johnson (1863-1929): **$200-$400.**

Walter Bush: **$300-$1,500.**

Nathan Rowley Horner (1882-1942): **$1,000-$6,000.**

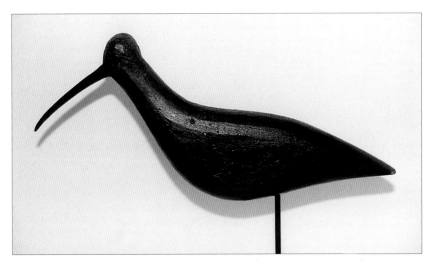

The "Flattie" Hudsonian Curlew is by an unknown New Jersey carver, circa late 1800s.
$750
Hank and Judy Norman Collection

This Hudsonian Curlew is attributed to Francis Sidney Townsend of Townsend's Inlet, Cape May, N.J., circa 1885. It is branded "F.S.T.N.J." for the carver and the state.

$13,000

Hank and Judy Norman Collection

A Harry V. Shourds Yellowlegs was made in 1910, Tuckerton, N.J. The original paint decoy was formerly in the Somers Headley Collection and now is in the Griff Evans Collection.

$4,000-$5,000

This Rhodes Truex hollow Bluebill pair, circa 1920s, Atlantic City, N. J., was repainted by Lem Ward (see Ward Brothers) in the 1970s.

$600-$800

Griff Evans Collection

Delaware River

Decoys of the Delaware River School have hardly any rivals in other schools as a group when it comes to the beauty of carving and painting. As a whole, the decoys made by the carvers of this school are considered by many, many collectors to be the most desirable from most aspects of collecting.

The method of hunting practiced in the area dictated that the decoys hunted over be made as much like the real thing as possible. The typical hunter in the area used a sculling boat to almost bushwhack the ducks. The hunter would set out his rig of decoys at known or likely feeding grounds, pull back upstream as much as three quarters of a mile, and wait for the ducks to pitch in and land. He then would very carefully and silently scull down to within killing range and fire away. Because of this method, the Delaware River decoy not only had to be good enough to decoy the birds down, but to still fool them once they had landed among the decoys. The latter requirement was to give the waiting hunter time to scull back down to his prey.

The decoys had to be extremely realistic in both carving confirmation and paint pattern. Most of them have heads squat down on the body with little or no neck showing. This conveyed an attitude to the live birds above of content ducks that sense no danger.

The decoys are full breasted and constructed in the two-piece hollow manner; few bottom board types were made. Heads are mounted directly to the body in the low head or sleeping position. They usually had glass eyes although the other types have been found. A very significant characteristic common to them is extremely well carved tails and wings. As a rule the paint patterns were extraordinarily realistic and often quite intricate.

As you go downstream on the river, you find that the makers paid less and less attention to the carving of wings and tails. But they did continue to pay close attention to the need for painting their decoys in the same realistic and characteristic pattern style.

John Dawson decoys are a bit different from his contemporaries in his paint patterns. An accomplished landscape artist, well known in his time, he apparently applied his knowledge of paint manipulation to his decoys. He would generally block out the main areas of color pattern and then go back and very meticulously render feathers and other characteristics with hundreds of tiny brush strokes.

Value Range FOR DELAWARE DECOYS

John Dawson (1889-1959): **$500-$4,000.**
Dan English (1883-1962): **$500-$5,000.**
John McLaughlin (b. 1911): **$500-$2,500.**

Some other makers of the Delaware River school are William Quinn (1915-1969) of Yardley, Pa., Charles Allen (b. 1893) of Bordentown, N.J., George D. Runyan, also of Bordentown, John Baker (b. 1916) of Edgely, Pa., and Jess Heisler (1891-1943) of Burlington, N.J.

A "Blair School" Bluebill Drake, hollow carved, dates to the late 1800s. Body halves are joined by four small dowels. There are repairs and touchups to paint but mostly original paint.
$1,700
Guyette & Schmidt, Inc.

Rich Anderson, Yardley, Pa., carved this oversized Mallard drake with William Quinn. It has traditional "V" wing carving.

$1,800

Guyette & Schmidt, Inc.

A sleeping Bluebill pair was made by Howard Bacon, Delanco, N.J., circa second quarter of the 20th century, with raised "V" wing carving.

$2,000

Guyette & Schmidt, Inc.

A "Blair School" Pintail hen dates to the first quarter of the 20th century. In original paint, it is worn, with a repaired neck crack and tail chip.

$400

Guyette & Schmidt, Inc.

A Delaware River Bluewing Teal hen is circa first quarter of the 20th century. It has raised wing tips and original paint.

$1,000

Guyette & Schmidt, Inc.

Larry McLaughlin, Bordentown, N.J., created this Bluebill drake. Dating from the early 20th century, it has original paint and minor wear.

$750

Guyette & Schmidt, Inc.

A rare and early Delaware River Pintail drake dates to the last quarter of the 19th century to early 20th century. By an unknown maker, it has hollow carving, "V" primaries and inserted hardwood tail, similar to work by John English. It has original paint with very minor touchup.

$27,500

Guyette & Schmidt, Inc.

John Blair Sr., of Philadelphia, created this swimming Black Duck in the last quarter of the 19th century. It has original paint and a small crack in the tail.

$6,250

Guyette & Schmidt, Inc.

A Mallard drake by John McLaughlin, Bordentown, N.J., is signed and original, with excellent condition and details.

$1,200

Guyette & Schmidt, Inc.

Susquehanna Flats

Of all the areas of the Chesapeake Bay, the Susquehanna Flats could be considered the one where market gunners and their sink boxes reigned supreme before the 1918 migratory bird legislation. These market hunters often used several hundred decoys in their rigs; consequently there were literally thousands of decoys made in the region. Although there are still many found, the huge numbers made are not evidenced by huge numbers surviving today.

The types of decoys made in the Susquehanna Flats school share similar basic construction techniques and decoy style. The difference between these decoys and those used in other schools of the Chesapeake can also be told by observing the species of wildfowl hunted. For example, the majority of decoys from the Susquehanna Flats are Canvasbacks, Redheads, and Broadbills. Farther down the bay the primary targets were puddle ducks such as Teal and Mallards. Keep in mind the enormous size of the bay; there can be a 300-

mile separation between schools of carvers on the Chesapeake.

The decoys of the Flats area are generally solid pine or cedar bodied with shelf carving for the nail-attached head. One exception to this is found on decoys by some makers from Havre de Grace. Earliest decoys had very good carving delineation between the face and bill, carved mandibles and necks, and forged iron keels or ballast weights. Later, when lead became more readily available, the weights were cast by pouring the molten lead into depressions in sand (sand cast) or natural or gouged out depressions in wood. Less attention was paid to detailed face and bill carving, but the overall conformation remained relatively unchanged.

Just about all decoys from this school have round bottoms and are broad-breasted. Many marsh duck decoys are found with a slight ridge down the back. Anchor line ties on earlier Flats decoys are usually of the leather thong type. But after around

1900-1920, the ring and staple type came into and remained in constant use all over the Chesapeake Bay.

John "Daddy" Holly of Havre de Grace, Md., is one of the most famous makers associated with the Susquehanna Flats. Holly had three sons: James T. (1855-1935), William (1845-1923), and John Jr. (1852-1927). James apparently operated independently of his father and brothers as a decoy maker. He was a craftsman who built fine boats primarily, but his decoys are also sought after. He is known most for the slim and sleek Black Duck decoys he fashioned, but he is known to have carved other species. He is thought to be one of the first to bring the scratch paint method to the Flats carvers.

His father, John "Daddy" Holly, carved and painted in several different styles over the years. He is, however, thought to have established the Havre de Grace style, with upswept tails and no neck shelf on diving and marsh ducks. Upon his death in 1892, his two other sons, William and John Jr., undertook to continue the decoy-making operation. They followed their father's patterns and style and this sometimes leads to confusion among collectors. Whatever the case, any decoy made by the Hollys is desirable.

There are two distinct styles to be found in the Susquehanna Flats School. The first is the Havre de Grace style. The other one, thought to have been founded by John B. Graham of Charlestown, is known as the Cecil County or Northeast River style. These decoys feature shelf carving for the head/neck and a straight tail protruding from the middle of the rear of the body.

Ben Dye of Perryville, Md., is one of the most respected carvers of the Cecil County style of the Flats. His heads were of exceptional quality with finely carved mandible, nails, ridges, and nostrils on the bills. His decoys tended to be smallish compared to the real thing. The tails tended to be of the small flat paddle type. His earliest blocks were decidedly flattened and the later ones are found quite rounded.

Samuel T. Barnes of Havre de Grace is as well known a name of the school as any. The one characteristic most easily used in beginning to identify a Barnes decoy is his curious flattening of the head from the face down the crown and onto the bill itself. His decoys otherwise exhibit the typical Flats characteristic in the Havre de Grace style. He is also known to be one of the earliest makers of cork-body decoys. They had pine heads and bottom boards.

R. Madison Mitchell began making decoys in 1924 by helping Sam Barnes in his shop. When Barnes died, Mitchell stayed on to finish unfilled orders. He apparently became more interested than just finishing up the orders, for he continued making decoys for more than 50 years! Although he hand fashioned them as Barnes had for five or six years, in 1931 he had begun to turn out bodies on a lathe after having rough cut them from cedar blocks. He then reverted to hand techniques with spoke shave, sandpaper, etc. The decoys were hand painted in high quality finishes. He added cast lead ballast weights after painting. The final touch was a staple and ring line tie.

The tradition continues today with Mitchell's students producing fine decorative ducks as well. Shown is a beautiful pair of Pintails in about one-half size that was made by Clarence F. Bauer in 1979, following in the training of Mitchell and the Havre de Grace tradition. Bauer watched Jim Currier make decoys in his shop and worked for Madison Mitchell for a number of years. The Pintails are in original paint and have Bauer's signature and date on the bottom of each. The drake measures about 12" and the hen 9.5" in length. They are about 4" tall at the head. A close look may show the dowel attaching the head where the paint is a little raised (see page 64).

Value Range FOR SUSQUEHANNA FLATS DECOYS

John "Daddy" Holly (1818-1892): **$500-$8,000.**
His goose decoys would be valued up to **$20,000.**
Ben Dye (1821-1896): **$150-$500.**
Joe Dye (circa 1910): **$2,000-$2,500.**

R. Madison Mitchell (b. 1901): **$150-$500** range
for Ducks, with Swans bringing **$1,000-$5,000.**
Sam Barnes (1847-1926): **$200-$600.**
John B. Graham (1822-1912): **$200-$600.**

John "Daddy" Holly, Havre de Grace, Md., carved this
Bluebill drake in the last quarter of the 19th century. It is
branded "BROWN BROS," old in-use repaint, with cracks
and scars.

$700

Guyette & Schmidt, Inc.

Madison Mitchell of Havre de Grace made this
pair of Widgeons. It is in good original paint.

$650

Guyette & Schmidt, Inc.

A Wood Duck pair by Madison Mitchell is signed and
dated 1983. They are all original.

$3,250

Guyette & Schmidt, Inc.

John Holly, Havre de Grace, Md., carved this Bluebill
drake. It is branded "H. E. & S." twice in the underside,
with old repaint and small body cracks.

$600

Guyette & Schmidt, Inc.

An R. Madison Mitchell Chesapeake style (high-neck) Bluebill drake, painted eye, is dated in the 1950s.

$500

Former Pitt Collection, Ducks Unlimited, Inc.

Captain Ben Dye, Cecil County, Maryland, made this Canvasback drake in the last quarter of the 19th century. It is branded "J. SLOAN," has old repaint, cracks in the neck and a rough tail.

$450

Guyette & Schmidt, Inc.

Joe Dye, Havre de Grace, Md., made this Bluebill drake. It is a rare early 20th century decoy in old repaint with small cracks and repairs.

$450

Guyette & Schmidt, Inc.

Clarence Bauer Pintails were carved in 1979 at Havre de Grace. **$400**

 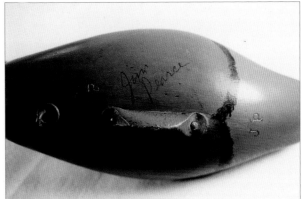

The R. Madison Mitchell Green-wing Teal drake is a one-nail version, late 1940s or early 1950s, owned by Jim Pearce, branded PP hunt club. In the second photo, the bottom shows the one nail and Pearce's label.

$500

Pitt Collection

Three photos show an R. Madison Mitchell Bufflehead drake with original keel that dates from the late 1940s or early 1950s. Details in the photos show it can be dated by the one nail both fore and aft as opposed to two nails found on later models.

$400

Pitt Collection

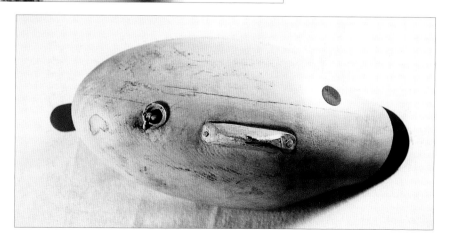

A James T. Holly Redhead drake, circa 1890, is in original paint, Havre de Grace, branded "G. B. G." and "D. G. Elliot."
$5,000-$6,000
Griff Evans Collection

Brands on the bottom of the "Daddy" Holly Redhead identify the maker.

This R. Madison Mitchell Widgeon drake is circa 1950s.
$350-$400
Pitt Collection

A James T. Holly Black Duck, circa 1900, Havre de Grace, is in original paint.
$6,000-$7,000
Griff Evans Collection

A Joe Dye Bluebill drake, Havre de Grace, made in 1910 is in original paint.
$2,000-$2,500
Griff Evans Collection

This Charles N. Barnard Canvasback drake, circa 1930s, Havre de Grace, is from the Gabler Rig in original paint. Note the extremely detailed and raised bill, typical of many Havre de Grace carvers.
$2,500-$3,000
Griff Evans Collection

A Charlie Bryan Coot, made in 1959, was one of 12 made for his son in Middle River, Md., in original paint.
$400-$500
Griff Evans Collection

Capt. John Smith's preening Black Duck in original paint, circa 1940s, is from Ocean City, Md.
$800-$1,200
Griff Evans Collection

John Glenn's Black Duck, made in 1946 in Rock Hall, Md., is in original paint.
$600-$800
Griff Evans Collection

A rare Richard Tilghman Goldeneye hen sink box decoy was made of iron in the 1920s in Talbot County, Md., and is in original paint.
$3,000-$4,000
Griff Evans Collection

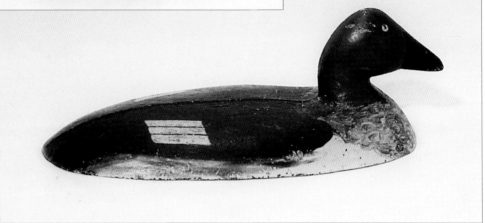

Richard Tilghman's Goldeneye pair made circa 1920s in original paint, is from Talbot County, Md.
$8,000-$9,000
Griff Evans Collection

Maryland Eastern Shore (Dorchester County)

A few examples from this school of makers are shown. In addition, there was a commercial decoy maker of note from Cambridge, Md., whose birds are well worth pursuit. Ed Phillips sold most of his decoys to hometown people and for a few gunning rigs. His decoys have not achieved the prominence of some other decoys of the Chesapeake Bay area because he did not produce them in nearly the numbers some of the other good carvers of the region produced. They are, however, excellent decoys.

The decoys are not quite so rounded on the bottom as others of the region, but are semi-rounded (not completely rounded nor completely flat-bottomed, similar to a Mason). The bodies are quite graceful and the necks usually exhibit a backward arch.

Almost all have carved eye representation and are very well made and painted. Phillips frequently used the scratch feather painting technique.

All of his decoys have a sheet lead ballast weight on the bottom and an anchor line tie made of sheet copper bent into a loop and attached with a copper nail, if the original is present. The bodies are solid as is characteristic of Chesapeake Bay area decoys. A dowel rod attaches the necks. He made Canvasbacks, Pintails, Widgeon, Black Ducks, Redheads and Canada geese.

A more recent carver in this region is Eddie Wozny and one of his Plover decoys is shown in the color section of the book, along with some other Phillips decoys. Other carvers of note include "Gunner" Al Meekins and Slater Robinson.

Value Range FOR MARYLAND EASTERN SHORE DECOYS

Value Ranges for Maryland Eastern Shore Decoys
"Gunner" Al Meekins (circa 1950s): **$500-$1,000.**

Ed Phillips (circa 1930s): **$700-$4,000.**
Slater Robinson (circa 1880s-1900): **$700-$2,750.**

An Ed Phillips Bluebill drake in original paint is circa 1930s, Cambridge, Md.
$2,000-$2,500
Griff Evans Collection

An Ed Phillips Black Duck in original paint is circa 1930s.

$3,000-$3,500

Griff Evans Collection

A Slater Robinson Bluebill is circa 1880-1900, from Dorchester County, Md.

$1,500-$2,200

Gary Campbell Collection

"Gunner" Al Meekins carved this Red-breasted Merganser drake, circa 1950s, in Dorchester County, Md.

$500-$800

Gary Campbell Collection

Capt. Ed Phillips (1901-1964), Cambridge, Md., made this Pintail drake, circa first quarter of the 20th century. This rare decoy with lifted head and an extended tail sprig is in original paint with minor wear; underside of the body has a small old touchup.

$10,500

Guyette & Schmidt, Inc.

The hen mate to the drake pictured on page 70, these birds are often called "Fence Post Pheasants" by collectors.

$500-$800

Gary Campbell Collection

A Capt. Ed Phillips Canada Goose, from the same era, has original paint some old in-use repaint on white areas, small cracks and a chip in the tail.

$2,950

Guyette & Schmidt, Inc.

A Capt. Ed Phillips Canada Goose is in the original "tiger stripe" paint style. There are thin cracks and one larger filled crack on the bottom.

$2,900

Guyette & Schmidt, Inc.

This Black Duck by Capt. Ed Phillips dates to the first quarter of the 20th century. It is rare, with original paint, small cracks, dents and scratches.
$900
Guyette & Schmidt, Inc.

A Capt. Ed Phillips Hollow Bluebill drake, from the early 20th century is in excellent original condition with only minor issues. Provenance: Somers G. Headly collection and so stamped.
$2,350
Guyette & Schmidt, Inc.

A Capt. Ed Phillips Redhead drake, from the same era, has original paint with only small cracks.
$1,600
Guyette & Schmidt, Inc.

Alvin "Gunner" Meekins, Hooper's Island, Md., carved this Merganser pair. They are in original paint with small cracks and minor wear.
$550
Guyette & Schmidt, Inc.

Crisfield (Maryland)

Just about all decoys from this school of carvers exhibit the same construction details. They are solid body decoys typical of the Chesapeake Bay birds, but here is where the first appearance of the true flat-bottomed decoy occurs in the bay. Typically Crisfield decoys are slightly oversize, narrow breasted, wide in the hip area, and flat-bottomed with a tail usually coming out of the top of the body as opposed to below, toward or at the middle of the rear end. The decoys were weighted with just about anything that might be handy to the maker at the time, so it is not a reliable characteristic.

The beginning of the fine decoys of the Crisfield School are thought to be found in the Sterling family and perhaps Elwood Dize products. The most famous of the school are the Ward brothers, Lemuel T. Ward Jr. (1896-1984) and Stephen Ward (1895-1976). Their father, Lemuel T. Ward, was a barber, but also a decoy maker, a waterman and a boat builder. Lem and Steve followed in their father's footsteps, also becoming barbers and decoy makers.

Lem Sr. died in 1926 and not long after that came very hard economic times for the nation: the Depression. After the outlawing of market gunning in 1918, it is likely that the hard times of the Depression increased demand for decoys to help individuals provide for their own meat through hunting, especially in the waterfowl rich Crisfield region. It is estimated that the Ward brothers produced as many as 10,000 decoys in the 50 years they were actively producing decoys.

The Ward brothers took the carving and painting techniques of their father and the other early Crisfield makers and refined them to a high art. Collectors recognize the Ward brothers today as the most deserving of note of all the Maryland makers. The carving and painting used on their working decoys was as good as much of the delicate work found on today's contemporary carvings. They are painted so beautifully that people began buying them, not for hunting over, but for use as decorative objects in the home.

It is known that Steve lamented the constant interruptions by those seeking their blocks, but that Lem became more and more interested in them as an art. Whatever the case, when demand for good hand-made stools waned in the 1950s, the Wards went into the making of decorative decoys in earnest and did not slow down until the early 1970s.

Other makers of note from the Crisfield School are Lloyd Tyler (1898-1971) and the Tyler family, Noah B. Sterling, Will Sterling, and Elwood Dize.

Value Range FOR CRISFIELD DECOYS

Ward Brothers: **$3,000-$76,750.** Two exceptional pairs brought **$15,000** and **$14,500** respectively. In 2000, a pair of Bluebills sold at auction for **$28,600**, a Pintail for **$27,500**, a Green-wing Teal for **$10,725** and a pair of Green-wing Teal for **$9,075**. At another 2000 auction, Ward brothers decoys hit a high of **$76,750** for a Pintail, **$74,250** for another Pintail, **$71,250** for a Goldeneye and **$43,000** for a pair of Canvasbacks. It appears current ranges at **$3,000** to **$6,000** for average birds would be accurate.

Sterling Family: **$500-$3,000 plus.**

Lloyd Tyler: **$500-$4,000 plus.**

Decoys have brought far in excess of these figures from time to time but the ranges are the norm for an average shape-working decoy. See specific values also given with the photos.

Lloyd Tyler, Crisfield, Md., created this Canvasback drake, signed at a later date by Tyler. It has original paint with minor wear, a chip missing from underside of the bill.
$350
Guyette & Schmidt, Inc.

An unknown Crisfield area Pintail drake, from the first or second quarter of the 20th century, is similar to the work of the Sterling Family of Crisfield, with old repaint and cracking.
$200
Guyette & Schmidt, Inc.

Lloyd Tyler, Crisfield, Md., made this Black Duck. It is in original paint with minor flaking and wear, repair to top of the head, small cracks.

$400

Guyette & Schmidt, Inc.

A Ward Brothers preening American Widgeon drake is circa 1960.

$20,000

Pitt Collection

This is a Ward Brothers Nuptial plumage Blue-wing Teal drake from 1967.

$4,000

Pitt Collection

The bottom of the Blue-wing Teal decoy shows the Ward signature and the 1967 date.

A Ward Brothers preening deluxe grade North American Pintail drake is from 1963.
$10,000
Pitt Collection

A Ward Brothers deluxe grade greater Scaup drake has no date but is found in the Ward Brothers book.
$8,000
Pitt Collection

The bottom of the Scaup decoy shows the Ward Brothers pedigree and details about the deluxe grade decoy.

A Ward Brothers Atlantic Brant was painted by Lem and carved by Steve in 1967.

$4,000

Pitt Collection

A closeup shows the head of the Atlantic Brant, made by the Ward Brothers.

A Lloyd Sterling Pintail drake in original paint is circa 1920, from Crisfield, Md.

$12,000-$14,000

Griff Evans Collection

A very rare summer plumage Old Squaw drake was the very last one of these made by the Ward Brothers in 1977.

$25,000-$30,000

Pitt Collection

Value Range FOR CRISFIELD DECOYS

A Ward Brothers Green-wing Teal drake, made in 1936, is in original paint.

16,000-$18,000

Griff Evans Collection

A Ward Brothers decorative standing Green-wing Teal made in 1953 was exhibited at the William Penn Memorial Museum in 1967.

$7,500

Griff Evans Collection

This Ward Brothers Canvasback pair, made in 1957 in original paint, is from the former collection of Norris Pratt.

$8,500-$10,500 for the pair

Griff Evans Collection

A Lloyd Tyler Canada Goose was made in Crisfield, Md., circa 1920s-30s.

$2,500-$3,500

Gary Campbell Collection

Virginia Eastern Shore

The majority of decoys from this region are of the solid-body, round bottom type with the remaining minority being hollow. There is quite a variety within this school; therefore the best way to familiarize you with its decoys is to discuss a selected group of representative makers.

Ira Hudson (1876-1949) of Chincoteague, Va., was the most prolific maker in the region. It is estimated that he produced more than 20,000 decoys in his decoy-making days. Hudson made a number of different types, both solid and hollow-bodied. He was a commercial decoy maker and the type, style, and sophistication of his products was largely dependent upon what his customers could afford. They ranged from very simply made and painted decoys to two- and three-piece hollow-bodied decoys with much detailed carving, but the majority are solid-body. His choice of wood was white pine, but Hudson decoys have been found in cedar, cypress, balsa, and cottonwood. Eyes were generally tack eyes or painted. He seldom utilized glass eyes. He often used the scratch feather painting technique. Carved neck notches or thumbprint carving are sometimes found on the back behind the neck.

In all the variations in type of decoy, his painting technique and style remained constant. After handling and studying several, the collector should be able to readily recognize it.

The usual method Hudson used to attach head to body was to place the neck down into a carved out hollow, although he used other methods such as the neck shelf carving. Hudson is also noted for using unusual head positions. Not always, but much of the time, he accomplished this by carving the heads from driftwood or roots.

Dave "Umbrella" Watson (d. 1938) was a commercial maker from Chincoteague, Va., whose style was a blend of Eastern Shore Virginia and New Jersey construction and styles. They were easily distinguished from the New Jersey decoys by the presence of delicate raised wing and tail carving detail. The Watson decoy is usually of the two-piece hollow body construction. A reasonable estimate of each would be 90 percent hollow and 10 percent solid body. The decoys were well sanded before painting. The painting was always well done and all his birds sport glass eyes placed in a carved eye groove. Most are carved from white cedar in two halves joined above the waterline.

Miles Hancock's (1888-1974) decoys were all solid body, constructed with flat bottoms. Most of his decoys were carved from cottonwood, a soft, easy to carve wood. He first roughed the shape out, then did his finishing with pieces of broken glass. He never sanded them before painting and his painting technique was not very refined. The result of this is rough but surprisingly effective overall. He supposedly never used glass eyes, sticking to tack eyes exclusively. There have been a few to show up with glass eyes, but these may have been later replacements by the users.

Charles Birch (1867-1956) of Willis Wharf, Va., made decoys that were quite similar to New Jersey decoys in general overall look. His decoys were the two-piece hollow body mostly, with a few solid decoys that still had the appearance of being hollow-bodied. There are two significant variances from the New Jersey decoys that make them easily identifiable as Birch products. All of his decoys will have a definite flat spot on the top of the body about three-fourths of the length back from the breast toward the tail. Another distinctive detail is the use of a reinforcing wooden dowel peg inserted from the bottom and visible from there. Birch always used a shelf carving to receive the head, nailed on pad weights, and his geese and swans had inlayed oak or hickory bills. The latter were inserted fully through the head and tightened in the back of the head by driving a spline into a split at that end of the bill piece.

Value Range FOR EASTERN SHORE VIRGINIA DECOYS

Ira Hudson: **$500-$3,000.** A fair number exceed this, but rarely exceed five figures.

Dave "Umbrella" Watson: **$500-$2,500.**

Doug Jester: **$300-$4,000.**

Charles Birch: **$400-$1,200.** Brant and goose decoys will frequently sell in excess of **$5,000** with the rare Swans bringing extraordinary prices at auction.

Miles Hancock: **$200-$2,000.**

A Miles Hancock Black Duck, circa 1940s-50s, from Chincoteague Island, Va., is a thick body model. **$900-$1,200**
Gary Campbell Collection

An Ira Hudson Brant has hollow construction and deep body design, circa 1920s-30s, Chincoteague Island, Va. **$2,500-$4,000**
Gary Campbell Collection

A Doug Jester Black Duck, circa 1930s-40s, is a very fat body model from Chincoteague Island, Va.
$1,800-$2,500
Gary Campbell Collection

A Canada Goose is attributed to Southey Bull, Northampton County, Eastern Shore, Virginia, circa 1900. Hollowed from top with thin board then applied, the head is two-piece construction, old working repaint with some cracks and chips. Provenance: consigned by Alma Fitchett, Northampton County. Fleckenstein shows the exact decoy in Southern Decoys.
$8,000
Guyette & Schmidt, Inc.

Ira Hudson, Chincoteague, Va., carved this hollow Brant. It has three-piece construction, original paint. Provenance: Used at Smith Island Gun Club, Eastern Shore, Va.
$8,750
Guyette & Schmidt, Inc.

An Ira Hudson Goldeneye drake is a very early bird. It is an old working repaint with some original paint still showing, small cracks and shot marks.
$2,250
Guyette & Schmidt, Inc.

An unknown maker carved this Canada Goose, Eastern Shore of Virginia, circa 1900. It has carved shoulders, old working repaint worn in places, checks on wood.
$150
Guyette & Schmidt, Inc.

A balsa Brant decoy, Elkins Hunt Club, is in original paint. It was featured in Southern Decoys.
$150
Guyette & Schmidt, Inc.

Dave Watson, Chincoteague, Va., carved a Pintail hen. It has worn old paint and numerous dents.

$400

Guyette & Schmidt, Inc.

Doug Jester, Chincoteague, Va., carved this Black Duck, circa second quarter of the 20th century. It appears to be all original with small dents.

$400

Guyette & Schmidt, Inc.

Miles Hancock, Chincoteague, Va., made this Bufflehead drake. It has worn old paint and small dents and cracks.

$250

Guyette & Schmidt, Inc.

Cigar Daisey, Chincoteague, Va., made this Brant decoy. Signed and dated 1960, it is a working decoy with original paint, cracks underside, some roughness on tail.

$600

Guyette & Schmidt, Inc.

Ira Hudson, Chincoteague, Va., carved this Black Duck, circa second quarter of the 20th century. There has been professional restoration work on this decoy.

$225

Guyette & Schmidt, Inc.

Charles Birch, Willis Wharf, Va., created this Canvasback drake, circa first quarter of the 20th century. It has hollow carving, old repaint, a crack in the neck, small cracks and dents in body.

$600

Guyette & Schmidt, Inc.

Cobb Island

Cobb Island, off the Eastern Shore of Virginia, is now uninhabited but was the home of the famous Cobb family of carvers. Nathan Cobb and his family settled on the island in 1833 as the result of a shipwreck. The family had sailed south from New England and, whatever their original destination, the island (subsequently named after them) became their home. They became market gunners, hunting guides, ship salvagers and, of necessity, decoy carvers. The decoys they made were unlike those of other Eastern Shore Virginia makers. They apparently adhered to the methods that were common to the area of their former home. Their decoys are much like those of Massachusetts.

Many of the Cobb Island decoys are found with the initial N or E and an occasional A carved on the bottom. The initials are of Nathan Jr., Elkenah, and Albert or Arthur.

Generally the decoys were made slightly oversize. They are two-piece hollow body mostly, but some were solid body. The ballast weights were sheet or flattened lead and always attached with brass screws. The head and neck are inlayed into the hollow body. It is significant to note that inletting into hollow bodies is unusual. Frequently this inlayed head and neck includes a portion of the breast as well. The bills on the greater proportion of the Cobb family's larger species of birds are inlayed into the head. Made of hardwood, they extend all the way through the head and are splined at the back of the head. You may note that Charles Birch of the Virginia Eastern Shore practiced this, but he was a later maker and probably emulated the Cobbs.

The Cobb birds are particularly noted for the many different lifelike attitudes of heads, with each decoy being different. This was accomplished by their extensive use of roots or driftwood to fashion the heads. The decoys are usually flat bottomed but some are found with round bottoms.

The Cobbs established quite an active hunting lodge on the island and catered to many, many hunters during their tenure on the island. The family and some employees were involved in decoy making, but apparently Nathan Cobb Jr. was the master. He was able to capture the very essence of a live bird with only the slightest carving gesture. His decoys were not in and of themselves perfect anatomical replicas of the birds; but they possessed a spark of life seldom captured by other carvers. Each of his birds was different. Nathan was able to use this to an exquisite degree. He did not so much carve individual birds as he created rigs. His individual birds, when used together, gave the impression of a flock of live birds rather than a bunch of decoys.

Split wing/tail carving is common to their birds, as is the use of glass eyes. There are, however, a goodly number with no eye representation at all. Painting was lifelike and effective but lacked sophisticated detailing.

Value Range FOR COBB DECOYS

There have been some extraordinarily high prices realized at auction, but most average decoys from the Cobb family would be valued between **$500** and **$5,00.** Decoys by Nathan Cobb bring considerably more on the average. His generally run between **$4,000** and **$10,000,** with some exceeding this considerably. A Nathan Cobb Brant brought **$101,500** at a 2000 auction.

Nathan Cobb, Jr., (1826-1905) Cobb Island, Va., carved this Black Duck, circa third quarter of the 19th century. It is hollow carved, with inlet head, carved eyes and "V" tail carving, from Elkenah Cobb's hunting rig. There is paint removed and "E" carved on bottom.

$11,500
Guyette & Schmidt, Inc.

Nathan Cobb, Jr., Cobb Island, created this Brant decoy, circa last quarter 19th century. It is hollow bodied construction, old working repaint, with "N" carved under tail, original hardwood inserted bill and split tail. Southern Decoys shows rig-mates to this bird.

$18,000
Guyette & Schmidt, Inc.

This Brant is attributed to Nathan Cobb, Jr., circa last quarter of the 19th century. It has solid body technique, black glass eyes, original inserted hardwood bill, old working repaint. Provenance: consigned by Alma Fitchett of Northampton County and found with the rig at Smith Gun Club. Southern Decoys shows the exact decoy.

$16,000
Guyette & Schmidt, Inc.

Elkanah Cobb made this Brant decoy in the last quarter of the 19th century. It is a hollow version, branded "E. B. COBB" on the underside. An old working repaint, the head is not original to this body.

$900
Guyette & Schmidt, Inc.

North Carolina

This school of carvers also includes a portion of Virginia just north of the state line called Back Bay. The decoys of the Back Bay area and those of coastal North Carolina are indistinguishable for the most part.

The North Carolina School is particularly noted for its slightly oversize Ruddy Ducks. Many have called them crude, but the overall appearance of most examples is pleasing. The most striking feature of the decoys is their very nicely shaped heads. None are finely finished but still they are effective. Eyes are usually not present or simply painted on.

Most makers concentrated on solid body, round or semi-V bottom decoys. One exception is the decoys of Ned Burgess who made his birds with flat bottoms.

There were also wire frame Geese and Swans made in the region. Although they do appear to be very nice decoys, they would have to be considered somewhat crude if compared to ones made by Massachusetts maker Joe Lincoln.

A significant characteristic common to most North Carolina decoys is the type of anchor line tie used. If you glance at the decoys in the accompanying photographs, you will note most of them have a prominent nail protruding from the lower portion of the breast. Less obvious is the actual line tie somewhat below and behind. The purpose of the breast nail is to provide a means of lengthening or shortening the anchor line. This was necessary because of the large tide fluctuations in the area. The hunter could choose his length by using a half hitch to the nail and letting the extra line simply hang beneath the decoy. A ballast weight that was often used in the Back Bay and upper North Carolina areas is shown on one decoy.

Some carvers of note from this school are: Lem (1861-1932) and Lee (1861-1942) Dudley, twins from Knots Island, N.C.; John Williams (1857-1937), Cedar Island, Va.; Ned Burgess (1863-1956), Church's Island, Va.; Mitchell Fulcher, Stacy, N.C., and Alvira Wright, town of Duck, Knots Island, N.C.

Value Range FOR NORTH CAROLINA DECOYS

Lem and Lee Dudley: **$2,000-$10,000.**
Ned Burgess: **$500-$1,500.**
John Williams: **$3,000-$6,000.**

Alvira Wright: **$4,000-$10,000**, some much higher.
Mitchell Fulcher: **$2,000-$10,000.**

Ned Burgess, Churches Island, N.C., carved this Mallard hen. It is very rare, created in the early 20th century. It has original paint and a small dent in back. It is featured in *Southern Decoys*.

$21,000

Guyette & Schmidt, Inc.

A North Carolina Teal has an inlet head with "K" carved under the bill. It is old in-use repaint, with repair to a neck crack.

$175

Guyette & Schmidt, Inc.

A North Carolina Canvasback drake may have been carved by Robert Morse. It is oversized in old repaint with small dents and flaking to wood in places.

$400

Guyette & Schmidt, Inc.

A pair of typical North Carolina Canvas over Wire Pintails are by an unknown maker. They have old repaint and are structurally sound.
$400
Guyette & Schmidt, Inc.

An unknown Swan from the Currituck area of North Carolina has old repaint and repair to the bill, but is structurally sound.
$400
Guyette & Schmidt, Inc.

South Carolina

Up to now books and periodicals have not paid much attention to decoys from South Carolina. This omission is understandable when you consider how few documented South Carolina decoys have been found and added to private collections. On the other hand, it is difficult to understand once you see the ones that have so far been uncovered, for they are striking in beauty, style, and size.

The origin of these decoys is still a bit hazy, but so far research in the area indicates that a family from around Georgetown, S.C., named Cains is responsible for some of them. There were at least two Cains brothers, Hucks and Saynay Cains, and possibly a third, Ball, who produced the decoys. One of them is known to have worked for Bernard Baruch on his plantation, Hobcaw Barony. Indeed some decoys attributed to the Cains brothers bear Baruch's brand BMB.

The most handsome of these decoys have an unmistakable style about them. The head and neck of the Mallards are gracefully carved in what is described as a snaky neck or swan neck (also seen in the Mason factory decoys on some models) with elongated bills and carved eyes. The head and neck are carved from one piece of wood and the body is of solid one-piece construction. Usually made of Tupelo gum or cypress, they have raised wing carving and, if you view just about any of them from above, you will note a distinctive heart shape formed by the wing carving.

Some of the decoys, particularly Black Ducks, are hollow bodied and often have glass eyes. It should be noted that it appears some of the Mallard decoys have been repainted as Black Ducks, and vice versa.

Value Range FOR SOUTH CAROLINA DECOYS

Once you have had the opportunity to personally examine these particular South Carolina decoys you will have no problem knowing that they are valuable. Collector value range is **$3,000** to **$10,000** with a few going much higher at auctions. A Hucks Cains Mallard sold for **$189,500** in 2000.

The Caines Brothers, Georgetown, S.C., made this very rare Mallard drake, circa turn of the 19th to 20th century. Carved with a peg placed to support a fragile bill, it has raised wings, tack eyes, working second coat of paint believed to have also been done by the Caines, and slight damage to the bill.

$35,000

Guyette & Schmidt, Inc.

Louisiana

Commercial makers produced thousands upon thousands of decoys, running the gamut from crude chunks of wood and decoys painted as if for a carnival midway to superb highly detailed and beautifully painted birds. It seems that everybody and his brother were making decoys. Louisiana makers probably produced a wider variety of species of wildfowl decoys than any other single region in the United States. It is therefore next to impossible to provide the collector with anything more than the broadest generalizations in describing any common characteristics for Louisiana decoys.

A few of the better known makers are: Victor Alfonso, Adam Ansardi, Xavier Bourg of Larose; Marc Alcide Comardelle, Jack and Robert Couret, William Duet, Gaston Isadore, Dewey Pertuit, Remie Ange Roussel, Jr., Nick Trahan, Nicole Vidacovitch of Sunshine; Clovis "Cadis" Vizier, Mark Whipple of Bourg; and the products of the loose partnership of three men who worked cooperatively: Charles Joefrau, Mitchel LaFrance, and George Frederick.

Value Range FOR LOUISIANA DECOYS

Xavier Bourg: **$300-$1,500.**

Marc Alcide Comardelle: **$1,000-$3,000.**

Jack and Robert Couret: **$1,500** for a Mallard hen in 2002.

Charles Joefrau: **$4,750** for a Mallard hen in 2002.

Dewey Pertuit: **$100-$300.**

Remie Ange Roussel Jr.: **$500-$1,000.**

Nicole Vidacovitch: **$400-$4,000.**

Clovis "Cadis" Vizier: **$500-$3,000.**

Marc Whipple: **$300-$4,000.**

Xavier Bourg, Bayou LaFourche, La., made this Pintail hen. It has relief wing carving, original paint with a tiny chip in the bill.

$400

Guyette & Schmidt, Inc.

Dewy Pertuit, Bayou LaFourche, La., carved this Mallard pair, circa second quarter of the 20th century. They have original paint with minor wear and a hairline crack in the drake's bill.

$1,000

Guyette & Schmidt, Inc.

Xavier Bourg, Bayou LaFourche, La., created this rare Pintail hen with relief wing carving, circa early 20th century. It has original paint, tack eyes missing, some in-use feather painting later added.

$500

Guyette & Schmidt, Inc.

A Mallard drake is attributed to Chester LeBouef, Port Sulfur, La. It has original paint, one glass eye missing, some shot marks.

$250

Guyette & Schmidt, Inc.

A Green-winged Teal drake was carved by Nicole Vidacovitch of Sunshine, La., circa 1930.

$4,000

Hank and Judy Norman Collection

A Coot was carved by Xavier Bourg (1901-1984) of Larose, La., circa 1950.

$1,500

Hank and Judy Norman Collection

This Pintail drake was made by Mark Whipple of Bourg, La., circa 1930s.

$4,000

Hank and Judy Norman Collection

Illinois River

The Illinois River School boasts some of the nicest hollow body working decoys to be found in the country. The norm was to construct them in two pieces that were hollowed out and then joined at a point above the waterline. They were carved realistically with much fine bill and face detail. Some of them even have hollow necks and heads. Just about all have glass eyes. Frequently the commercial makers would have ballast weights made for them with their names cast into the strip lead weight surface, making their products easily identified if the original weight is present.

Most of the decoys have a rounded semi-V bottom. The Illinois River birds were also sleek and adorned with the strip ballast in an attempt to keep them from being "hung-up" in fast moving detritus found in the river. Many of them have been found with a coat of shellac or varnish. It is theorized that they felt, because the waters they hunted in were usually muddy or murky, that orange shellac made them more visible to the live bird.

The Mallard decoy is the most commonly found species in the area, for that was the dominant bird in the Mississippi Flyway. Painting was very realistic with the comb feather painting technique frequently applied.

There were at least 140 carvers in the Illinois River School, from Beardstown to Joliet. But, among them all, Robert Elliston (1849-1915) has been credited by some experts as having originated what is today known as the Illinois River style of decoy making. He started making them about 1880 and it is thought that he made several thousand before his death in 1915. He fashioned them from white pine in two halves, hollowing each out and joining them so that the joint would be above the waterline when floating. Heads were generally very sloped down to a detailed carved bill. Eyes were glass and placed anatomically correctly on his earlier decoys and later he placed glass eyes high on the head. His bodies were made flat-backed, narrow at the shoulders and rear-ending in a flat paddle-type tail.

Painted by Elliston's wife Catherine, they exhibit beautiful accuracy. She used fine brush and comb in wet paint methods to render the feathers. She was obviously quite accomplished. As with typical examples from this school, they were made with long lead keel weights, often with the weight manufacturer's name and The Elliston Decoy stamped or cast into it.

Bert Graves (1887-1956) was another master of the Illinois River School. He made decoys from the late 1920s to the early 1940s. That he was influenced by Elliston is a foregone conclusion. Like Elliston, he placed glass eyes high on the head. His early decoys very much emulated Elliston's. His bodies were a little thicker and have a rounded back. It is known that Catherine Elliston painted Graves' decoys after her husband died. Graves' early decoys painted by her are considered the most desirable although the later ones, painted by Graves' sister-in-law, are also quite nice.

Charles B. Walker (1876-1954) of Princeton, Ill., worked as a house painter and only made decoys part-time. It is thought that he made fewer than 500 in his lifetime. His output was largely Mallard drakes and hens, though other species such as Pintails have shown up. His works are fine examples of decoy making. The breasts on his decoys do not protrude as much as those more typical of this school of carvers, but are rather flattened. They are all hollow, two-piece white pine in construction. Some are found with carved wing details. Some have round bottoms, while others have the typical flat bottoms. His weights were not the typical lead keel type, but rather comprised two pieces. The paint patterns are excellent, rendering individual feathers by brush on the earlier models. Later the combing method was utilized, sometimes even combining the two methods. Most of his decoys were made for the

Princeton Game and Fish Club at Goose Pond.

Another extremely important Illinois River carver is Charles Perdew and his painting partner-wife, Edna. Charles Perdew not only made beautiful decoys, but also produced calls commercially, both waterfowl calls and crow calls. All of his items are very collectible and command some premium prices in today's market.

Some other carvers from the Illinois School are: Oscar Alford, Beardstown; Glen J. Cameron, Chillicothe; Anton Chiado, Granville; Thomas Chiado, Spring Valley; Walter Dawson, Putnam; Leonard Doren, Pekin; Harold Haertel, Dundee; George Kessler, Pekin; Charles Ruggles, Henry; Charles Schoenheider, Peoria, and Forest J. Stiles, Savannah.

Value Range FOR ILLINOIS RIVER DECOYS

Robert Elliston: Range for average decoys, **$750-$2,000.** Exceptional decoys: **$3,000-$20,000.**
Bert Graves: **$450-$3,250.**
Charles Perdew: **$1,000-$5,000** is a fair average range, but one needs to be aware of much higher values as well. Mallards sold for **$15,000** each.
Mario Piolotti: **$600-$3,000.**
Charles B. Walker: **$1,000-$6,000.**
Perry Wilcoxson: **$1,000-$2,000.**

Here is a Charles Perdew sleeping Mallard hen repainted by Clara Steele of Henry, Ill.
$1,000 +

Some very rare circa 1930s Charles Perdew miniatures are shown flanking a carved duck call by Perdew.
$750-$1,500 each

An Al Riese Pintail was one of 600 made, circa 1940s. He was in business as Tru-Dux Wood Products Company from 1938-1942 and 1946-1948 in Long Grove, Ill. (Chicago area).
$1,500
Pitt Collection

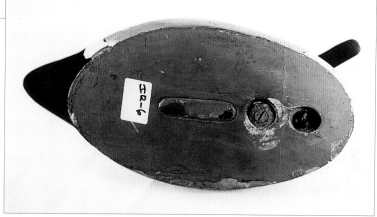

The bottom of the Al Riese Pintail shows the anchor ring and ballast.

This Charles Perdew Mallard drake, never rigged, was found in a safe deposit box in Florida.
$15,000
Pitt Collection

This Charles Perdew Pintail Drake was thought to have been done in his later years, as the paint is a little thicker due to failing eyesight.
$5,000
Pitt Collection

A Charles Perdew Mallard hen, never rigged, is mate to drake.
$15,000
Pitt Collection

A metal strip on the bottom of the Mallard hen marks it as a Perdew, made in Henry, Ill.

A preening Carolina Wood Duck was made by Virgil Lashbrook, Pekin, Ill., circa 1960.
$1,300
Pitt Collection

The maker's mark is carved into the bottom of the Lashbrook Carolina Wood Duck.

A sleeping Green-wing Teal was made by Virgil Lashbrook, Pekin, Ill., circa 1960.
$1,500
Pitt Collection

Details of the Green-wing Teal are on the bottom, including carver Virgil Lashbrook's signature.

This Pintail drake was carved by Clarence Jacobsgaard (1911-), Gardner, Ill. He only carved for 20 years and it is thought he did no more than 200 decoys total.
$3,500 due to rarity

This is a very early Robert Elliston bird, circa 1890s. Elliston is one of the premier early Illinois River carvers and lived in Bureau, Ill.
$15,000-$20,000
Pitt Collection

A Pintail drake, circa early 1950s, was carved by Cline McAlpin (1919-1969), a Chicago carver. He made only about 1,000 decoys in his lifetime.
$1,500-$2,000
Pitt Collection

A Green-wing Teal was also made by McAlpin.
$1,500-$2,000
Pitt Collection

A Magnum size Illinois River drake Mallard was carved by premier early carver Mario Piolotti (1900-1964) of Spring Valley, Ill., circa 1940.
$3,000+
Pitt Collection

Robert Elliston, Bureau, Ill., made this Blue-wing Teal hen, circa 1880.
$12,500
Guyette & Schmidt, Inc.

Charles Perdew, Henry, Ill., carved this Mallard drake, circa 1930s.

$2,500

Guyette & Schmidt, Inc.

Charles Perdew made a Pintail with three-piece construction, some repairs and repainting.

$1,000

Guyette & Schmidt, Inc.

Heck Whittington, Oglesby, Ill., created a hollow Mallard drake. It has original paint.

$3,200

Guyette & Schmidt, Inc.

Ignatius Staichowiak, LaSalle, Ill., created this Pintail drake. It has original paint.

$1,600

Guyette & Schmidt, Inc.

Missouri

I have only one photo of a documented Missouri decoy, a Mallard drake by Ben Yeargen (1896-1974) from North St. Louis, Mo. He was one of the best and one of the few documented carvers making working decoys in Missouri. I am sure we shall learn more as time goes on, but for now his example must suffice as an example of Missouri carvers.

A Mallard drake by Ben Yeargen was carved in 1932.

$850

Hank and Judy Norman Collection

Value Range FOR MISSOURI DECOYS

Little documented sales data exists in this area; however, values will tend to be in the general range of **$300-$1,500** for most decoys from the Missouri region.

Indiana

Very little has been documented about Indiana decoys. It has been reported that Indiana did not have a decoy carving tradition due to the early drainage of the Kankakee drainage system in the north. However, I cannot agree as Indiana was populated from south to north and many early setters along the Ohio and lower Wabash rivers would have been involved in subsistence hunting for waterfowl.

In addition, even if a major school of carvers does not exist for southern Indiana, and I believe it must, many Hoosiers were great sport hunters beginning in our era of more modern carvers in the 1930s and beyond. There were many game call companies and fishing lure companies located in Indiana during this period. One would have to assume that there were also carvers working in the period from the 1930s until the 1960s in Indiana, just like its neighboring states. Thanks to the help of Hank Norman, I have two examples of Indiana carvers: Bernard Ohnmacht (1889-1975) of Lafayette, Ind., and Paul Lipke of Whiting, Ind. Whiting is also home to a small modern duck call company.

Value Range FOR INDIANA DECOYS

Shown is a Black Duck by Bernard Ohnmacht made circa 1930. This is one of only seven known Black Ducks to have been made by Ohnmacht. This one is stamped #4 on its keel slot. Also shown is a Blue-winged Teal drake made by Paul Lipke in about 1940. The Black Duck is valued at **$3,000** and the Teal at **$4,000.**

A Black Duck by Bernard Ohnmacht was made circa 1930.
$3,000
Hank and Judy Norman Collection

A Blue-winged Teal by Paul Lipke dates to about 1940.
$4,000
Hank and Judy Norman Collection

Ohio

Maybe I was first attracted to Ohio for its cork duck decoy tradition, but for certain a major school of carvers existed in the western section of Lake Erie, carving fine ducks in the 1930s and beyond.

The cork tradition is epitomized by the work of William T. Enright (1913-1979) from Toledo. I have shown one of his Black Ducks from my own collection, valued at about $500. John Sharon was greatly influenced by Enright and also produced many collectible ducks from this region. The earliest decoy carver was likely Ned John Hauser (1826-1900) from the Sandusky area.

One other carver of note in Ohio is Charles Klopping of Point Place, Toledo. Shown is one of his Canvasback drakes made about 1935. It would bring about $1,500 in today's market.

Value Range FOR OHIO DECOYS

William T. Enright: **$500-$2,000.**
Ned John Hauser: **$1,000-$3,000.**

Charles Klopping: **$500-$3,000.**
John Sharon: **$300-$1,000.**

Shown is a William T. Enright Black Duck, circa 1935-40.
$500-$700
Lewis Collection

A closeup of the head shows details of the Enright Black Duck.

Charles Klopping carved this Canvasback drake, circa 1935.
$1,500
Hank and Judy Norman Collection

An early Bluebill Hen with flapping wings was found in Ohio. The carver is unknown.
$2,000
Guyette & Schmidt, Inc.

Michigan

Decoys from this school comprise at least two major types found on the eastern side of the state. One type was made for hunting in the heavy waters of the Great Lakes and the others were those made for use in more calm waters and shallow marshes. I believe that there was a variation found on the west side of the state along Lake Michigan, typified by birds from the Grand Traverse Bay region and used on the large lakes such as Torch, Crystal and others. These are not unlike the east coast birds in Michigan, but I am sure we will ultimately type them in a separate school. Also, we are still learning more about small factory decoys in Michigan, two of which were located along the shores of Lake Michigan. There is a folk type of decoy in use in the Upper Peninsula that has not been discussed in any detail. These varied from crude chunks of wood carved from telephone poles to nicely done birds made from native cedar.

Similar to the Upper Peninsula fish decoys, the duck decoys were first designed for use and secondly appearance. If you find a decoy with found items for eyes, it may be from the Upper Peninsula. Also, look for the possible influence of Native American carvers on decoys if any are found with wood burned details. After all, our first American decoys were Tulle Canvasbacks and I am certain that we need to do more research on Native American decoys to see what recent influences could be found. Many fish carvers have been influenced by, and many great fish carvers are, Native Americans. It is reasonable to believe that the same is true in Michigan, Wisconsin, and Minnesota for duck decoys.

The Great Lakes decoys were made large with hollow bodies and big keels. They were generally hollowed out from the bottom and closed up with bottom boards. There are lots of unusual keels to be found on Michigan decoys with some of them being downright ingenious. The other types are constructed in the same manner, but are usually smaller in scale, lack the large heavy keels, and use a very thin bottom board. By the time decoy making had worked its way this far west from the Atlantic seaboard, it was about 1880. Makers in this part of the country had the experience of their Eastern predecessors from which to draw on, many sources for fine materials, and good tools available to work with. The band saw and glass eyes are two good examples of this. It is therefore no surprise that the decoys of the Midwest are, for the most part, very finely made and finished. Just about all decoys from the region have

good quality glass eyes. Most are hollow body types with bottom boards, but there are some very nice solid body birds to be found as well. Some makers also used cork in fashioning bodies and mounted them on bottom boards for stability and durability.

As a whole, the decoys of the region are beautifully constructed and painted. The collector would do well to concentrate his efforts in the whole region including Michigan, the St. Clair Flats, Wisconsin and the Illinois River. There are probably quite a few decoys as yet not found (West Michigan styles and Upper Peninsula makers) and there were a few makers who are known to have produced literally thousands of them in their combined carving careers.

Ken Anger (1905-1961) of Dunnville, Ontario, may or may not belong with the listing of the Michigan makers. The fact is that even though he lived and worked in Ontario, much closer to Toronto than Detroit, Anger's blocks are much more similar to those of the Detroit makers than those made by Toronto carvers. Furthermore, they are quite similar to those of Detroit makers Ben Schmidt and Neil Smith. I would most definitely include him in the Michigan style.

Anger used a rasp extensively in fashioning his decoys and developed the technique to such a fine art that, when combined with his painting, he was able to achieve a realistic soft feather-like texture. It is his trademark. He was so adept at it that collectors have dubbed him the rasp-master. Most of his decoys are made of two pieces of hollowed out blocks of red cedar joined by glue and two screws. They are mostly flat bottomed with heads carved from basswood and attached to the body by a screw from below. They exhibit nicely rendered wing carving. There are two different styles of Angers to be found. His early (pre-mid 1930s) style was a low and gracefully flattened body, while the examples made after that have a higher, fatter look to them. They were made to float higher in the water than the older style. The other characteristics, however, remained the same.

Value Range FOR MICHIGAN CARVERS

Ben Schmidt: $250-$5,000. On the low end are the repaints and the working ducks. Most people figure that a Ben Schmidt decoy of any quality is worth $1,000 and I would agree. I would put his goose decoys at double his ducks. Also, special positions and superb paint would also increase the value.

Ken Anger: $1,000-$10,000. His decoys have seen a major increase in value in recent years.

Walter Strubling: $500-$3,000.

Four Ben Schmidt decoys and part of a fifth line a shelf in a display from the Pitt Collection.

Bluebill drake, $1,500; Widgeon hen, $9,000; Redhead pair, $2,250

A pair of very rare Green-winged Teal is by Sibley & Co. of Whitehall, Mich. These could go under the factory section but, as this is my only example, I placed them here due to the early patent of 1899.

$27,000 for the pair

Hank and Judy Norman Collection

Tom Singleton, former conservation officer from the Upper Peninsula of Michigan, carved this fancy Mallard hen, a contemporary example of a decorative decoy, circa 1990. He also carved other birds, including hummingbirds, and fish decoys.

$400

Lewis Collection

Floyd Joseph Bruce, Gaylord, Mich., famous carver of Michigan fish decoys, also carved a very limited number of duck decoys. This is one of his Redhead drakes carved in 1959.

$500

Lewis Collection

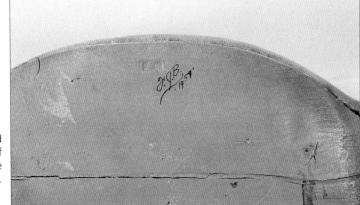

The bottom of the Redhead drake shows the initials of Floyd Joseph Bruce and the 1959 date of the carving.

This is a Floyd Joseph Bruce 1969 Canvasback drake.

$500

Lewis Collection

Here are details from the FJB Canvasback bottom.

A closeup shows bill details of the FJB Canvasback.

Tom "Savvy" Kruse, Watton, Mich., carved this Bluebill drake. He is an example of a hunter who started carving his own ducks in Michigan's Upper Peninsula. It was carved from hand-picked Michigan cedar from local swamps in the same style used for hunting by the carver. He has been carving the decorative versions in about one-half size for the past few years and is constantly improving his painting and detail work. This is a technique well developed by Frank Lewis in New York State, e.g., carve all the birds alike and then make the species by the painting. Tom carved his own ducks for hunting for the past 20 plus years prior to making any decorative decoys.

$125+
Lewis Collection

Close-ups show the head and tail of the Bluebill carved by Tom Kruse.

Value Range FOR MICHIGAN CARVERS

This is a Tom "Savvy" Kruse Canvasback drake.

A Kruse Wood Duck drake was carved in 2000.

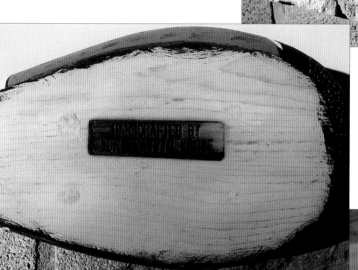

Tom Kruse marks his decoys with a plate on the bottom.

This is my favorite Kruse decoy, a decorative Canada Goose on a duck sized body.

A beautifully done Jonathon Jones hand-carved decorative glass-eye owl sits on a unique take-apart stick stand that inserts into the owl's body. This was purchased from an estate sale in Michigan in the mid-1990s and, from the patina and data surrounding the find, I would guess it to be circa 1960.

$500+

Lewis Collection

The Kruse Canada Goose is shown next to the Wood Duck drake.

A Kruse Bufflehead was carved in 2000.

Floyd Joseph Bruce carved this Pintail hen in 1965.

$500

Lewis Collection

Pat Kane's decorative one-half size Canada Goose was carved in 1990. This Midland, Mich., carver makes beautiful decorative decoys and is also a collector of fine decoys.
$250
Lewis Collection

A gorgeous decorative Woodcock nestling in the day lillies was carved by Frank Sarns (1912-) of Morley, Mich., circa 2000.
$250-$400

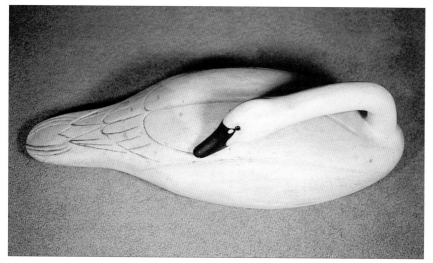

The B.J. initials on this Swan are the mark of Michigan carver Donald Pawlaczyk.

A "B. J." decorative Swan was carved in 1990. B.J. is Donald Pawlaczyk from Au Gres, Mich. This beautiful modern Swan is reminiscent of an East Coast bird by a famous carver (Crowell). The carving is excellent and the lines are very beautiful on this decorative item.
$300-$500
Lewis Collection

A folk art Pheasant rooster, circa 1960s, by an unknown maker, was found in a Michigan estate sale.
$50+
Lewis Collection

A rare Ben Schmidt Widgeon may be one of a kind.
$1,250
Guyette & Schmidt, Inc.

Here is a Ben Schmidt Black Duck.
$800
Guyette & Schmidt, Inc.

A Ben Schmidt Canvasback hen has its bill broken and repaired.
$350
Guyette & Schmidt, Inc.

Ed "One Arm" Kelly, Monroe, Mich., made this Redhead drake.
$3,000
Guyette & Schmidt, Inc.

George Sibley, Whitehall, Mich., carved a Pintail drake.
$750
Guyette & Schmidt, Inc.

St. Clair Flats (Mount Clemens and Toronto Schools)

For the most part, decoys from the banks of St. Clair Flats are very light, well-constructed flat-bottom, hollow-body birds with thin bottom boards (some as thin as 1/4"). Some even boast hollow necks and heads. They are finely sanded and finished, and sport glass eyes. There were many fine low heads and sleepers made in the area.

Lake St. Clair is on the United States and Canadian border with the border running north/south through the lake. There are, therefore, American and Canadian carvers in the school. Serious collectors divide the St. Clair Flats into two separate schools: the Toronto School and the Mount Clemens School. Decoys by makers from both sides of the lake have definite but subtle differences.

Canadian carvers were frequently given short shrift until about 20 years ago. They were apparently particularly adept at carving Canada geese decoys (that probably should not be a surprise), but they carved many other species also. A particularly noted carver from Toronto was George Warin. A boat builder and commercial decoy maker, he fashioned several styles of Canada's both solid and hollow-bodied, but also carved Blacks, Bluebills, Canvasbacks, Redheads, Mallards, Pintails and Ringnecks. These were usually in the style of typical St. Clair Flats carvers. They are characterized by a finely carved bill, but with no details carved in the bills. They were exquisitely painted with fine detail. Many will be found marked G. & J. Warin Makers Toronto or G. & J. Warin Builders. The J. is his brother, James, who was a partner in the boat building business. It is generally held that James had little or nothing to do with the decoy business. It is thought that there were about 2,000 decoys made in the years from 1870 to 1900.

Another Toronto maker of note was Tom Chambers (1860-1948). He managed the marsh for the St. Clair Shooting Company from 1900 to 1930. Like Warin, he made a very stylish Canada Goose decoy as well as many others. Also like Warin, he made some with solid bodies, but most are in the St. Clair Flats style. The majority of his decoys were Canvasbacks and Redheads, but you can find most of the other species common to the area. They are characterized by detail carving of the bill with diamond-shaped nostrils. Some of the later decoys he made are found with Thos. Chambers Maker on the bottom. I love the style and symmetry of Chambers birds and find them outstanding.

Some other St. Clair Flats makers are: Robert C. McGaffey, Ontario; David Ward, Toronto; William Finkel, St. Clair Flats; Robert Gilbert, Hamilton, Ontario; James R. Kelson, Mount Clemens; Zeke McDonald, McDonald Island, Mich.; Danny Scriven, Detroit; Phineas Reeves and sons, Charles and John, Port Rowan, Ontario; Davey Nichols, Smith's Falls, Ontario; Tobin Meldrum, Fair Haven, Mich.; Frank Schmidt, Detroit, and John R. Wells, Toronto.

Value Range FOR SOME ST. CLAIR FLATS CARVERS

Thomas Chambers: **$1,000-$6,000.**
Robert Gilbert: **$350-$500.**
James R. Kelson: **$1,000-$1,500.**

Davey Nichols: **$350-$1,000.**
Phineas Reeves: **$200-$500.**
Ralph Reghi: **$200-$500.**

Frank Schmidt: **$500-$1,500.**
George Warin: **$750-$1,500.**

James R. Kelson's Redhead drake is in a sleeper position, circa 1940. This Mt. Clemens carver used balsa and carved many fine birds in sleeping positions.
$1,000
Lewis Collection

This is a Frank Schmidt drake Black Duck.
$800
Lewis Collection

The bottom of a Black Duck shows the St. Clair Flats keel style.

An unknown superb wooden Black Duck has Bach or Schmidt style feathering details, Ben Schmidt and Illinois River style weight, and St. Clair Flats keel style. Although it appears to be a Black Duck, the bill color and green wings indicate a possible very large Teal. This may be a Ben Schmidt solid duck or by one of his protégés such as Neil Smith.
$1,000
Lewis Collection

A small cork decoy has a very detailed wooden head. It is a Ring-bill or Bluebill hen with initials stamped under the mandible of J-M for Jim McDonald, McDonald Island. It has a thin St. Clair Flats style bottom board, Nate Quillen style of resting duck, extremely detailed head with nares, carved nail, and glass eyes.

$350-$500

Lewis Collection

Close-ups show the detailed carving on the cork decoy and the initials stamped under the mandible.

Robert Gilbert Bluebills have original paint and are small, hollow with thin bottom board. Circa 1930, Hamilton, Ontario.

$700-$900

Griff Evans Collection

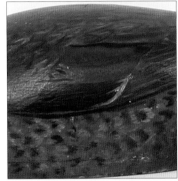

William Hart, Belleville, Ontario. Hart lived from 1875-1949 and was a superb carver. This is a hollow carved swimming Green-wing Teal hen with original paint, some professional repair to the neck and a tiny tail chip and a great cocked head to the decoy.

$55,000

Guyette & Schmidt, Inc.

John R. Wells, Toronto, Ontario, carved a Bluebill drake, circa 1900. It has solid body construction, JA & C brand, comb painting on back, original paint, small chip and shot marks.

$1,100

Guyette & Schmidt, Inc.

George Warin, Toronto, Ontario, is credited for this hollow carved Teal. It is in old Belleville style repaint, with a small chip and shot marks.

$500

Guyette & Schmidt, Inc.

Sanford Gorsline, Demorestville, Ontario, made this Black Duck, circa 1880s. It is hollow carved with original paint, "RJ" and "JRA" stenciled on the bottom.

$8,500

Guyette & Schmidt, Inc.

A late 1800s St. Clair Flats Canada Goose is by an unknown carver. It has thin shelled construction, hollow, original paint with professionally restored/replaced bill.

$5,000

Guyette & Schmidt, Inc.

Tom Chambers, Long Point, Ontario, created a Canvasback drake, circa 1900. It is hollow carved, short bodied style, mostly mint but 20 percent of combing on the back has worn through to black paint on the back.

$7,000

Guyette & Schmidt, Inc.

Davey W. Nichol, Smith Falls, Ontario, carved a Black Duck, in a rare hollow low head variety. It has excellent original paint.

$1,400

Guyette & Schmidt, Inc.

Davey W. Nichol, Smith Falls, Ontario, made this Black Duck. It is a virtually unused mint example.

$800

Guyette & Schmidt, Inc.

J. R. Wells, Toronto, Ontario, made this Black Duck, circa first quarter of the 20th century. It has solid body style, paint appears original, moderate wear with small dents.

$700

Guyette & Schmidt, Inc.

An Ontario Bluebill pair is by an unknown carver. It has relief wing carving, fluted tails, original paint with small chip and shot marks. The hen had eyes replaced.

$350

Guyette & Schmidt, Inc.

Wisconsin

With the exception of factory-made decoys, there were few commercial makers in the Wisconsin School. Most of the decoys of the area were made by individual hunters for themselves and perhaps a few for friends. There were nevertheless many, many fine decoys made in Wisconsin. This is similar to the Upper Peninsula of Michigan. In other words, there are more folk birds and relatively localized carvers of birds.

Decoys from this school are generally oversize renditions of diving ducks species. They are usually found in solid-body construction, but there are some very nice hollow-body examples to be found as well. Whatever the construction technique, they usually have exaggerated body features such as big, long necks and hump backs. Most sport glass eyes. There are some well-known makers in addition to many who are still being discovered today. Paint styles or patterns are usually very similar to factory birds widely used in the Midwest.

There are many makers from this school who turned out nice blocks, but there are two who stand out in quality and numbers fashioned: August "Gus" Moak (1852-1942) of Tustin and Frank G. Strey (1890-1966) of Oshkosh.

Moak's birds are hollow cedar and he used bottom boards that were slightly convex. The bodies were the typical hump back and necks were long. The heads are distinctive in that there is a deep V carved separating the bills from the foreheads. There are very obvious carved nostrils and mandibles.

Decoys made by Frank Strey are big, solid blocks. The cheeks are pronounced as the result of his carving out elongated recesses for the eyes. In later years he did not carve the cheeks quite so deep and he had begun to use a rasp to give the

Here is a nice example of miniatures from Wisconsin, circa 1930s. These diminutive little decoys are only about 5″ in total length, with excellent painting.

$300 for a pair

Lewis Collection

surface a textured look.

Additional carvers include Howard Homer and Joseph Geigl, both expert in the art of painting cork decoys. In addition, collectors should be aware of decoys by the Milwaukee Museum School. Warren Dettman was on the staff of the museum and is known to have taught others how to carve, including WPA employees, to make decoys to be used by the museum in collecting specimens for its various displays. Some attribute some of these decoys to the Christie brothers of Saginaw Bay, Mich. But most were likely done by Dettman or one of his protégés.

Unique to one of the photos shown is the set of plans that have not been previously reported next to the second Mallard shown. The plans were published by Deltacraft (Delta Tools) of Milwaukee and they were designed by Ed Hamilton. It is definitely the pattern for this decoy. This plan may establish Hamilton as one of the carvers; this would be a new name to the school. As Hank Norman noted to me, it is hard to understand how a group of decoys of this quality, from a relatively modern period, and associated with a major public museum, can go unidentified. We certainly need to learn more about all of the carvers and the history of this tradition.

Value Range FOR WISCONSIN DECOYS

Joseph Geigl (circa 1930s-early 1950s): **$300-$2,000.**
Howard Homer (circa 1930s-1940s): **$300-$1,500.**
"Milwaukee School Decoys": **$500-$5,000**, depending on carver.
August "Gus" Moak (1852-1942): **$1,000-$10,000.**
C. C. Roberts/J. J. Rheinschmidt (circa 1930s-1940s): **$500-$7,500.**
Frank Strey (1890-1966): **$500-$3,000.**

A Canvasback drake by an unknown Wisconsin carver dates from the first quarter of the 20th century.
$400
Guyette & Schmidt, Inc.

A Mallard drake from the Milwaukee Museum School, circa 1938, is signed "N. Trader" on the bottom.
$3,000
Hank and Judy Norman Collection

A Scaup (Bluebill) drake, circa 1885-1890, is also by Gus Moak. It would be valued as the Canvasback. Moak decoys are highly desirable early examples of the Wisconsin School.

$5,000-$6,000

Pitt Collection

A Mallard drake, circa 1935, is attributed to Warren Dettman and the Milwaukee Museum School. See the text on this carving tradition but note the decoy pattern in the photo.

$3,500

Hank and Judy Norman Collection

A Yellowlegs by Ben Shostak of New London, Wis., is signed and dated 1974.

$750

Hank and Judy Norman Collection

A Canvasback drake was carved by premier Wisconsin carver Gus Moak, Tustin, Wis. (1852-1942), circa 1885-1890. This beautiful decoy sold at Guyette & Schmidt, Inc. for $4,400 in 2000 and would now be valued at $5,000-$6,000 or more.

$5,000-$6,000

Pitt Collection

A Bluebill pair of Evans factory decoys, circa 1920s, were made by Walter Evans, Ladysmith, Wis. (1872-1948).
$8,000
Pitt Collection

A beautiful cork Black Duck is by Howard Homer, Diamond Lake, Wis., circa 1950. The bottom has H H carved in it. Many of Homer's decoys were so marked, or signed, but not all of them were.
$800+
Lewis Collection

Here is the Howard Homer base to the Black Duck decoy.

A beautiful cork hen Mallard is by Howard Homer, Diamond Lake, Wis., circa 1950. Also, there is a carved H H in the base board.
$800+
Lewis Collection

Here is the Howard Homer base to the Mallard hen decoy.

A cork Bluebill is by Howard Homer, circa 1950.

$300-$400

Lewis Collection

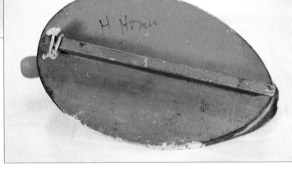

The bottom of the cork Bluebill identifies the carver as Howard Homer.

A Bluebill pair by Howard Homer, circa 1950, was purchased by the author. The drake is signed.

$600-$800, pair

Lewis Collection

A great little decorative one-half size Mallard drake, marked "Ballard" on bottom of the tail, with a felt-covered bottom and glass eyes, was purchased in Wisconsin, circa 1960s.

$300

Lewis Collection

A Blue Goose, of wood with glass eyes and original paint, was carved by C. C. Roberts and J. J. Rheinschmidt for relatives, employees, and friends, circa 1930s. This is one of only 200 decoys made by these famed fishing lure makers (makers of the Robert's Mud Puppy).
$3,000
Lewis Collection

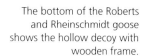

The bottom of the Roberts and Rheinschmidt goose shows the hollow decoy with wooden frame.

Roberts and Rheinschmidt developed a pulp over wooden frame process to lighten large decoys. This is a very rare sleeping/resting pose of a Canada Goose of pulp, hollow on wooden frame, with glass eyes and original paint, circa 1930s.
$3,000
Lewis Collection

A very large wooden goose has a pulp insert on top, three-fourths of the way between the back of neck and tail, to lighten this large decoy made for Lake Michigan hunting. The decoy has glass eyes, bill details and is in original paint, circa 1930s. This is the only one known to still exist.
$3,000+
Lewis Collection

Here is a comparison of the resting goose and large goose from left.

Here is a comparison of all three geese from above.

Roberts/Rheinschmidt pulp-bodied geese with steel legs and feet and carved wooden heads have glass eyes and carved details. With original paint, only two are known to exist. They made these large geese for field hunting and they are very realistic and actual life size. The legs are removed, as is the head, for transportation. The pulp over a wood frame body makes for a lighter decoy. They have excellent painting and details.

$3,000+ each

Lewis Collection

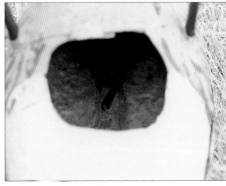

The No. 7 is painted inside the metal goose.

The most unique of all Roberts/Rheinschmidt decoys, No. 7 of the dozen tin field Canada geese made as an experiment. The decoys worked fine but were very hard to form. The body is all metal with a wooden insert dowel piece on which the neck is placed, connected by a single steel rod protruding from a dowel. The head and neck are carved from one piece of wood with glass eyes and details. This is in original paint and is one of only two known to exist.

$7,500+

Lewis Collection

A Roberts/Rheinschmidt oversize, magnum plus, Canvasback hen is the only one known to exist. Like the one goose earlier, the middle of the back of the bird is pulp to save on weight of the massive decoy. It is still a ton!

$3,000

Lewis Collection

The drake Canvasback is the mate to the hen. Note these are both still rigged ready for Lake Michigan waters.

$3,000

Lewis Collection

The Canvasback pair is displayed.

Here is a Roberts/Rheinschmidt regular size pair of all-wooden Canvasback decoys, with feather details, carved bills, glass eyes. Note that the decoys are actually rigged together as a pair.

$1,500 for pair

Lewis Collection

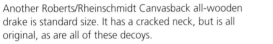

Another Roberts/Rheinschmidt Canvasback all-wooden drake is standard size. It has a cracked neck, but is all original, as are all of these decoys.

$700

Lewis Collection

Here is a size comparison of the super magnum and the regular size Canvasbacks.

A one of a kind Roberts/ Rheinschmidt papier-mâché over a light frame Canada Goose has two steel leg inserts, but no legs left and no face details. This is a very light decoy.

$500

Lewis Collection

A one of a kind Snow Goose was made by Roberts/Rheinschmidt in a similar fashion to the Canada Goose, but has no leg standards or even a place to insert them. This decoy is extremely light and well made and is intended to sit directly on the ground. I do not think this decoy would have withstood the test of the rough handling of the hunter. It's a very unique decoy. Also shown is a "Scotch" goose call, No. 1605 (see calls).

$1,250 due to unusual species and rarity

Lewis Collection

A magnum Black Duck was made of cork with thin bottom board by Joseph R. Gigl (1882-1962) from Fremont, Wis. Gigl (also spelled Geigl in some references) carved and painted many decoys for sale. He was an outstanding painter as can be seen by this example.

$1,000-$1,250

Lewis Collection

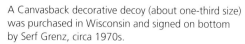

A Canvasback decorative decoy (about one-third size) was purchased in Wisconsin and signed on bottom by Serf Grenz, circa 1970s.

$200

Lewis Collection

A hollowed, two-piece glass eye wooden decoy is one of a dozen found in the Hayward area, maker unknown. I sold the rest of this string in 1997 for $300 plus each.

$500-$700

Lewis Collection

My wife's favorite decoy, maker unknown, is similar to Moak and many early Wisconsin decoys. This decoy was purchased in an antique store in Traverse City, Mich., many years ago and could also be a West Michigan bird. It is a solid body, no eyes, neck held on by a single bolt through body, bobtail design. It appears to be original paint and has great lines.

$1,500+

Lewis Collection

A rare Roberts/Rheinschmidt all-wood, highly detailed Mallard hen decoy is a little more than life-size. We were told that only four of these were made, two pairs. One resides with a friend and the two drakes remain in the family. As were all of the decoys made by these men, they were working decoys. This is in original paint, well worn.

$1,500+

Lewis Collection

A close-up of the Mallard hen shows details of the bill carving and nice painting.

A laminated Bluebill drake from Wisconsin is by an unknown maker but may be associated with the Milwaukee Museum School. The bird is constructed of four laminated boards. The third board has a carved tail, the second board has a shelf for the head to attach, the top board has wings carved into it. The decoy has tack eyes painted.

$200-$300

Lewis Collection

By an unknown carver, a decorative Wisconsin or Michigan Canvasback has very nice form and bill details, no name or data, circa 1980s.

$125

Lewis Collection

Pacific Coast

Although not foolproof, the type of wood used to fashion a decoy is a good clue to decoys from the West Coast or Pacific flyway. The wood of choice for most makers of the area was redwood. Often they used ponderosa pine for heads. Another good way to identify a West Coast decoy is by species. For instance, the Pacific Coast Black Brant has a different plumage pattern than that of the Brant that migrates through the eastern flyways. The Swan I show from my own collection is believed to be a Pacific Coast bird. It is made out of redwood with beautiful eye and mandible details, but the maker is unknown to me.

Generally, the hand-carved decoys of the Pacific Coast are solid bodied and sport tack eyes. Many have a similar look about them. There are many notable exceptions to these generalities as elsewhere. Some of the makers who worked after 1900 (some still carving) were very talented. The beautiful late 1930s Mallards, Canvasback, and Teals of Harry L. Cook are good examples.

The Pacific Coast School, as we use it here, encompasses the whole of the United States West Coast from northern California to Washington (and extending north into Canada). About 20 percent of the pre-World War II decoys found in the region are hand-carved. The remaining 80 percent of the decoys found are factory-made, being primarily Masons.

Perhaps the dean of the Pacific Coast decoy makers was Richard Ludwig "Fresh Air Dick" Jantzen of the San Francisco area. He produced thousands of decoys in his 20-odd years of carving. He carved just about all the species hunted. His blocks are almost always characterized by slightly hump-backed bodies of redwood with distinctly carved wings and tail. The heads may or may not be mounted on a shelf, but all are puffy cheeked, and have glass eyes and nicely carved bills. The bodies are found both solid and hollow. Unfortunately for the collector, his style was so respected that many other carvers copied it. My Swan may indeed be a Jantzen or a copy of one of his decoys.

Horace Crandall (1892-1969) of Westwood, Calif., is another carver of note in the Pacific Coast School. His decoys differ from most of the other products of the region. They were very slender and graceful, almost to the point where they might be considered elegant. They had upswept tails and a fragile slim neck. Toward the end of his carving career he began fashioning his decoys with carved upsweeping wings similar to those of Jantzen. The bodies were solid pine.

Some other carvers in the region worthy of note are: Frank Bay (1896-1980) and brother, Jack Bay (1882-1941) of Astoria, Ore.; Charles Bergman (1856-1946), also of Astoria, and Luigi Andreucetti (1898-1978) of the Sacramento, Calif., area.

Value Range FOR PACIFIC COAST DECOYS

Richard Ludwig "Fresh Air Dick" Jantzen: **$750-$5,000.**
Harry L. Cook: **$200-$650.**
Horace Crandall: **$750-$2,000.**

This is likely a Pacific Coast Swan. It is four-piece wooden board construction held together with redwood pegs; all wood is redwood. It has great detailed eyes and appears to be original paint. Maker unknown.

$4,000-$5,000

Lewis Collection

A close-up of the Pacific Coast Swan shows the detailed eyes.

Chapter Three:

Factory Decoys from the Vintage Period

During the last half of the 1800s, the popularity of
the sport of waterfowl hunting increased dramatically.
This, coupled with the appearance of the market hunter
and his requisite large rigs of decoys and the advent
of the duplicating lathe, made it economically feasible
for the establishment of factories for the commercial
manufacture of decoys. Hundreds of operations were
established, a few of which became large and successful.
Several small operations also achieved success.

I have used this early production of factory decoys
up until the banning of live decoys and baiting in 1935,
to demarcate what I call the "Vintage Period" of
factory decoys. It includes the production runs of
such companies as Stevens, Peterson, Dodge,
Mason, Evans and the early Pratts. The next

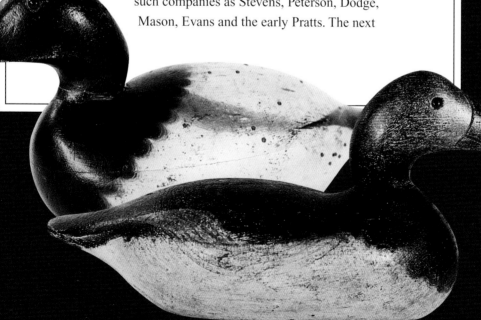

chapter will take up post-1935 factory production.

The use of the word factory can be misleading as used here. It does describe larger operations such as Mason's Decoy Factory. But we are also including any commercial operation location devoted to the manufacture of wooden decoys in which the duplicating lathe is an integral part of its production, or the production, lathe or no, on an assembly line. This latter could encompass many, many makers, but only those that have been routinely accepted as factory decoys by collectors are included. Most of these have been accepted as factories by virtue of extensive commercial advertising of the decoys.

Factory-made decoys made by the best-known companies were all quite similar to each other. And there was a relationship between many, with one buying out another. Mason, and probably many others, would make atypical decoys on special order, but their regular lines all performed their tasks in pretty much the same manner in most conditions. Therefore a small degree of standardization was practiced, albeit by accident.

Manufacturing operations were in a position to make innovations in decoys not practical to hand makers. Some of the innovations, such as the folding tin shorebird decoys, were successful and some were little more than comical. A decoy that flapped its wings was once patented, a dubious achievement at best, but a most collectible decoy today. And today, with advanced computer technology, we have the Robo-ducks that will ultimately be banned due to the unfair advantage given to the hunter.

Metal-bodied decoys with wood bottom boards and the folding tin shorebirds had appeared by the mid-1860s, and rubber decoys arrived about 1867. There were even some honking decoys produced by factories.

The art of the manufactured wooden decoy, however, was carried to its highest form by the early factories and this is where they finally concentrated their efforts.

The collector can encounter factory decoys just about anywhere, for they were made by the thousands (especially around Detroit) and shipped to just about all points of the compass. A notable exception is New England. There seems to be a shortage of factory-made decoys in that part of the country. The reason may be the reputation New Englanders have for being handy, educated in fine craftsmanship, industrious, and possessing innate Yankee ingenuity. However, I think a better point could be made with a two-fold hypothesis that there simply were far more local carvers in the area, as it was the beginning of decoy carving in America. And secondly, some regions of the New England area have been notoriously lacking in excess capital to buy factory goods when locally available. These two reasons make far more sense to me.

While hunting for factory decoys, it might be judicious to keep in mind another theoretical possibility. It would not be unreasonable to think that some employees of factories carried their vocation home and made decoys in home workshops. There were many talented people working in these factories (especially painters) and there would be nothing to prevent them from making decoys. It is most reasonable to assume that some of them might have produced birds that were almost, if not completely, identical to the factory product. Further, my research on fishing lure production makes it very clear that there were many "lunch hour specials" and other products made by creative employees just for fun and the sake of creativity. It would be very likely this same behavior carried over into the making of duck decoys at factories.

The new wildfowl laws of 1918 struck a fatal blow to most of the decoy manufacturing companies, and factory after factory went out of business almost overnight. The laws eliminated the market hunters, thus their huge demand for decoys simply vanished. Then, with the banning of live decoys and baiting in 1935, we had a reinvigoration of decoy making, but it came too late for the classic factories.

J.N. Dodge

Jasper N. Dodge (1829-1909) of Detroit, Mich., went into business about 1883, when he bought an existing decoy-making operation owned by George Peterson. One should become familiar with the Peterson-Dodge-Mason evolution, as it is likely the most important evolution in factory decoy production. Peterson had been in business since 1873. The Peterson products were very fine, usually solid body birds with glass eyes. Although Dodge did not use Peterson's original patterns, he did use many of the existing techniques. His decoys were also generally solid bodied but, he also manufactured some hollow decoys in the St. Clair Flats style.

Early Dodge decoys had unusual eyes. The eyehole was drilled out and a tack placed in the hole, resulting in slightly recessed tack eyes that appeared very much like glass eyes. Later he adopted the glass eyes. There is usually evidence of Dodge's extensive use of putty filler where the neck joins the body. Dodge also carried on the breast swirl style of painting developed by Peterson. This swirl style was later used extensively by the Mason's Decoy Factory in Detroit. The swirl style may be one of the most characteristic traits of the Detroit factory birds over a 50-year period.

Dodge advertised that he would make decoys "... after any model furnished without extra charge." It is therefore possible to find many different types, styles, and species made by the company. He went out of business in 1908, but there has been no evidence uncovered, to date, that he produced decoys past 1905.

Value Range FOR J.N. DODGE DECOYS

Merganser and Canada Goose: **$1,000-$6,000.**
Record-breaking Dodge Swan: **$17,600 (1991).**

Other species: **$300-$5,000.**
Rare decoys such as Barrow's Golden Eye: **$10,000 plus.**

A Dodge Widgeon drake has original paint, circa 1890s.
$2,500
Pitt Collection

A close-up shows details of the head of the Dodge Widgeon drake.

A very rare Dodge Barrow's Golden Eye drake is one of only four known to exist. This is the same bird as shown in the Dodge decoy book.
$10,000+
Pitt Collection

A Dodge Widgeon hen, circa 1890, has original paint, small shot marks and a crack in the bill.
$950
Guyette & Schmidt, Inc.

A Dodge Black Duck, circa 1880s, has its original paint, reglued neck crack, cracks in the underside.
$700
Guyette & Schmidt, Inc.

Evans Duck Decoy Company

Walter Evans (1872-1948) of Ladysmith, Wis., began making decoys in 1921 and continued in business until 1932 when illness forced him to cease operation. In the beginning, the factory consisted of two lathes in his garage. His success was rapid, for just a couple of years later he had moved into a large building in Ladysmith and employed a number of people. He offered three different types or grades of decoys in various species. The largest grade, the Mammoth, was offered only in solid bodies. But the other two, the Standard and Competitive, were offered in both solid and hollow bodies. The Competitive grade was not sanded, but rather left with the ridged lathe blade marks around the body. The others were very nicely sanded and finished.

The hollow bodies were fashioned by two different methods. One is the familiar two-piece hollow body, in two more or less equal halves, but the other method was rather unusual. He would take a solid body and drill a 1 1/4" inch hole through the front of the breast longitudinally into the body. He then plugged the hole in front and finished the bird.

All heads were hand carved and sported quality glass eyes. His method of preparing his decoys for painting was effective, rendering the finish very durable. Many are found today with very good original paint as a result.

The decoys have a Mason look to them and, indeed, it is said that he was inspired to go into the business of decoy making after finding a Mason premier grade Mallard. Being a woodworker by trade, he decided that he could do as well.

Evans frequently rubber-stamped the words Evans Decoy on the bottom of these flat bottom decoys. This stamp is not always found, as he, like most other makers, individuals or factories, was not particularly diligent in placing his brand on his products.

Numbers of birds he produced are not known, but a widely circulated photograph of him at work in his shop pictures about 150 Mallard and Canvasback decoys in various stages of completion. With this evidence it can reasonably be assumed that in 10 or 11 years he must have produced at least a minimum of 1,000 decoys, perhaps many more. However, it should be noted that the author lived in Ladysmith for two years buying and selling duck decoys and only once found a pair of Evans decoys for sale at a local flea market. In other words, regardless of his production, the decoys do not turn up often even in his hometown.

Value Range FOR EVANS DECOYS

The range for Evans decoys runs from **$750-$5,000** for most birds, with some exceptional examples bringing more and working repaints bringing less at times. Most of the decoys shown from the Pitt collection would be valued at **$4,000** each.

This is an Evans Double Blue, Blue-wing Teal.
$4,000
Pitt Collection

Here are Evans Competition Grade Canvasback and Bluebill drakes. There is an Evans stamp on the bottom of the Canvasback and original paint.
$1,200
Guyette & Schmidt, Inc.

This is an Evans Canvasback hen (drake is on page 130).
$5,000-$6,000
Pitt Collection

An Evans Magnum Mallard pair dates to the second quarter of the 20th century. They have original paint, with a slight touchup.
$1,600
Guyette & Schmidt, Inc.

An Evans Bluewing Teal drake bears an Evans stamp, original paint with touch up on the speculums and white area of the head, and filled crack at the factory.
$1,200
Guyette & Schmidt, Inc.

A Magnum Evans Bluebill drake has an Evans stamp, all original.
$1,300
Guyette & Schmidt, Inc.

An Evans drake Canvasback.
$5,000-$6,000

This Evans Bluebill pair (with bottom left) are a beautiful set.
$9,250
Former Pitt Collection, Decoys Unlimited, Inc.

The other Evans Bluebill is at left and a close-up of the pair is at right.

Hays Decoys

J. M. Hays Wood Products Company, Jefferson City, Mo., circa first quarter 20th century. This company began sometime around 1920 and Henry A. Fleckenstein's *American Factory Decoys* has a brief history of both Hays and Benz and the likely relationship between the two companies. The decoys are somewhat Mason-like and the lead weight used on the decoys was stamped with the maker's name which helps if the weight is still present. Fleckenstein indicated that it was unknown if Benz preceded Hays or vice-versa but I believe Benz is from the second quarter of the 20th century. I have placed the company in the next chapter for that reason.

Mason's Decoy Factory

Of all the factory-made decoys, the ones made by Mason are the most famous. There are more Mason decoys sitting around in living rooms and collections than any other decoys made in the country. Mason's was located in Detroit, going into business around 1895 and continuing until 1924. It made five grades of decoys. The best was labeled Premier, then came Challenge, Detroit grade (called Standard grade Glass Eye by most collectors), Standard grade Tack Eye, and Fourth Grade (also known as Standard grade Painted Eye). The company called the last three No. 1 Glass Eye, No. 2 Tack Eye, and No. 3 Painted Eye respectively. There are other names such as the Challenge Grade Hollow model that was usually a special order.

Weights of all sorts are found on Masons, but there was a standard weight used by Mason. Workers did not attach them at the factory, but shipped them separate in the same box. The buyers had to attach the weight themselves.

Premier Grade Masons had very fine bill and face carving, including a nicely carved nail at the end of the bill. This nail carving was not present on any of the lesser grades. The nail on the Challenge Grade decoys, for instance, was merely painted on.

Premier Grade characteristics are: finely carved bills with the all important carved nail representation; two-piece hollow bodies normally, with flat bottoms; glass eyes, and very beautiful paint, including the well known Mason swirl pattern on the breast. Look at some of the photos and you will see that all Premiers have a triangle carved on the bill, the nail is carved in detail, the nares (nostrils) are carved as well, and glass eyes are always used.

Challenge Grade Masons are characterized by either solid (most of them) or hollow bodies, depending upon how the hunter ordered them; bill carving not nearly so pronounced as on the Premier Grades (the triangle is not present); good paint but also not quite so elaborate as the Premiers; most significantly, a painted black dot to represent the nail, not carved as in Premiers; and glass eyes.

Standard Grade or Detroit Grade Masons have glass eyes; no bill carving at all, but details represented by painting. They are all smaller than the Challenge or Premier Grades.

The No. 2 Tack Eye (Mason terminology) is exactly as it says. It is quite nearly the same as the above Standard or Detroit grade, but has tack eyes.

The No. 3 Painted Eyes is the same as the No. 2 except it has painted eyes. This was the most economical grade in the line.

There are a number of non-standard or atypical Masons about, but most of them were special order decoys (some fine examples of Seneca Lake and Back Bay decoys are illustrated in this chapter from the Pitt Collection). The Mason style of construction and painting was apparently derived from the earlier products of two earlier Michigan factory type decoys made by George Peterson and his successor, Jasper N. Dodge. They were in business in excess of 20 years prior to the Mason factory. Peterson started in 1873 and sold to Dodge in 1884. Mason operated from 1895-1924.

Value Range FOR MASON DECOYS

Merganser, Brant, and Canada Goose decoys have all brought far in excess of the value ranges listed here at various auctions, but what is listed here reflects normal averages for decoys in all grades. Mason decoys are getting out of reach of many new collectors and the prices of Masons vary widely. Most of them were not marked, and it is still possible to find Masons in antique stores and at auctions without them being so identified. However, most Masons today will start at a few hundred dollars and go into the thousands, with most collectible grade birds starting around **$700-$1,200.**

A Mason Premier Grade Wood Duck drake broke all Mason records when it sold for **$354,500** in 2000 at an auction. At the same auction, its companion, a rare Premier Grade salesman's sample of the same duck, sold for **$24,000**. These are exceptional and rare prices for exceptional and one-of-a-kind decoys. Most Masons can still be purchased for sums affordable to the more advanced collector and some Masons are still found for a few hundred dollars that would be fine additions to any collection.

A beginning value range for collectible common Mason duck decoys would be **$700-$1,200** for most decent birds. This would not even be a beginning price for special order birds, branded birds, or magnums and special poses.

A Mason Premier grade Widgeon drake is circa 1915.
$11,000
Hank and Judy Norman Collection

A Mason tack-eyed Dowitcher (Robin Snipe) and a tack-eyed Yellowlegs by Mason are circa 1910.
$1,750 each
Hank and Judy Norman Collection

Value Range FOR MASON DECOYS

A Mason Standard Grade glass eyed White-wing Scoter was used as a confidence decoy.
$800-$1,200
Pitt Collection

Here are Mason Premier Grade Black Ducks.
$5,000+ each

 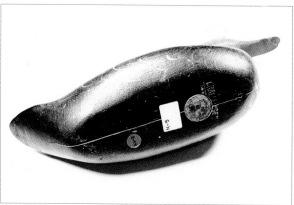

This Mason Black Duck is Challenge Grade. The second photo shows the bottom of the decoy.
$2,500-$3.500
Pitt Collection

The Mason Standard Grade Black Duck has glass eyes.
$1,000-$1,500
Pitt Collection

This drake Blue-wing Teal is a Mason Premier Grade decoy.
$10,000+
Pitt Collection

Here is a Mason Premier Grade Blue-wing Teal hen.
$10,000+
Pitt Collection

A drake Blue-wing Teal is a "butterball"
Mason Standard Grade with glass eyes.
$8,750
Pitt Collection

This is the hen Blue-wing Teal Mason Standard Grade, with glass eyes. A second photo shows the decoy's bottom.
$5,000+
Pitt Collection

The Blue-wing Teal drake is a Mason Standard Grade, with painted eyes.
$1,200-$2,000
Pitt Collection

Tack eyes mark these three Mason Standard Grade Blue-wing Teal drakes.
$5,500 each
Pitt Collection

This Green-wing Teal drake is a Mason in the Premier Grade.
$10,000+
Pitt Collection

The Mason Standard Grade Green-wing Teal drake has painted eyes.
$1,000-$2,500
Pitt Collection

This Back Bay Widgeon drake is a Mason Premier Grade decoy.
$5,000-$10,000
Pitt Collection

This Back Bay Widgeon drake is in Mason's Challenge Grade.
$3,500+
Pitt Collection

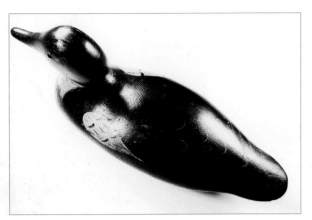

A Red-breasted Merganser drake is in the Mason Standard Grade, with glass eyes.

$1,000-$1,500

Pitt Collection

A Redhead drake in Mason Premier Grade is the low-head version.

$5,000+

Pitt Collection

This Mason Standard Grade Old Squaw drake features glass eyes.

$1,000-$2,500

Pitt Collection

A Wood Duck drake in Mason Standard Grade has glass eyes.

$2,500-$4,000

Pitt Collection

Painted eyes mark this Mason Standard Grade Wood Duck drake.

$2,500-$4,000

Pitt Collection

A Bufflehead drake in Mason Standard Grade has glass eyes.

$1,000-$1,500

Pitt Collection

Value Range FOR MASON DECOYS

Here is a Mason Oversize Back Bay Premier Grade Redhead drake.
$7,500-$15,000
Pitt Collection

A close-up shows the detail on the head of the Mason Redhead drake.

This hen is a Mason Oversize Back Bay Premier Grade Redhead decoy.
$7,500-$15,000
Pitt Collection

The Mason "snake-head" Pintail drake, in Standard Grade with glass eyes, is a very rare configuration.
$32,000
Pitt Collection

The Mason Standard Grade Pintail Drake has glass eyes.
$2,500-$4,000
Pitt Collection

A close-up shows the "snake-head" of the Pintail drake.

Here is a Pintail hen in Mason Standard Grade, with glass eyes.
$2,500-$4,000
Pitt Collection

A Widgeon or Bald-plate drake is in Mason Standard Grade with glass eyes.

$1,500-$3,000

Pitt Collection

Here is a Mason Standard Grade, painted eye Pintail drake.

$1,000-$2,500

Pitt Collection

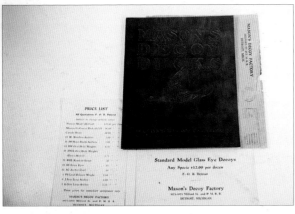

An original Mason Decoy Ducks catalog dates from 1923.

$300+

Pitt Collection

A Mallard hen with glass eyes is a Mason Standard Grade decoy.

$1,800-$2,500

Pitt Collection

This is a Mason Challenge Grade Mallard drake.

$3,500-$5,000

Pitt Collection

A Mallard Drake with glass eyes is in the Mason Standard Grade.

$1,000-$1,500

Pitt Collection

Painted eyes mark the Mason Standard Grade Mallard drake.
$700-$1,200
Pitt Collection

A Bluebill hen in Mason Challenge Grade has the standard head.
$3,500-$5,000
Pitt Collection

Both male and female are alike in the Mason Atlantic Brant Challenge Grade. The photos also show reinforcing dowel and a brand.
$7,500-$15,000
Pitt Collection

Here are details of the Mason Challenge Grade, standard head Bluebill.
Pitt Collection

The low neck version of this Bluebill drake is in the Mason Premier Grade.

$7,500+

Pitt Collection

This Bluebill is in the Mason Oversize Premier Grade.

$7,500+

Pitt Collection

Here is the bottom of the Bluebill Mason Oversize Premier Grade decoy.

Pitt Collection

A small body Bluebill drake was made by Special Order in the Premier Grade by Mason.

$2,500-$4,000

Pitt Collection

A low head Bluebill hen is in the Mason Challenge Grade.

$6,000+

Pitt Collection

Here are details of the Mason Special Order Premier Grade small body Bluebill drake.

Pitt Collection

Value Range FOR MASON DECOYS

Here is a low head Bluebill hen in Mason Premier Grade.
$6,500+
Former Pitt Collection, Decoys Unlimited, Inc.

Painted eyes mark the Mason Standard Grade Bluebill drake.
$700-$1,200
Pitt Collection

This Canvasback drake is in Mason Standard Grade, with glass eyes.
$1,800-$3,000
Pitt Collection

A Canvasback "snake-head" drake is in Mason Premier Grade.
$15,000+
Pitt Collection

A Canvasback hen is in Mason Challenge Grade.
$3,000-$5,000
Pitt Collection

Here is the drake Canvasback in a Mason Challenge Grade decoy.
$3,000-$5,000
Pitt Collection

Factory Decoys from the Vintage Period **141**

A Canvasback hen in Mason Standard Grade has glass eyes.
$1,200-$1,800
Pitt Collection

A Back Bay Canvasback drake is in Mason Premier Grade.
$5,000-$7,500
Pitt Collection

One of the Mason Special Orders is this Seneca Lake Premier Grade Canvasback drake.
$20,000+
Pitt Collection

This is the Seneca Lake Canvasback hen in a Mason Special Order Premier Grade.
$20,000+
Pitt Collection

A Redhead drake is in Mason Premier Grade.
$5,000-$7,500
Pitt Collection

This is the Redhead hen in Mason Premier Grade.

$5,000-$7,500

Pitt Collection

This is a very rare, special order Mason Challenge Grade decoy with the colorful extra blue on the wings. It's a Double Blue Blue-wing Teal drake from the Pitt Collection.

$10,000-$12,500

A Mason Greater Scaup drake (Bluebill) dates to the first quarter of the 20th century. It is Premier Grade, with original paint, missing eyes, cracks and dents.

$400

Guyette & Schmidt, Inc.

A rare Widgeon drake, Premier Grade, produced by the Mason factory early in the 20th century has original paint, several tiny dents, with original newspaper wrapping visible.

$55,000

Guyette & Schmidt, Inc.

A Mason Decoy Mallard pair, in Premier Grade, is circa first quarter of the 20th century. It has original paint, minor roughness to tail tips, the hen has two small cracks in underside of bill.

$13,000

Guyette & Schmidt, Inc.

Peterson Decoy Factory

The Peterson Decoy Factory was the predecessor to the far more famous Dodge Decoy Factory. It was founded by George Peterson circa 1873 and lasted until 1884. See the discussion concerning the sale of the Peterson company to J. N. Dodge under the Dodge entry in this chapter. This was one of the very first attempts at factory decoy production in America. The evolution from Peterson to Dodge to Mason is obvious to the collector when examining these beautiful early wooden decoys. The characteristics of the Peterson birds still are highly visible in the Mason decoys, including the more rounded bottoms and ovular shape of the sides. To me, the most obvious difference is that the Peterson heads are almost a little too large in proportion to the body, at least a little larger than most Mason heads. Regardless, a Peterson is a beautiful decoy and a prized addition to any collection due to its rarity.

A Peterson Widgeon drake, circa last quarter of the 19th century, has original paint, with neck filler missing.
$1,200
Guyette & Schmidt, Inc.

A Challenge Grade Peterson Black Duck, circa late 1800s, is rare, with original paint, small dents and cracks.
$5,000
Guyette & Schmidt, Inc.

William Pratt Manufacturing Co.

This Joliet, Ill., company was established as a hardware manufacturing company in 1893 by William Pratt. He continued with the company until his retirement in 1933. The company did not begin producing any large number of decoys until 1921, with the first samples being done in 1920. In 1924, when the Mason Decoy factory went out of business, Pratt bought out its production line and expanded the decoy making enterprise. But the company never approached the quality of Mason decoys. By the issuance of its 1925 catalog, Pratt could list a full complement of decoys, decoy anchors, live decoy supplies, and even a duck call. Most of Pratt's decoys exhibit the rough ridging left by the lathe blades.

They called this a feather-finish model, but this was more likely a way to glamorize their lack of sanding and finishing the decoys.

Because Pratt most likely picked up some Mason inventory with the purchase, collectors sometimes find nice Mason bodies with Pratt heads on them or Masons with a little different paint pattern than a true Mason. Other types of decoys made by Pratt include the metal Hurd Decoy and the Profile Goose Decoys. Pratt also made a Crow similar to a Perdew Crow.

The Animal Trap Company of America (Victor) eventually bought out Pratt. One unusual thing is its clever use of fake names in advertising decoys so the company knew where orders were being generated. The Pratt name never appears in many years of an advertising review.

I have left the Pratt decoys in this chapter even though they also go into the modern era past 1935, because it did indeed start during the earlier era and also because it bought out the Mason company and stock. The Pratt decoy is a transitional bird between the heyday of classic decoy manufacturing and the modern era of factory birds. It seems only fitting that the Pratt examples are duck decoys of fine shape and contour, but not finished as nicely as their predecessors. This is a good example of the transition to modern mass production of decoys for a sporting market apparently not as concerned about quality as price. It offered various degrees of quality over the years. The company was sold in 1937 to the Joslyn Manufacturing & Supply Company, which soon thereafter sold the decoy making operation to the Animal Trap Company of America (see next chapter).

Value Range FOR PRATT DECOYS

Most Pratt decoys will sell for $300-$1,000 with only exceptional examples bringing more. The most valuable Pratt decoys will be the rare species and perhaps some of the nice Mason-bodied birds from the early years of Pratt. A pair of similar Buffleheads sold for $4,200 in 2006.

A rare Pratt Bufflehead drake has its original paint.
$550
Guyette & Schmidt, Inc.

Sperry Decoy Factory

This factory has little written about it to date. It was known as Paul A. Sperry, Manufacturer, New Haven, Conn., in advertisements circa early 1920s. See Henry A. Fleckenstein Jr.'s *American Factory Decoys* for a reproduction of a 1923 advertisement from *Field & Stream Magazine* showing two decoy examples. The company made both cedar wood decoys and balsa wood decoys and only sold directly to the consumer, cutting out the normal jobbers and retailers, according to its own advertising. Decoys were advertised as having flat bottoms painted with "non-glint" paint to eliminate shine and glitter on the birds.

A Sperry Merganser drake is oversized, with original paint.
$1,100
Guyette & Schmidt, Inc.

H. A. Stevens

Harvey A. Stevens lived and worked in Weedsport, N.Y. He died in 1894 and his brother, George W. Stevens, apparently carried on for a while, for there have been some decoys found with his initials in the brand. Stevens decoys were marked H. A. Stevens, Weedsport, N.Y., by use of stencils, so if you find an original paint model, it should be easy to identify. If you are not so lucky, there are other reliable ways. He almost always manufactured his decoys with an inlaid lead weight (poured into a drilled circular hole) and a line tie staple recessed in a similar hole. Tails are paddle type and glass eyes were the rule. Paint was fairly thick and the comb-feather technique was used extensively. Heads were screwed into the body from the top, resulting in a hole plugged with a piece of dowel.

Stevens decoys are classified as factory decoys because the Stevens brothers advertised nationally to sell their decoys and provided some full-time employment for others. However, Stevens decoys made from 1880 to 1902 were all hand-carved rather than turned on a lathe. The most unusual form is the rare long-bodied, round-bottom style with strong comb painting shown from the Norman Collection.

Value Range FOR STEVENS DECOYS

The collector value range for Stevens decoys is from **$300 to $2,000**, with a few bringing **$2,500-$6,000**. The record Widgeon sold for $18,150 in 1990.

This is a rare Redhead drake by Harvey Stevens, circa 1890.
Note the comb painting on sides and back.
$6,000
Hank and Judy Norman Collection

Chapter Four:

Modern Factory Decoys

This chapter is devoted to what I call the "modern" factory decoys.

I am an unabashed "Baby Boomer" born in 1947 and have a decidedly different concept on collectibility than did collectors writing similar works even a few years ago. I believe that a lot of nice items exist from the modern era, deserving our attention and our collecting.

It is tough to discern where to break off the vintage from the modern in decoy collecting. For fishing items I have used 1940, and it made great sense given the changes World War II brought to fishing. However, for decoy production, a more suitable year is 1935. The reason to select 1935 is because it demarcates the year that both the use of live decoys and the use of baiting were outlawed by the federal government under the

Lacey Act Amendments. Market gunning was, of course, outlawed in 1918 and other provisions of conservation had begun, including the Waterfowl Stamp Act of 1934. However, not since the use of hundreds of decoys by the market gunners prior to 1918 was there as much impetus for the renewed production of duck decoys until the live "callers" were outlawed in 1935. Until they were made illegal, the average gunner could do little better than use a few live English Call Ducks to do the double duty of decoying and calling in live game. However, after 1935, hunters once again created a market demand for both duck decoys and duck calls.

In addition to the legal changes that set the stage for renewed decoy and call production, the time period also saw the introduction of many new materials and manufacturing techniques. Some of these changes were brought upon companies by the outside forces of World War II. Other changes were born of opportunities afforded by inventions in the making of modern plastics. The result of all of these historical forces working together was the birth of many new manufacturing companies, some of which were long lived and some of which only contributed to the body of sporting memorabilia for a short time. It was this time period that led to expansions in the use of rubber, plastics, cork, mass production techniques and mass marketing techniques, all of which left an impact on the hobby of decoy collecting.

There are many excellent references for decoy collecting on the market. However, I know there is a need for a detailed reference for items of this so-called "modern" age. It is my intention to cover important changes in the big companies, introduce the readers to some of the lesser known companies, and provide a history of the changes that ultimately led to the closing or selling off of most major companies by 1970.

It is not hard to figure out why more collectors are now starting to concentrate on the modern items: the pricing of vintage items is driving them to another part of the hobby. How many decoy collectors can really hope to amass a 200-plus Mason collection? However, pricing of some modern items is also surprising as indicated by the Lititz, Pa., Victor D-9 I sold online for $60 plus shipping/insurance.

I have also met many collectors who relate to the modern items the same as the older collectors related to the vintage items. Those items bring back childhood memories. "Modern" duck decoys have come of age. The point is simple: what appeared at the edge of the hobby five years ago has now become central to the hobby. Without an interest in "modern" items, most of the new members would not have anything to collect, and frankly would be priced out of a most fascinating hobby.

Dating Techniques of Modern Sporting Collectibles

One of the most puzzling areas for any collector new to the field of collectibles is how to reliably date an item. Here are some thoughts:

1. Catalogs and magazines are invaluable aids to dating items. However, the catalogs themselves are too expensive for the average collector to acquire just for dating purposes. Magazines, on the other hand, are very affordable and can assist one in determining the first year of production of an item, short production run identification, and trends in manufacturing. I have identified many decoys and related items by scanning through old magazines and seeing the "only" advertisement ever run by a small company. It is common to find magazines from the '50s for only a few dollars each in mint condition.

2. Club literature of the various decoy and call collector clubs is another wonderful source of data. In addition, old issues of newsletters and club magazines can assist one in identifying "unknown" items. There has been a bias in most decoy publications toward the older, pre-1935 items but more interest is being shown in articles on such companies as Herter's and others in recent publications. This will serve as another important source of information for the collector in the future.

3. Packaging is a big clue in dating items if you are lucky enough to find a decoy or game call in its box or on its card. The first thing to look at is the address to determine if a Zip Code is present. Zippy introduced the Zip Code for the U.S. Postal Service in 1963 and the Zip Code started appearing immediately on some packaging. However, the lack of a Zip Code may also simply mean that the company used up "in stock" packaging first or failed to comply with new postal regulations. The lack of a Zip Code is not a guarantee that an item is pre-1963, but it is one possible indicator. Also, I have noticed that many companies used the Zip Code on a coupon or mailing label, but not on the front of a package or catalog for the first few years of the '60s. So, again, beware. Lack of Zip Code was often only a sign of a company being slow to react to new postal regulations and/or the layout department was not being creative, using old copy for catalogs and advertisements.

4. Material is one of the most important clues for dating decoys. Rubber was commonly used as early as 1930 on decoys. However, the newer synthetic materials did not really take hold until after World War II in most instances. Molded fiber was first used in 1939 and was popular throughout the early 1950s, when Styrofoam and Tenite started taking over the market share. Wooden decoys after 1935 were apt to be made out of lighter wood, as quality cedar was in short supply. Even major fishing lure companies had problems getting enough. Also, the war years made many materials scarce, if not illegal, for use in sporting products. Herter's made thousands of wooden decoys, but the wood was a very light balsa material and not cedar in most cases. Rubber became popular with some companies again after the war era, but most decoys eventually became polyethylene based. Of course, we also have great decoys combining materials, such as Herter's graphically printed canvas over cork and Johnson's folding decoys beautifully printed and mounted on fiberboard. By the mid-1950s, most decoys were Styrofoam (Herter's called them Durlon), Tenite, polyethylene, light wood, cork, or a combination of materials. Herter's reintroduced quality cedar decoys as "antique decoys" in the 1970s and these are quite collectible due to their beauty and fairly small production runs. However, if you have one dated from the 1800s, it is not old, but only an advertising ploy of the company.

5. Package colors and materials also evolved and are an obvious indication of approximate time of manufacture. The two-piece cardboard shot shell box did not live too long into the '30s for most companies. Calls likely came in two-piece cardboard boxes until the early 1950s. However, in general, one finds many smaller companies going to a solid two-piece plastic rectangular box without hinges or hinged one-piece plastic boxes as early as the later '40s or early '50s. Part cardboard and part cellophane boxes were also common for calls. Then the slide top boxes became very common by the mid-'50s for most call companies. Eventually, calls were coming in bubble packs with little resemblance to the earlier beautiful packaging. Items can usually be dated to a range of years by the package type and/or color. Of course, addresses on the packaging may also help date a company if one knows the various locations of the company.

6. Handling items for which you already know the dates is the most important way to date an item. You can learn to compare by examination of similarities and differences. This is one of the main advantages of the sporting collectible and decoy shows. You are able to walk around, pick up items, ask questions, make comparisons, learn, and not spend a cent. Most people who do the shows also enjoy helping one learn about the items they have for sale. So go, ask, learn, and maybe even buy an item or two. I no longer go to shows in anticipation of selling, as I believe the Internet is a far superior tool for that avenue. However, I still enjoy seeing thousands of decoys, shell boxes, game calls, etc., in one spot and it is a great social activity.

7. Company Names and Packaging. One way to help date an item is to examine its packaging and note the full company name, which often changed through the years, and the complete address of the company. As we learn more about the modern items and their production, it will become easier to place an item in time once we can place it in space. For example, where was your Animal Trap product made? What other company names appear on the item?

8. Benchmarks include literature or advertising introducing an item as "NEW." But beware. Some companies used the designation "NEW" for more than one year to sell their products. Catalogs, magazine advertisements, company brochures, call box inserts, separate wholesaler fliers or advertisements, and company histories can all be useful. I think that the wisest investment the new collector can make is that once a direction for the collection has been decided upon, purchase the company catalog for the particular year of the beginning of the collection. Then, attempt to follow the changes in following years through catalogs and advertising in trade magazines and popular literature. Research and collecting must both have a beginning. Once you have this foundation, the rest of your collection is built on the strength of knowledge of your product.

9. Oral History. I long ago learned the importance of paying attention to oral history. Seek out "informants" when attempting to learn the history of an area or subject. This is no different in decoy and sporting collectible history. It is most important to the future of decoy history and sporting collectibles that we document all we are able to about the history of items by seeking out individuals with knowledge. We must write down what they have to say while the information is still available. I have learned much through discussions with collectors, decoy carvers, call manufacturers, jobbers and retailers in the trade. I can only hope that others are also documenting all they are able to while it is fresh in the minds of those involved.

10. Patents, Trademarks, Trade Names and Copyrights. One final way to date an item is to complete a patent search for the item on the U.S. Patent and Trademark Office Web site found at http://www.uspto.gov. The site is quite easy to use and will result in finding great details on an individual piece. Sometimes the only information we have about an item is the patent number printed on it. Entering the number in the search process will result in a complete history of the item. There are limitations on certain searches unless you know the patent number. Keep in mind that the patent year only indicates when the patent was actually granted. Sometimes this was years after an item was "used in commerce." It is also possible to conduct trademark, trade name, and copyright searches for items. However, this is a bit more complicated than entering the patent number. Trademark and trade name searches are conducted through the U.S. Patent and Trademark Office. Copyright searches would be completed through the Library of Congress, the organization in charge of protecting copyrighted material in the United States. You can go from the http://www.uspto.gov site to the copyright site but the address for copyrights is http://lcweb.loc.gov/copyright/ and it tells one how to go about searches. Also, keep in mind that if you are printing items for publication, some of the materials on the U.S. government sites are protected by copyright. You will need permission to reprint certain items for publication.

"The Modern Era"

The modern era, beginning in 1935, has ushered in a whole new field of collecting that this book can just barely touch upon: collectibles made for the collectibles market. I include in this list: limited edition art prints; limited edition wood carvings that are not actual decoys but still represent the decoy makers' art; original art work in oil, acrylic, bronze, ceramic, etc.; books of a rare or limited production nature in the field of sports and decoys; limited edition duck calls; limited edition knives, and the list goes on. For the lack of vintage items, we certainly do not lack current classics on which to concentrate.

I cannot say, without a crystal ball, which of these newer items will really become rare or collectible in the long run. However, there are many items on which we can spend our money when we can't find the right Mason decoy for our collection. All of these items also have a place in the hearts of collectors.

The Modern Decoy Companies

Here is a grouping of modern duck decoys, including a Victor D-16, Victor D-9s, Plasti-Duk decoys, an inflatable unmarked drake Mallard, and more.

Animal Trap Company of America (Victor)

This company produced mass quantities of duck decoys under the names Victor and Animal Trap. Its history is still not totally clear. However, we know that the company acquired a previous maker or makers located in Pascagoula, Miss., and also acquired the Pratt Decoy Company of Joliet, Ill. Pratt had earlier purchased the Mason Decoy Company and thus Animal Trap became an owner in the Mason line; however, it never produced the Mason type decoys.

The company did produce wooden, fiber and plastic decoys of note. The wooden ones were made originally in the Mississippi operations, but apparently continued in Pennsylvania. Company addresses eventually included Mississippi, Pennsylvania and Ontario, Canada. Victor was one of the three big fiber duck producers. It also invented and produced what many consider the finest of the early plastic ducks, the D-9. A Victor D-9 drake Mallard recently sold online for $60. This decoy was marked with the "Majestic Decoys" trademark in a flying duck on one side of the keel.

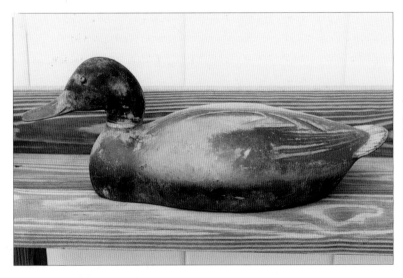

The Victor D-9 drake Mallard is considered the finest of the early plastic ducks.

There is much confusion surrounding the products of this company. The reason is the obscure history or evolution of the company and its relationships to companies it purchased. It is also clear that the Mississippi operations ceased production during the war years to manufacture military items, which was true of nearly every factory in the country.

There were various companies making decoys in the Pascagoula area, but the two better known were the Victor Company and the Pascagoula Decoy Company whose decoys were sold under the trade name "PADCO." The Victor Company products from Mississippi, when marked, carry the stamp "VICTOR" and later, "ANIMAL TRAP CO. OF MISSISSIPPI, Inc." The following advertisement in the 1947 *Shooter's Bible* illustrates the problem:

Mississippi Wood Decoys

We are pleased to advise that the popular line of DEPENDABLE Tupelo Mississippi DUCK DECOYS is again available in two well known grades: SUPREME and STANDARD. In four species—Mallard, Pintail, Blue Bill and Black Duck; packed 8 drakes and 4 hens, in cartons containing 12 decoys each. The following prices are Per Dozen, in Cartons of 12, f.o.b. Pascagoula, Mississippi. BRAND DESCRIPTION PRICE SUPREME (Extra light, smooth finish) $24.00, STANDARD (Regular weight, rough finish) **$15.00**.

The decoys shown in the advertisement appear to be Victor wooden decoys and the eight drakes/four hens per carton was Victor's common practice. Note that Carry-Lite and some others shipped six drakes/six hens per carton. I would guess that the lighter Supremes are balsa and thus finish smoother with the same equipment and the Standards are a heavier wood and do not finish as nicely. But, are they PADCO or Victor? My guess is Victor.

Although the paint patterns used by the two different companies were somewhat different from each other, the lathe-turned bodies were almost identical. They are crude looking but nicely shaped. Both companies left the ribbed or ridged look imparted by the duplicating lathe blades, ostensibly to give the decoys some representation of feathers. It could just as easily be said that the marks were left to save time and money in the finishing process.

The degree to which the grooves or ribs are apparent was probably due to the type of wood from which the decoys were made. Generally speaking, the harder the wood the more obvious the ribbing. Wooden dowels attached heads, some being left loose for changing head position or transporting them without damage.

Painting was done by spraying, perhaps with some handwork on the wing details and heads. Hundreds of thousands of these birds were made and sold through several companies' sales catalogs, such as Sears and Roebuck and Montgomery Ward. They became tremendously popular after the end of World War II. They are probably the most commonly found wooden decoys in the country.

I think that the decoys have doubled in the last 10 years to about $200 for a common duck in excellent shape. However, a large number of them are on the market, keeping the prices down for now. I would think this a good investment, however, for a beginning collector as they are available and a nice collection could be built at a reasonable cost. They will appreciate, just not as rapidly as a Mason or an Evans.

Value Range FOR ANIMAL TRAP (VICTOR) DECOYS

Papier-mâché decoys: **$75-$250.**
Plastic decoys: **$10-$75.**
Wooden decoys: **$50-$300.**
Salesman samples/miniatures: **$50-$100 each.**

A pair of Animal Trap Mallards from Pascagoula, Miss., features hollowed out bottoms, circa 1940s-early 1950s.
$125 each
Pitt Collection

This Animal Trap/Victor D-11 Canvasback is from Lititz, Pa.
$25-$40
Pitt Collection

These are Mississippi era hollowed out wooden Victor Mallards.

$250/pair

Former Pitt Collection, Decoys Unlimited, Inc.

The bottom of a Victor Mallard shows how the decoys were hollowed out.

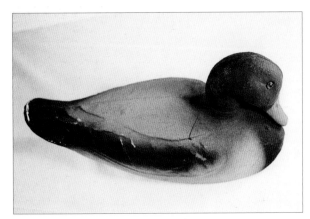

Tru-Life papier-mâché bird is from the Lititz, Pa., era of Animal Trap Co. Victor.

$75-$125

Pitt Collection

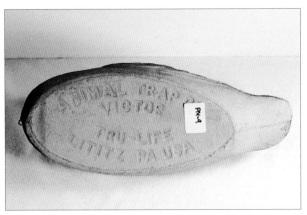

The bottom of a Tru-Life decoy has the Animal Trap and Victor labels.

A Victor Model D-10 Scaup drake shows the cross keel to wrap an anchor rope, developed in the mid-'50s.

$40-$60

Pitt Collection

A more difficult species to find is the Victor Model D-11 Pintail drake.

$25-$40

Pitt Collection

This Victor oversized D-11 Mallard drake has a cross keel.

$25-$40

Pitt Collection

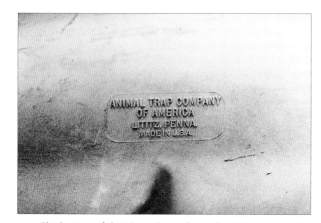

The bottom of the Victor decoy shows the Victor trademark along with the name and address of the Animal Trap Company.

A pair of Bluebills are Victor Model D-9s.

$75 a pair

Lewis Collection

This Victor D-100 oversize Bluebill hen decoy is newer, dating after the purchase by Woodstream, circa 1970s.

$10-$25

Lewis Collection

This Animal Trap Co. of America Pintail hen, Model D-9, was made in Lititz, Pa., circa mid-1950s.

$25-$40

Lewis Collection

This is a Victor Model D-9-R drake Mallard, marked "Woodstream, Lititz, Penna," copyright 1967. This is a patent pending model and thus unique even though a Mallard drake. Note the gaudy new paint scheme.

$25-$40

Lewis Collection

Here is a Victor Model D-9 Pintail hen, circa late 1960s. It has a cross anchor rope wrapping system.

$25-$40

Lewis Collection

A D-16 Mallard drake of the Animal Trap Co., Lititz, Pa., dates to the late 1960s.

$25-$40

Lewis Collection

A Victor papier-mâché Owl decoy is circa mid-1950s.

$75 +

Lewis Collection

A Victor Model D-9 Bluebill hen is circa 1967.

$40-$60

Lewis Collection

This Victor Model D-9 Mallard hen shows the anchor, circa 1967.

$25-$40

Lewis Collection

Armstrong Decoys

Armstrong Decoys from Houston, Texas, were interesting little canvas over stuffing decoys that were from our early modern period. Shown is a pair of Mallards in nearly perfect shape. One of the problems is finding these in nice shape.

Value Range FOR ARMSTRONG DECOYS

Most Armstrong decoys will bring at least **$125** in decent shape with the more unusual species demanding double that value.

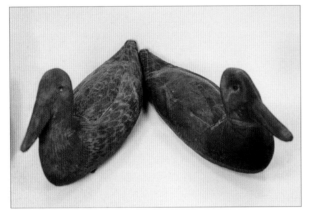

A Mallard hen and drake were made by Armstrong Decoy Company, circa 1930s.

$125 each

Lewis Collection

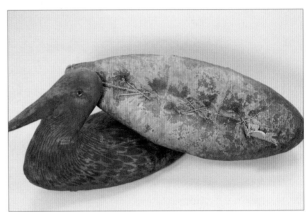

Sewing details are shown on the bottom of Armstrong decoys.

A grouping of Armstrong decoys includes two Canada Geese. The rest are Pintails and Mallards, with some tip ups. This is a great sale buy.

$700

Guyette & Schmidt, Inc.

B and J Manufacturing Co.

This is what I would label a "classic" modern decoy that was manufactured by B & J Manufacturing Company of Chicago, Ill. This bird had wings that moved by wave action when a line was pulled by the natural breeze/wave combinations. It was made in both papier-mâché and hard rubber; the one shown is rubber. It was developed under U.S. Patent number 2747316 by F. J. Benedetto, filed Aug. 17, 1953, and granted May 29, 1956.

The line drawings in the patent application show the anchor attached to a line and the bird moving around in different positions of waves to show how the wings would work in the natural conditions. Of course, today we have Robo-Duck and some others available from Cabela's that work on advanced computer principles and concepts of magnetism. There were earlier duck decoys with movement principles as well. But this is my favorite one for showing how our new post-war technologies culminated in a neat contraption to lure ducks to the blind.

Value Range FOR B&J DECOYS

These nifty modern decoys will sell for **$200** to **$500**, depending on model, condition, and if accompanied by boxes and paper instructions.

A B&J movable-wing duck was made in the mid-1950s.
$250
Pitt Collection

The B&J movable-wing duck is shown with wings open.

Benz Lifelike Decoys

Benz Lifelike Decoys was based in Jefferson City, Mo., circa late 1930s. See the entry in the Older Factory section on Hays Decoys for a discussion of the relationship between the two Jefferson City companies. I believe the Benz birds are newer and date from circa 1937, plus or minus a few years. I base my conclusion on the circular reproduced in Fleckenstein's *American Factory Decoys* that in my opinion dates from Dec. 6, 1937. Most circulars, and even boxes for fishing lures and game calls, have date codes and I think the code 12637 is simply the time of printing the circular. I also believe the print style and design is more typical of the later 1930s than of a period prior to 1920. Of course, one other indicator is the lower prices received for the decoys at auction. However, as Fleckenstein so clearly states, we know little about these two companies compared to the major Detroit decoy factories.

A Bluebill drake by Benz Decoys has original paint and small dents.

$250

Guyette & Schmidt, Inc.

A Superior Grade Model Benz Green-wing Teal drake has its original paint with small cracking underneath.

$600

Guyette & Schmidt, Inc.

Carry-Lite Decoys

Carry-Lite began producing fiber molded decoys from pulp as early as 1939. However, due to the war era, production did not become significant again until the late 1940s. A review of *The Shooter's Bible* for 1947 shows what Carry-Lite had to offer right after World War II:

#710 STANDARD MALLARD Realistically painted in a dead flat waterproof paint; most of the decorations finished by hand; packed 6 drakes and 6 hens to the shipping container; weight approximately 14 lb. per carton.

Sold only in full dozen lot, **$12.00**

They also offered in the same configurations, for the same prices, the following:

#711 PINTAIL
#712 BLUEBILL
#713 CANVASBACK
#714 BLACK DUCK

All prices were F.O.B. Milwaukee, Wis., home of Carry-Lite Decoys. Carry-Lite also offered two sizes of its Horned Owl decoy, the #651 at 10 1/4" from tip of tail to top of horn and the #652 at 14 1/2" from tip of tail to top of horn. It also had a Goose decoy about 24" from tip of tail to breast. Finally, the Crow decoy was also available and measured 16" from beak to tip of the tail. Any of the foregoing could be purchased individually or by the dozen. The advertisement explaining the duck decoys also indicated that glass eyes were used on all duck decoys.

These earlier Carry-Lite Decoys can be differentiated by a label affixed to the bottom of them showing a pair of duck hunters standing in marsh grass with four ducks landing into their spread of 11 Carry-Lite Decoys (one must be hiding). Carry-Lite Decoys is at the top, following the contours of the oval label. Later Carry-Lites are identified by the indentations being clearly marked as shown, with either regular beaks or Dura-Beaks.

Carry-Lite produced an extremely large number of fiber birds and they are common. However, some species are not common and finding them in pristine condition can be a challenge. Clearly, with all the fiber birds, damage is common on the bills, wing edges, and tails. Also, Pintails and many other less common birds are difficult to find. Remember that about 90 percent of all decoys used by hunters were Mallards and it is clear that the other species are less common. Bluebills were the next most common species, followed by Canvasbacks and others. Again, the catalog pages on pages 62-63 really demonstrate the birds at their best.

Value Range FOR CARRY-LITE DECOYS

Papier-mâché Decoys: **$75-$250.**
Plastic decoys: **$10-$75.**
Salesman samples/miniatures: **$50-$100 each.**

The company also produced goose decoys and some decorator ducks and salesman samples. All of these are more difficult to find. The photos show some examples of Carry-Lite birds.

Carry-Lite DECOYS

De Luxe Mallards: 1 doz. case assortment supplied with THE HEAD OF EVERY DUCK TURNED IN A DIFFERENT DIRECTION.

NO TWO ALIKE! Adds greatly to realism. Attracts birds more readily. An exclusive Carry-Lite feature so far as we know.

No. 800 DE LUXE MALLARD HEN

No. 800 DE LUXE MALLARD DRAKE

No. 850

DUCK MINIATURES

Attractive as desk ornaments . . . or can be used as a floating bath-tub toy for small children. Universal appeal. Stock some.

No. 735 ANCHOR REEL ATTACHMENT

More AND Better DECOYS

For 1941, we have not only added several new numbers to our line, as illustrated on this page, but improved production processes assure even better decoys than last year's excellent product.

Carry-Lite Features: Hollow-molded by a special process which not only assures extremely light weight, but also realistically reproduces feathers and lines of the actual duck. Carry-Lite natural design and coloring BRINGS THE BIRDS where other types of decoys fail, according to enthusiastic sportsmen who "bag the limit" with Carry-Lites. They are waterproofed both inside and outside. Will not list or tip; guaranteed to right themselves when tossed into the water. No weights needed for balance (additional weights are detrimental to the use of these decoys). Finished in dead flat paints, in natural colors. Most of decorations done by hand. Glass eyes are used throughout.

New Crow and Owl Decoys: As every outdoorsman knows, crows and owls are mortal enemies. Crows attack owls by day, owls rob crows' nests by night. Crow and Owl Decoys, mounted on fence posts or "planted" in the ground, bring on the Crows!

Weights and Packing: Carry-Lite Duck Decoys packed 8 drakes and 4 hens to shipping container weighing less than 14 lbs.

No. 650 CROW

No. 651 SMALL OWL 10¼" High

No. 652 LARGE OWL 14½" High

No. 653 GOOSE (Approx.) 32" x 24" Large, attract realistic . . . use on land or water. Should a "live" numl

DEALERS: Order from your regula sporting goods or hardware jobber. Com plete stocks available.

Carry-Lite DECOYS

MOLDED CARRY-LITE DECOYS

2601 N. 30th ST., MILWAUKEE, WIS

Carry-Lite papier-mâché Crow and an owl crow hunting kit are displayed in the box.

$300+

Pitt Collection

One of the early decoys imported was the modern Carry-Lite Italian made Goldeneye decoy. Similar Carry-Lite lines are still carried by Cabela's and others. See the unique dealer samples from this company on the following page.

$10-$25 depending on age

Lewis Collection

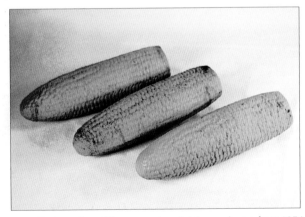

Here are Carry-Lite rare papier-mâché corn decoys from 1954. A second photo shows the hollow cores.

$50 each

Pitt Collection

Details of a Carry-Lite hen Mallard are shown.
$125
Lewis Collection

Wood Duck salesman samples from the Italian exporter of Carry-Lites to the U.S.A. are displayed. All salesman samples are hard to come by so even these plastic ones are of interest. They were purchased online more than five years ago for $50 each.
$50-$75 each
Lewis Collection

Details and a shot of a Carry-Lite drake Mallard, circa 1955, show the prices per decoy and per dozen on the bottom of the decoy along with company name imprints. These extra pricing details make this decoy worth a little more.

$175-$200
Lewis Collection

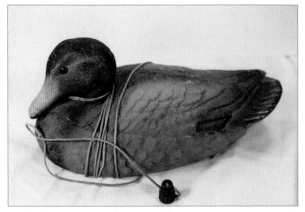

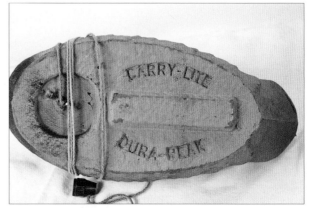

The Carry-Lite Dura Beak version of a drake Mallard has an improved toughened beak that does not break, in theory. (They do break in reality however.)

$75 due to commonness of Mallard drake
Lewis Collection

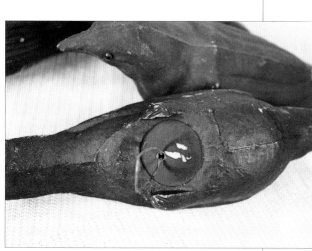

Carry-Lite Crows were made of papier-mâché.
$25-$50 each
Lewis Collection

A Carry-Lite Owl needed repairs.
$50
Lewis Collection

This Mallard pair of Carry-Lite Dura Beak models are well used. Note the raised keel version in the second photo of these.
$25 each in this worn condition
Lewis Collection

Dunster Sporting Goods Company

The Dunster Sporting Goods Company of Seattle, Wash., produced a very nice fiberboard folding goose decoy called a Dupe-A-Goose, similar to the Johnson's Folding Goose. The decoys may even have been produced by the same company for Dunster and Johnson. I have detailed the photos comparing the two in the Johnson's section. The company advertised fairly heavily in the late 1940s and early 1950s and gave an address of 16824 Pacific Highway, Seattle 88, Wash. A 1945 address was 462 No. 34th, Seattle 3, Wash.

According to a 1947 advertisement, it also offered a Dupe-A-Duck decoy in Mallard, Pintail, Scaup, Canvasback and Black Duck. It also distributed floating goose, feeding goose and stake-out goose decoys. The goose decoys were available in Canada (all types) goose. The regular stake-out decoys were available also in Snow, Blue and Speckle belly styles. One unusual item that would be nice to find was the company's "Duck Hunting Kit" consisting of a wooden carrying tote similar to a "carpenter's tote" that appears to have had the company name stenciled on its side. This held 18 duck decoys and was available in 1945. The values for these decoys would be about the same as for the Johnsons listed below.

General Fiber Company

The General Fiber Company of St. Louis produced nice fiber decoys beginning in 1946, according to an advertisement that claims them to be new that year. They produced many ducks, geese in at least two sizes, and even Swans under the Ariduk brand name. The Ariduks seem to me to be the best made of all the fiber birds and usually retain their condition well. Of course, this is also because they are newer than some of their counterparts found in the field. I have a Swan shown that clearly has the body of a goose, and would be a Snow Goose if painted properly, but is instead painted with the black bill of a Swan.

Value Range FOR ARIDUK DECOYS

Papier-mâché decoys: **$75-$250.**
Salesman samples/miniatures: **$50-$100 each.**

An Ariduk Scaup female, in pristine condition, is a harder decoy to find than the drake, circa early 1950s.
$175
Pitt Collection

The bottom of the Scaup decoy shows the Ariduk logo.

The value of this Ariduk Swan from St. Louis is only $50 due to a repaired bill broken by movers in a recent move. In good shape, this should command more than $200 due to the rarity of type.

$50-$200

Lewis Collection

An Ariduk Mallard drake is a rarer version that was made for Sears, Roebuck & Co.

$175

Pitt Collection

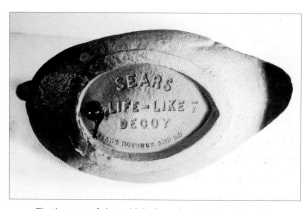

The bottom of the Ariduk decoy has the Sears brand.

The bill is green on this Ariduk Black Duck.

$125

Lewis Collection

The bottom of the Ariduk decoy has more company details.

More difficult to find is an Ariduk made for J. C. Higgins (Sears), known as a Higgins Life-Like Black Duck. Various details are shown on the second photo.

$175

Lewis Collection

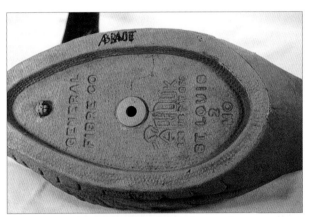

This Ariduk small Canada Goose dates to the mid-1950s. Details are shown on the bottom of the decoy.

$225

Lewis Collection

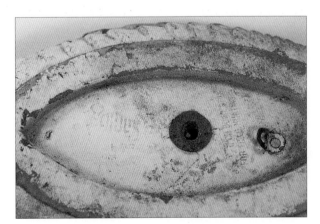

A photo shows details from the bottom of a large Ariduk Canada Goose.

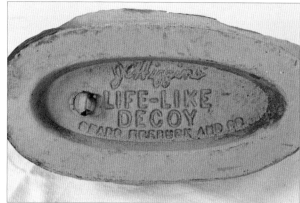

This is a J. C. Higgins Ariduk Mallard drake.
$175
Lewis Collection

Fairfax Decoys

Fairfax decoys were new in the mid-1950s (1954 for McGuire, likely 1955 for Fairfax) and apparently fairly short-lived. It was a low production company, producing high quality plastic decoys in many species. I have only a couple of them. They appear to be very well made and I would like to find examples of all of the species in excellent shape.

A most interesting thing about the decoys is the confusion names can cause. I have a section under J. S. McGuire, but it is one and the same company. Apparently he placed his name on the keel of the first decoys produced in 1954 to gain copyright protection. But then, in full production, they became "Fairfax," named after the company of which he was president, "Fairfax Engineering Co." of Kansas City, Kansas. This was only discovered by the 1955 advertisement. So if you have a decoy with just J. S. McGUIRE on it, it is an early one. The Fairfax decoys all appear to be clearly stamped on the keels with model numbers and data. They were called FFD for Fairfax Featherlite Deluxe.

Value Range FOR FAIRFAX DECOYS

The range for these plastic birds would be **$25-$150.**

Value Range FOR FAIRFAX DECOYS

The bottom of the Featherlite has details about the decoy.

A Fairfax Deluxe Featherlite Pintail drake is from the Pitt Collection.

$50-$75

Another Fairfax Deluxe Featherlite Pintail drake is in rougher shape.

$25

Lewis Collection

A Personal Message to Duck Hunters

From J. S. "Mac" McGuire, President, Fairfax Engineering Co.

"We believe ducks know ducks better than we hunters do. They can see far better than we can. You've had bunches headed straight in—then flare and leave. Wild ducks can spot ordinary decoys much farther than any shotgun range.

It is our obligation to you hunters to design Feather-Lite Deluxe decoys so near like ducks that you can bring 'em right on in to the gun! We invite your most critical inspection—THAT YOU MAY DECIDE—how well we meet that obligation.

"AS NATURAL AS NATURE"

You know the best decoys of all are live wild ducks—resting—feeding or loafing—completely relaxed and unafraid. At rest their heads are low and pulled back—Feeders have their heads higher and forward. Loafers may be looking to one side or another. Hens have different feather patterns and the proud drakes are much larger. Feather-Lite Deluxe decoys have all of these features. "JUST LIKE DUCKS."

Ducks can tell when other ducks are happy—and they surely know when other ducks are scared. All Feather-Lite Deluxe decoys are completely free from the strained necks and snaky heads of scared ducks. The bodies are high—not low like hiding ducks—or wide like enemy turtles. Much care has been given to every detail of happy ducks—YOU WILL AGREE.

Only a Live Duck Is More Natural—They Have to Fly to Be Better

Please visit your local FEATHER-LITE DELUXE DECOY DEALER. He is an alert and progressive asset to your community. Feather-Lite decoys in his store shows he looked far ahead to your hunting pleasure and satisfaction. He has other things you need and they too are the best the market affords. We can serve you best through him—BECAUSE HE HELPS MAKE YOUR TOWN A GOOD PLACE TO LIVE.

YOU DO NOT have to accept substitutes from other dealers. It's your hunting, your fun, your money at stake. You know your decoy spread is the "Welcome" sign in front of your blind. Make that "WELCOME" big and warm with Feather-Lite Deluxe Decoys that pull ducks FOUR ways. 1. THE DECOYS ARE RIGHT. 2. THEIR ACTIONS ARE RIGHT. 3. THEIR REFLECTIONS ARE RIGHT. 4. EVEN THEIR SHADOWS ARE RIGHT."

SEE YOUR FEATHER-LITE DECOY DEALER TODAY OR SEND YOUR ORDER NOW—DIRECT TO ME
J. S. McGUIRE, 2957 CHRYSLER ROAD, KANSAS CITY, KANSAS

FEATHER-LITE DELUXE DECOYS are made in six species—MALLARD, PINTAIL (SPRIG), BLACK (BLACK MALLARD), CANVASBACK, GREATER SCAUP (BLUEBILL-BROADBILL), AND REDHEAD. They are only $17.45 per half dozen plus parcel post. Even 4 drakes and 2 hens set close in will LIVEN UP YOUR SPREAD AND IMPROVE YOUR HUNTING.

You can examine these decoys for little more than it costs to park your car. Simply send your check or money order for $17.45 plus parcel post for 7 lbs. for 4 drakes and 2 hens of any of the six species. If you wish—return them promptly and we will immediately refund your purchase price. No C.O.D. please.

Copyrighted 1954—J. S. McGuire   Offered for sale only as non-mechanized waterfowl decoys

Look Decoys Over Carefully Before You Buy—The Ducks Will Before They Come In

A full-page ad in the 1955 edition of *Hunting & Gun Annual* shows a "personal message to duck hunters" from Fairfax president J.S. "Mac" McGuire.

Herter's, Inc.

Herter's is the perfect company for this chapter. It exemplifies a company that responded to changes in technology, the ability to mass-market its products, and changes in manufacturing for the masses, with quality still in mind. It is also perfect because it fits our time line of the modern era of 1935 and beyond to a tee. Herter's started in the early 1930s as a small fly-tying operation and quickly expanded, producing thousands of catalogs for mail order. It eventually opened retail outlets in six different locations within five states.

Catalog references will be given to 1893, but this was not the same man or company. It was his father's clothing and dry goods store founded in Wasceca, Minn., circa 1893. However, George Herter of Herter's, Inc. never let that fact stop him in promoting his sporting goods to the public. Actually, some of the collectible Wood Duck decoys called "Ancient Cedar Wood Decoys" by Herter's that were marketed from 1966-1977 have the date of "1893" on their base. This led some collectors to think that they indeed have a rare old Herter's. Actually, these were not really decoys: not rigged, flat bottomed, no keels or weights, and decorative only.

Herter's is a perfect illustration of responses to technological changes and marketing changes. The company did not resist technological change, but embraced it with gusto. It then made products marketed by the millions to sporting consumers throughout America and the world. A thorough study of Herter's and an understanding of its product changes made from 1935 through its demise in 1977 would give the decoy collector an excellent base of knowledge that could then be applied to other decoy companies of the same time period.

Herter's, Inc. made classic wooden decoys, wooden decoys out of much lighter balsa materials, decoys made out of Tenite (the Model 50s are superb), decoys made out of Styrofoam (Herter's called it Durlon), decoys made out of cork and cork with a wonderful printed material over stretched, silhouette decoys, shell decoys, shore birds, crows, owls, and even a rabbit decoy of Tenite in the 1960s. Herter's also made every type of game, duck and goose call imaginable. In addition, Herter's had a complete line of decoy paints that many considered second to none. They are now collectible due to the nice packaging and rarity of unused paints. A collection of just Herter's birds and related items would take one a lifetime to complete.

Some of the finest examples of decoys made by Herter's are the cork-bodied decoys with a wooden bottom board and a stretched material over the bodies that had been printed in the colors and designs of the birds. Shown are examples of both duck decoys and a goose decoy. The Canada Goose came in at least two sizes as did the duck decoys. Some of these decoys are already fetching up to $1,500. One of the Black Ducks recently sold for only $46. But it was in rough shape and the seller had no idea what it was when he/she listed it for sale. A fair price would normally be $700-$1,500.

One nice thing about Herter's is that we can still afford to buy the catalogs. Herter's sent out tens or hundreds of thousands of catalogs around the country and the world. One can find most years quite easily. Also, Herter's produced specialty decoy and game call catalogs for a number of years and these are also readily available at a reasonable price. A good selection of catalogs would be necessary to fill in all of the possible variations of Herter's decoys. For instance, the Durlon ducks were first available with wooden heads and Styrofoam bodies for only a limited time. Then, they had Tenite heads and Styrofoam bodies. Of course, the wooden-head versions are in greater demand by collectors due to their rarity.

Many of the Herter's early decoys are desirable to collectors. But by far, the most highly sought are the wooden Owl and Crow decoys. They made great Owls, actually using grizzly bear claws for the beaks of the Owls. Their Owls, for instance, usually exceed $2,000 to $3,000 when put up at auction and Crows often compete. I have shown one of the rarest of the owl decoys, the one that is clutching a crow in its talons. This decoy will sell for $3,500 at a minimum,

often more. This is without a doubt the Herter's decoy in greatest demand today.

The most common of the Herter's birds found today have solid balsa bodies and cedar heads. Most of these would be from prior to the early 1950s when Herter's very successful Models 50 and 59 Tenite decoys starting taking over the sales numbers. Also, the Durlon ducks were good sellers beginning in the early 1950s and the balsa birds were dying out. It was not until Herter's reintroduced cedar decorative birds in the 1960s that wooden ducks did much in sales. However, some wooden decoys were marketed throughout the period.

I would say that the most collectible Herter's are (in order of demand): the wooden crows and owls; the early fabric over cork decoys from the 1930s; the early balsa/cedar duck and goose decoys from the 1940s and early 1950s; the decorative "ancient cedar decoys" from the 1960s/1970s; the crows and owls made from materials other than wood; the shore birds by Herter's; early Tenite Model 50s and 59s; early Durlon birds with wooden heads; early calls by Herter's; and, nice box examples when there were still two-piece cardboard boxes. Now that Cabela's has purchased Herter's and plans some decoy production again, only time will tell what we shall seek in the future.

Of course, there are rare and common examples in each of the above categories. And there are items we are still being surprised by as we more carefully study the evolution of the company.

Here is a Herter's Model Perfect Owl and Crow Wooden Decoy, circa 1945.

$3,500+

Hank and Judy Norman Collection

Value Range FOR HERTER'S DECOYS

Due to the wide product variety of the company, it is difficult to give a precise range, but the following should be used as a general guideline:

Wooden Owl Decoys: **$1,000-$4,000.**
Wooden Crow Decoys: **$500-$2,000.**
Balsa Duck Decoys: **$100-$200.**

Balsa Goose Decoys: **$150-$350.**
Ancient Cedar Decoys: **$200-$500.**
Model 50s and 59s: **$25-$100.**
Durlon/wood head: **$25-$100.**
Calls: **$20-$4,000.**
Catalogs: **$5-$50.**

A Herter's oversize cork Mallard drake has a balsa head, circa 1950s.
$125+
Pitt Collection

Two examples from the Pitt Collection are Herter's cork with canvas wrap Black Duck drakes.
$700-$1,500

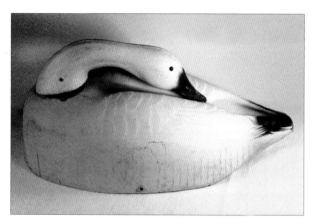

Herter's shell Snow Goose in original paint has heads that are interchangeable and movable for different poses.
$50
Pitt Collection

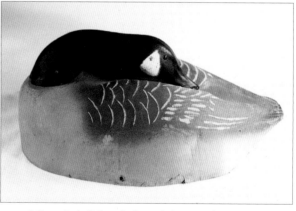

A Herter's shell Canada Goose is in original paint.
$50
Pitt Collection

A Herter's cork Canvasback has a wooden head, circa 1950s.
$125+
Pitt Collection

This is a Herter's Ancient Wooden Decoy American Eider.
$150
Former Pitt Collection, Decoys Unlimited, Inc.

A Herter's Model 50 Mallard hen in original paint shows the encapsulated keel and the Herter's markings on the bottom.
$50-$100
Pitt Collection

William R. Johnson Company

The William R. Johnson Company of Seattle, Wash., was a prodigious producer of fiberboard decoys from the 1930s until the 1950s. The decoys were manufactured by printing photographs etched onto copper plates placed onto a special water-resistant paperboard and then made waterproof by dipping the finished product into wax. This company must have advertised more than any other decoy company in the modern era, with the exception of Herter's. One cannot pick up a fall month of a major sporting magazine without finding a Johnson Folding Decoy advertisement.

The decoys sell for about $15 each. The company also made geese, which usually sell for about the same amount. The photos show some advertising, bags for shipping and storage, and geese and ducks. They are not rare, but are great additions to any collection of factory birds.

Value Range FOR JOHNSON'S AND DUNSTER FOLDING DECOYS

The goose decoys should be valued at **$25-$60** and the ducks at **$15-$30**. The advertising items and bags for shipping could bring easily as much.

Details compare Johnson's folding Canada Goose decoys with Dupe-A-Goose decoys by Dunster.

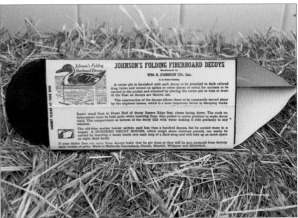

Here are some Johnson's Folding Duck and Goose decoys as well as the bag for a dozen of the decoys.

$15-$60 each

JOHNSON'S FOLDING GOOSE DECOYS JUDGED THE FINEST

By competent, impartial judges the Wm. R. Johnson folding Goose Decoy was chosen first in actual competition with other folding decoys at the Seattle Sport Show.

Johnson Folding Decoys lead, too, in actual use. More hunters use Johnson folding decoys than any other make.

Over thirty years of experience in making decoys assures you that Johnson Folding Decoys are well made, will withstand many seasons of hard use, and more important, they DO bring in the birds.

A COMPLETE LINE OF FOLDING DECOYS

Regular or Feeder Goose Decoy..

Floating Duck Decoy...

Stakeout Duck Decoy..

WM. R. JOHNSON CO., INC.

3131 Western Ave.   Seattle 1, Wn.

An advertisement shows Johnson's Folding Goose Decoys.

A brochure advertises the advantages of Johnson's Folding Decoys.

K and D Decoys

The K. and D. Decoy company of Minnesota produced a nifty little set of decoys that were usually sold by the dozen in a wooden box. The decoys had heads that came off and were then inserted into the bottoms of the decoys for storage and transportation. A Bluebill example is shown. These decoys usually command at least $100 each in prime shape. The shipping carton is also a nice addition to a collection.

Value Range FOR K AND D DECOYS

These decoys will bring from **$100-$300** depending on the species and if packaging is present. The shipping crate itself would also be valued and would increase the price of decoys.

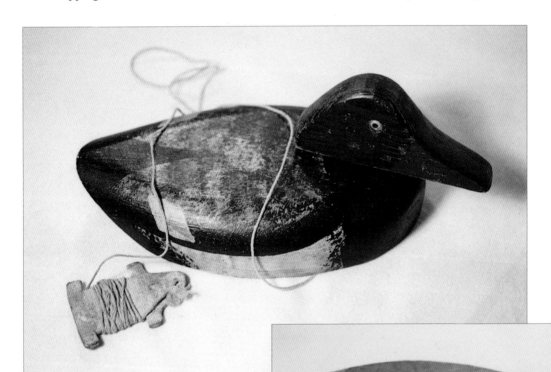

Bluebills were made by K. and D. Decoy company.
$100
Pitt Collection

The heads of K. and D. decoys were removable and could be stored in the bottom of the decoys.

L. L. Bean

The L. L. Bean company is well known to nearly every American household due to its catalog mail order business. The company has been sending out catalogs for nearly a century. The company did not always sell decoys. However, for a period, it did sell some beautiful cork decoys similar to Herter's and some others. The L. L. Bean decoys can be distinguished, normally, by a wooden insert into the tail of the decoy not usually found in other models. Because all the decoys are cork, there has not been as much demand for these decoys. However, demand will increase, as earlier decoys are even harder to locate.

Value Range FOR L. L. BEAN DECOYS

Most L. L. Bean decoys will bring **$150-$250**. Some unusual species may command a premium.

An oversize female Scaup was made by L.L. Bean.
$175
Pitt Collection

J.S. McGuire Company

As discussed under Fairfax, this is really a short-lived predecessor of Fairfax, only for 1954, to protect the copyright of J. S. McGuire, the inventor of the decoys and president of its later producer, Fairfax Engineering Co.

Value Range FOR MCGUIRE DECOYS

There is little sales data on this company but the decoys appear to be rare. I think that we need to get a better handle on the numbers but I am fairly sure these are a very low production run and doubt many exist in collections. For this reason I would rate them about five times more collectible than most plastic decoys, being worth **$25-$150** depending on species and condition.

A strip on the bottom of the decoy reads: "Copyright 1954 J.S. McGUIRE."

A well worn female Mallard McGuire decoy dates from 1954.
Details are on the bottom of the decoy.
$25 in this shape
Lewis Collection

Neumann & Bennets, Inc.

The brand name Plasti-Duk was produced by Neumann & Bennets, Inc. located in Berkeley, Calif., and later in Oregon. Some of the Plasti-Duk products have a copyright date on them, giving us at least the beginning of their history. A Model 22 Pintail drake I have was made in 1956. A photo shows a S10 "Pat Pend" model Mallard drake. This duck sold for $25 online due to the "Pat Pend" designation and its excellent condition. As on many of the plastic decoys, there is often a wealth of data printed on one or both sides of the plastic keel.

Value Range FOR PLASTI-DUK DECOYS

As with Victor and Carry-Lite, most of these plastic ducks will run from **$25-$75**.

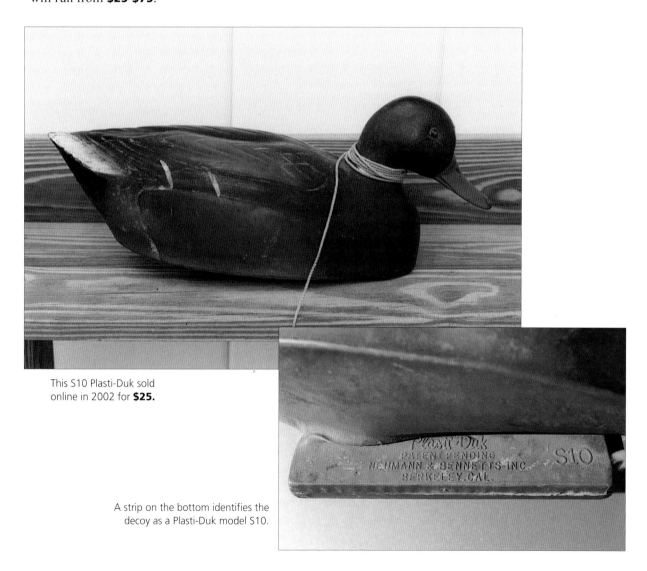

This S10 Plasti-Duk sold online in 2002 for **$25.**

A strip on the bottom identifies the decoy as a Plasti-Duk model S10.

A newer Plasti-Duk Mallard drake was made in the 1960s.
$10-$20
Lewis Collection

A Plasti-Duk Model #17 Pintail drake is copyrighted 1956.
$40-$60
Lewis Collection

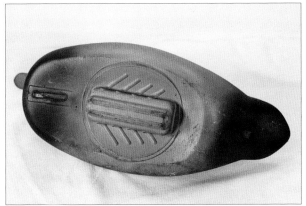

A Plasti-Duk Model #13 Mallard hen has copyright 1956 on the keel. The factory was located in Berkeley, Calif.
$25-$40
Lewis Collection

A pair of Plasti-Duk Model R 15s Bluebill decoys is marked patent pending.
These early patent pending models should bring a premium.
$40-$60
Lewis Collection

A Patent Pending S-10 Mallard drake is another Plasti-Duk decoy.
$25
Lewis Collection

This Plasti-Duk Mallard drake has no dates. It is a newer version with more pliable material and more feathering details molded into the decoy, circa 1970s.
$10-$20
Lewis Collection

An unmarked Mallard drake inflatable decoy was likely made by Plasti-Duk, circa 1960s.
$10-$20
Lewis Collection

An unmarked Plasti-Duk is circa 1960s.
$10-$20
Lewis Collection

A Plasti-Duk Mallard pair has pliable lead weights and is newer with feathering details. One is marked MM on the keel and one is marked D on the keel, circa late 1970s.
$10-$20 each
Lewis Collection

This is an oversize Mallard drake from the late 1960s.
$10-$20
Lewis Collection

A.W. Randall Co.

The A. W. Randall Company was located in Nahant, Mass., and that is all I have about this Owl. It still has its original hang tag and has a pre-Zip Code address on this Styrofoam type Owl decoy. The tag said it was used to rid pigeons from eaves, to scare away certain birds in the garden, keep away seagulls, and to be used by crow hunters as a decoy with a crow-call. It has a little hole in the bottom for a stick and is two-sided just like the early metal Owl decoy that it looks like.

Value Range FOR RANDALL DECOYS

There is insufficient sales data on these to have a range, but I would rank this decoy as fairly scarce and would value the owls at **$250-plus**.

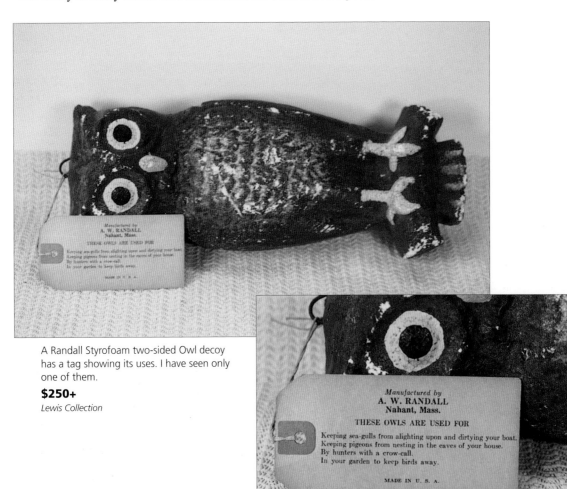

A Randall Styrofoam two-sided Owl decoy has a tag showing its uses. I have seen only one of them.
$250+
Lewis Collection

Real-Lite Co.

The Real-Lite Decoy Co. was located in Kansas City, Mo. It developed its decoys under U.S. Patent number 2622360 by Henry J. Bertram, filed on July 29, 1948, and granted by the patent office on Dec. 23, 1952. One can see these decoys were in development during our classic evolution into newer materials for decoy manufacturing and right after the war.

Some of the claims made about the patent were related to the superior quality of the eyes being visible through a transparent plastic material, the fact that the decoy could be painted in a superior fashion due to its composition, and a new way of manufacturing the keel. The patent application referred to previous patents granted from Oct. 27, 1874, to Dec. 25, 1945. A quick trip to the U.S. Patent Office via the Internet gets one all of this data as fast as your computer can load it once one enters the number in the search box. Then one only needs to push the print icon to have a permanent record of this decoy company.

Value Range FOR REAL-LITE DECOYS

A harder-to-find plastic decoy from the early period would bring **$75-$125**, with common and worn decoys being worth far less in the **$10-$25** range.

Here's an example of a Real-Lite Decoy, with a Real-Lite logo and details on its bottom.
$75-$125
Pitt Collection

J.W. Reynolds Decoy Factory

Located in Forest Park, Ill., the J. W. Reynolds Decoy Factory produced a very clever silhouette decoy patented by the company in 1925. These consisted of three duck silhouettes carved and placed onto a spring-loaded floating wooden framework. The normal practice of the company was to include two drakes and one hen with the two drakes trailing the hen on the end of the "Y" when unfolded. The company also made an unusual set of three Redhead drakes. The company referred to these as the "Illinois River Wooden Folding Decoys."

As with other companies, the Mallards are the most common and the Redheads fairly rare. The frame is often found with the stencil "J. W. Reynolds Patentee Forest Park, Ill." My thanks go to Hank Norman for providing the photos and information on these nice decoys. See also the Canvasbacks shown in Chapter Two under the Maryland section.

Value Range FOR REYNOLDS DECOYS

These decoys will normally sell for **$175 to $300** per set of three, depending on species and condition.

A J. W. Reynolds set of three Mallards includes two drakes and one hen, circa 1925.
$175
Hank and Judy Norman Collection

A J. W. Reynolds set of three Redheads is very rare because it is all drakes, circa 1925.
$200
Hank and Judy Norman Collection

Unknown Turkey Decoy

An unknown Styrofoam stick-up Turkey decoy dates to the 1950s. This great looking bird is similar in material to the Randall Owl decoy, maybe even made by Randall, but no data has been found. The decoy itself is not marked, but was a working decoy with some wear. Photos show the decoy with some shot shell boxes from Western for size. I still use it for hunting the largest of our game birds.

Here are details of the stick-up Turkey decoy.

A Turkey decoy is compared in size to some shell boxes.

$125-$175

Lewis Collection

Tuveson Manufacturing Co.

Tuveson Manufacturing Co., St. James, Minn., operated in the first third of the 20th century. There were a number of cork and cedar decoy advertisements for this company dating to the late 1920s and early 1930s. Its most famous decoy was called a Tuveson Flyer, a flying decoy set on rods. According to the advertising, the decoys were available "…in every species" and the decoy was also patented. The exact dates of the entire production run are unknown at this time, but a "Flying Tuveson" is a great addition to any collection. A pair sold for $2,000 in 2006.

Tuveson Goldeneye hen and Bluebill drake decoys are cork-bodied with wooden bottom boards. The Goldeneye has a Pratt Factory weight added. Both are in original paint.
$150/pair
Guyette & Schmidt, Inc.

Wildfowler Decoys, Inc.

The Wildfowlers Decoys company began doing business in 1939 in Old Saybrook, Conn. The earliest decoys had bodies of white pine and heads of white birch. For the first two years or so, the bodies were fashioned by hollowing them out from the bottom and carefully inlaying the bottom. This proved to be too tedious and time consuming so the company modified the process to simply fit a full bottom board to the hollowed out body. All made after 1941 will exhibit a bottom board. All the decoys will have inlaid heads and a keel. Some time shortly after the end of WWII, balsa became readily available again and they switched to dense balsa bodies. Pine bodies were still offered, but only on special order. Some sources say that heads may also be found made of cedar and pine.

It is reported that the Old Saybrook factory produced up to 15,000 birds per year in its 18 years of operation there. There were two grades of decoys available. The best was designated "No. 1" and the second, "No. 2." The difference was the detail in the paint finish. The No. 1 had more feather detail than the No. 2 grade. The No. 1 also had a smoother finish than did the No. 2 grade. All sported glass eyes.

Many were marked with the stamp (on the bottom) reproduced in an accompanying photo. Notice the complete name "Old Saybrook..." in the stamp. At some later date, the "Old" was dropped from the stamp. Although this attractive stamp makes identification and dating fairly easy, unfortunately many decoys were made without the stamp. It is known that Wildfowler made several thousand decoys for Abercrombie and Fitch without the stamp. It is safe to assume that it made them for resale to other companies as well.

In 1957, the company was sold to Robert H. "Rab" Staniford and moved to Quogue, N.Y., on Long Island. The brand remained the same, but the location on it was changed to "Quogue, L.I.N.Y." These decoys were still made of dense balsa with the pine heads; however, the heads were no longer inlaid.

In 1961, the company was sold and moved yet again. It was bought by Charlie Birdsall, who moved the operation to the head of Barnegat Bay in Point Pleasant, N.J. He changed the location portion of the brand stamp accordingly. The latest sale was to Amel and Karen Massa in the mid 1970s. It is located in Babylon on Long Island, N.Y.

Value Range FOR WILDFOWLER DECOYS

The collector value range for Wildfowler decoys is from **$300 to $1,500**. A wood duck sold for **$1,760** in 1995. The Wildfowler factory birds are rapidly gaining in value as they gain in collector desirability.

A Wildfowler Pintail hen, with glass eyes, was made in Quogue, Long Island, N.Y., circa 1960. The matching drake is on the next page.
$450/pair
Former Pitt Collection

This is a Wildfowler Pintail drake with glass eyes. It was made in Quogue, Long Island, N.Y., circa 1960. Details are on the bottom.
$450/pair
Pitt Collection

A Wildfowler Green-wing Teal hen was made in Point Pleasant, N.J., circa 1970s.
$500+
Pitt Collection

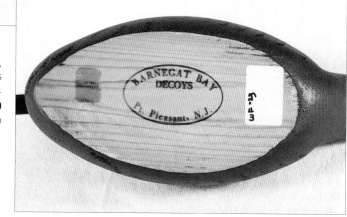

This is a Wildfowler Green-wing Teal drake, circa 1970s. A company logo clearly marks its origin in Point Pleasant, N.J.
$500-$750
Pitt Collection

A Wildfowler Blue-wing Teal drake from Old Saybrook, Conn., dates to the 1950s.
$750-$1,000
Pitt Collection

This Wildfowler Special Order Pintail drake was made on a diminutive Swan body, maybe for Abercrombie & Fitch, in the Point Pleasant, N.J., factory.

$1,500+

Pitt Collection

This Wildfowler Special Order Pintail hen was crafted on a diminutive Swan body, maybe for Abercrombie & Fitch, at Point Pleasant, N.J.

$1,500+

Pitt Collection

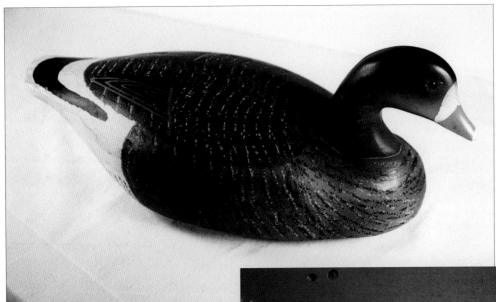

A very rare Speckled Body Goose (white fronted) by Wildfowler was one of only six dozen made in Point Pleasant, N.J., circa 1970s. Its bottom shows the company logo.

$2,000+

Pitt Collection

Value Range FOR WILDFOWLER DECOYS

Although unmarked, this Wildfowler White-wing Scoter drake may have been made for Abercrombie & Fitch.

$500+

Pitt Collection

A Wildfowler Atlantic Brant was made in Point Pleasant, N.J., circa 1970s. A second photo shows the bottom of the decoy.

$700-$1,200

Pitt Collection

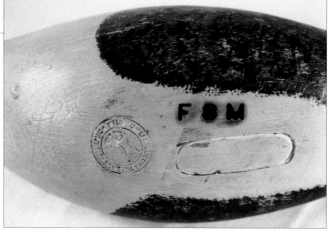

Two Blue-wing Teal were made by Wildfowler.
$500-$1,000
Pitt Collection

This is a pair of Wildfowler Green-wing Teal.
$500-$1,000
Pitt Collection

Chapter Five:

Duck Calls
and other Game Calls

Many decoy collectors also possess a few duck calls. Many of the collectors are or were waterfowl hunters and this addition of other hunting paraphernalia would be a natural adjunct to a nice decoy collection.

Here is a basic guide to this particular collecting discipline, a primer if you will. The basic thrust is for those who might develop an interest in collecting old duck and other game calls.

I have broken this part into two chapters, adding one on modern calls and other game calls. The designation of modern calls really includes two types of calls, the factory-produced calls and the call makers following a more classic approach who are still in business. In the second chapter, I cover primarily the factory calls that most collectors will easily find and be able to identify.

The development of the art and science of call making

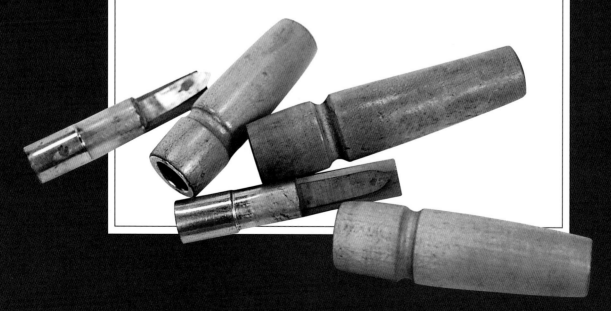

has reached high pinnacles. The calling contests and contestants have constantly demanded finer and finer instruments. This has resulted in the high quality, technologically advanced calls produced by makers today. Unbelievably, they are still improving them. The final quality of a call is found, however, in the ability of the hunter to use it. A fine call does not a fine caller make, and used wrong it only lessens your chances at bagging a limit, or any birds at all. Bad calls can, at the very least, make friends unhappy and nearby hunters downright angry. The latter have been known to express their dissatisfaction in most unpleasant words and actions. If you persist in driving the birds away, the friends may become hostile, making it very difficult to find hunting companions.

Although quality and versatility of the sounds capable of being made on a call can certainly have a bearing on its collectibility, this is more important with contemporary calls than with the old ones. Most of the old calls that survived probably were as effective as was needed or required at the time or they probably would not have survived. However, sound quality is something many collectors also admire in a call and they would prefer a quality sound over an inferior one.

Identification and Evaluation of Calls

Many calls are starting to get a track record of sales. I think it's safe to say that calls by even the lesser-known makers will easily bring $50. Others will command several hundred dollars in many cases for highly detailed checkering, painting, fancy or unusual wood or materials. Many calls by makers such as Perdew have brought five figures, and many more calls now sell in the four-figure range. Values have been established and one will have to do further research online and at auctions to keep abreast of the rapidly changing pricing on calls.

As with duck decoys, a quick tour of online sales will educate one in a hurry. Also, attending sporting collectible shows and auction sales will increase one's awareness of call prices. The only thing for certain is that calls have gone up in price about four-fold, at least, since the mid-1990s. It is very likely that game call collecting is currently about where lure and tackle collecting was about 15 years ago. The associations are just now starting to grow and expand in numbers. Awareness of this interesting hobby is rapidly growing nationally. This growth and exposure will result in increased demand for calls and increased prices. The future is likely bright for this facet of collecting.

Their history, construction and use are, of course, fundamental to appreciating calls. But the beauty and rarity of the fine call is the primary motivation for collecting it. The quality of the sound one is able to produce on the call is of secondary importance in collecting. One must give it some emphasis for, after all, that is the reason for their existence in the first place. What I am saying is that the quality of sound can be de-emphasized because the advances in call-making have improved to such a degree as to make many of the old calls pale in comparison. One could argue further that few, if any, makers would go to the trouble of fashioning a call that would nowadays be considered collectible, if he could not produce the requisite sounds with it.

Once you have seen and handled a number of the finer collectible calls, you will begin to be able to recognize what is good and what is not. There is no substitute for experience. You can read this book and study the photographs and it will give you a good basis on which to build. But hands-on is the byword here. There are a number of things that influence the value and collectibility of a call. Here are a few of them:

MAKER—This is the most important factor in the valuation of calls. Is he a well-known maker? Was he a recognized and accomplished decoy carver? The second point is important because it then creates double demand by crossover collectors.

CONDITION—Collectors differ on the importance of this factor, but all agree that the call needs to be in decent condition. As with any collectible, a very rare example is desirable in just about any recognizable condition. Finish and appearance would weigh heavily here. Also, quality of the wood or the presence/absence of burls and so on may become an important consideration.

PATENT MODEL—This is the extremely rare instance where you come across a call that is exactly like the drawing in the original patent application in every detail. Also, some models are available with "Patent Applied For," "Patent Pending" or some other such nomenclature, making it special. Then, of course, one may also have calls without any numbers and ones that have the patent numbers on them.

SPECIAL OWNER—You might encounter a relatively common call that was owned by a famous individual or was used to win a world championship-calling contest or to bag a world record. Whatever the circumstances, a thing called "provenance" comes into very important play. Provenance is a provable record of origin and ownership. It is a written, provable record of an unbroken chain of ownership from the time of the incident of a famous person's ownership. It is not always written, but should have a sound oral history at the very least.

QUALITY, AGE, UNIQUENESS, BEAUTY AND RARITY—All of these factors are self-explanatory.

Identification of Calls

In the pages following are descriptions and photographs of selected calls of some of the known call-makers from the various regions. Not all known call-makers are represented. I wish I could have included all makers from all regions, however, that would be an encyclopedic work beyond the scope of this introductory text. The makers are grouped by the type of call made without regard to where the maker lived or worked.

Construction and Nomenclature of Calls

Most of you who are interested in collecting calls are already intimately familiar with the construction details of at least the calls you have used over the years. A few of you have never used a call, nor ever owned one to clean and maintain. A few others have never hunted. The latter are interested only in the uniqueness, beauty and collectibility of this fine example of American folk art. So, a few notes and diagrams regarding construction details and nomenclature follow. Names of the parts have changed over the years and differ from region to region as well. This can be very confusing.

EXAMPLES:
Stem = Stopper = Plug = Keg = Bill
Insert = Bill = Sounding Board = Tone Board
Reed = Tongue
Wedge = Wedge block = Stopper

Because hunters and collectors almost universally use Stopper and Insert interchangeably, they will be used so in this work. In the interest of alleviating any confusion due to the above examples it is best to standardize the names of these parts in this book. The following diagrams of the four major types of calls should help you avoid any further confusion.

Some clarification of the Insert (Stopper)/Stem/Sounding or Tone Board relationship is necessary to understanding their location and construction with regard to one-piece and two-piece styles.

The one and two in the style names do not refer to the number of parts in a call but rather to whether the Insert (Stopper) is made of one or two pieces. Figure 3 and Figure 5 show the parts of a typical one-piece style and how they go together. Note that the Insert is made in one piece. Now take a look at Figure 2. Note that the Insert consists only of the Tone Board. In order to assemble the call, the Reed must be placed on the Tone Board, the Wedge on the Reed, and then pushed into the part named the Stem. This assembly is then inserted into the Barrel to complete the call. The Stem in this particular instance is made of metal,

but it could be made of any other material.

These diagrams also serve to illustrate the differences between the Rounded or Curved Radius Sounding or Tone Boards and between the straight and curved reed.

Materials for call bodies typically used over the years have been Bakelite, plastics, hard rubber, all sorts of woods and metal. Wedges have been made of cork or some other wood mostly and reeds are plastic, metal or hard rubber. Sometimes the use of particular material in a call is somewhat like a maker's signature. It can be a great help in identifying a call in some instances, in others, useless. When significant, these characteristics will be covered in individual listings.

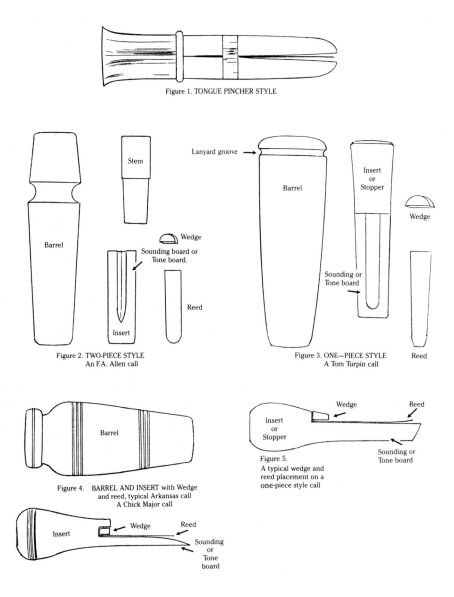

Figure 1. TONGUE PINCHER STYLE

Figure 2. TWO-PIECE STYLE
An F.A. Allen call

Stem

Wedge

Sounding board or Tone board.

Barrel

Reed

Insert

Figure 3. ONE—PIECE STYLE
A Tom Turpin call

Lanyard groove

Barrel

Insert or Stopper

Wedge

Sounding or Tone board

Reed

Figure 4.   BARREL AND INSERT with Wedge and reed, typical Arkansas call
A Chick Major call

Barrel

Insert

Wedge

Reed

Sounding or Tone board

Figure 5.
A typical wedge and reed placement on a one-piece style call

Insert or Stopper

Wedge

Reed

Sounding or Tone board

A History of Duck and Game Calls

Until just a few years ago there was precious little written material with regard to the origins and early history of the development of bird calls in America. What little we have now is, however, a valuable asset to the collecting of these calls.

Primitive Times (Pre 1850s)

This would be the time before we have any concrete, demonstrable evidence of a man-made object, fashioned expressly for the luring of wild game to within a killing distance by imitating the calls or sounds. At some point in time in early North America, some pre-historic being likely may have successfully mimicked the cry of a wild animal with his own vocal cords and mouth in order to lure it in. It is also likely that early humans would develop the talent for using whatever might be at hand for imitating game sounds. Certainly the American Indians developed this to a high degree. They are known to have used whistles and reeds. (Have you ever placed a blade of grass between your thumbs and blown a shrill call?) Certainly any people capable of creating the beautiful decoys found in the Lovelock Cave excavations in Nevada were sophisticated enough to have fashioned some sort of calling device.

Early History (1850s-1935)

The areas of most concentrated activity in this period of the development of commercial call making were the Illinois River basin and the Reelfoot Lake area in Tennessee. There are distinct differences in the style of call from each of these regions.

Collectors and writers have been able to trace production calls back to 1854 or slightly before. There appears to be a Tongue Pincher style of duck call clipped or otherwise attached to the left breast pocket of a hunter's coat in a Currier and Ives print dated 1854. The print is titled "Wild Duck Shooting/ A Good Days Sport." It is a stone lithograph of a painting by Arthur Fitzwilliam Tail (1819-1905). It is not clear if this is a European call or an early American attempt at call making.

The earliest evidence of American production of a duck call is a patent issued to Elam Fisher of Detroit in 1870 for a Tongue Pincher type call.

There is a scarcity of information about this period of time, but there was apparently a surge of interest and activity among call makers then. And there seems to have developed some amount of competition among them. There is evidence by the Fisher patent and advertising claims by Fred A. Allen of Monmouth, Ill., and Charles W. Grubbs of Chicago, that each was the first to offer a production duck call commercially. Grubbs claimed in a 1928 advertisement that he did so in 1868. The authors of Decoys and Decoy Carvers of the Illinois River, Paul W. Parmalee and Forrest D. Loomis, state in their book that: "Allen's Nickel-Plated Duck Caller" was made for private use in 1863 and "...was considered to be the first duck call to be mass produced in Illinois." Whatever the case, it is ample evidence of commercial call-making activity at that early date. It is important to note here that the Allen call was the first to have utilized a barrel, thus creating a resonant chamber for the call. His Nickel Plated Duck Call is recognized as a significant development in call making. Examples of it are highly collectible.

So far as can be determined, it looks as if no one got the bright idea to advertise his or her products until the early 1880s. It seems almost absurd that it would not occur to these folks for 10 or 15 years, but so far a search of old magazines and catalogs has not turned up any ads for calls. They took up advertising with a vengeance from the early 1880s on.

There were some distinctly different styles invented and refined during the Early History period. The Illinois Style and the Reelfoot or Glodo Style were the first to be developed, followed closely by the Arkansas Style and concurrently, the Louisiana or Cajun Style utilizing bamboo or cane (as it is known in the South) instead of wood or other substances. Refer to the Construction and Nomenclature section for details regarding the differences between these different styles.

There were many variations and experiments in the development of the styles. One that has survived through the years is that of Victor Glodo of Reelfoot Lake. All the others made contributions of varying importance, but the Glodo or Reelfoot Style is the one that survived intact. Glodo moved to Reelfoot Lake around 1890. Until recently it was thought that Glodo was a French Canadian, but we now know that he came from a call-making family that hailed from the Fountain Bluff Area of southern Illinois. His calls were of the two-piece type using a wooden wedge block, a flat tone board and a curved metal reed. The Glodo and Reelfoot Style of duck call is the most widely used style of metal reed design in call making today. The fact that he was the first maker to decorate his calls (he was the first to use checkering) makes him the father of the American duck calls as a folk art in the estimation of most aficionados.

This important era, the Early History Period, in the evolution of duck call making can be laid out more clearly in the following chronology:

1854-1870

First patent of the Tongue Pincher Style duck call. It was characterized by a straight reed sandwiched between two rounded or curved radius tone boards bound together; no barrel. An 1854 Currier and Ives lithograph possibly illustrates this type. Elam Fisher-1870, Charles Schoenhieder-1880.

1863-1870

Early Illinois River Style. This style is characterized by a curved metal reed, a single straight or flat tone board (two-piece stem and insert), a half-round cork wedge block, and a barrel. First known use of the barrel to create a resonant chamber is attributed to Fred A. Allen. Others making this style call were Charles W. Grubbs of Chicago, who claimed he was making them as early as 1868 and advertised his calls at least as early as 1892, and George Peterson, who was in business in 1873 making decoys and perhaps duck calls. Jasper N. Dodge bought out the Peterson business 10 years later, about 1883. The Early Illinois River Style continued to be made into the 1900s, though the variation known as the Later Illinois River Style had been developed and was being used in call making, also in the 1900s. The Later Illinois River Style, however, is more appropriately discussed in the next period of this chronology.

Victor Glodo of Reelfoot Lake originated the Reelfoot or Glodo Style. It is characterized by the use of a curved metal reed held to a straight, one-piece (combination stem and insert) tone board by a wooden wedge block inserted into a barrel. Glodo was the first to decorate duck calls. He used checkering. Herter's calls are more recent examples following in the Glodo tradition.

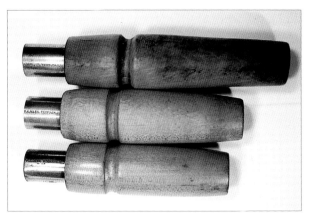

Three F. A. Allen calls are from the author's collection. Reed details are also shown.

$125-$200 each

Lewis Collection

Reed details are displayed from the three F.A. Allen calls.

1880's-1920

The Tongue Pincher Style continued to be made into the 1910s by Fisher and Schoenheider. Others who joined them in the making of them were the Bridgeport Gun and Implement Co. (B.G.I.) in Connecticut, a company named Red Duck Calls, and the N. C. Hansen Company of Zimmerman, Minn. They all made their calls in the Elam Fisher design. The Hansen Company was still advertising these calls (albeit modified) in the late 1940s. Early Illinois River Style calls continued to be made into this period by Charles H. Ditto of Keithsburg, Ill., (he made other styles also) and James W. Reynolds, Chicago, who became more known for his Double Duck Call patented in 1906. Charles H. Perdew of Henry, Ill., also produced calls in the Early Illinois River Style.

A Perdew Crow Call is valued at **$500.**
Lewis Collection

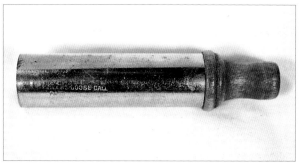

Another early call maker is the Fullers Goose Call.
$150-$200

The patent and reed details of the Fullers Goose Call are shown.

The Later Illinois River Style was developed during this period (c. 1903). This is the era when the hard rubber call and reed were developed. August L. Kuhlemeier of Burlington, Iowa, was the first to patent this, but may not have been the inventor. For some unknown reason, the Later Illinois River Style was characterized by a return to the older rounded radius or curved tone board and straight reed (both of hard rubber, frequently). They also used cork wedge blocks. The call made by Philip Sanford Olt represents this style developed to a high art. His company, P. S. Olt, Pekin, Ill., developed a call dubbed the D-2 that, with some minor changes, has been successfully made and sold since 1904. The company was recently closed. I have included more on the impact of the P. S. Olt in the next section on modern calls.

Reelfoot or Glodo Style duck calls. Victor Glodo died in 1910, but the style he developed was continued by Tom Turpin of Memphis, Tenn.; J. T. Beckhart, Swiftwater, Ark.; John "Sundown" Cochran, Samburg, Tenn., whose son John "Son" Cochran continues to make calls in this classic style and form today; and G. D. Kinney of Hughes, Tenn.

In addition to the classic duck and goose calls of the early years, shorebird and dog whistles make an interesting addition to any decoy collection.

A lot of eight shorebird and dog whistles are circa 1885-1915.
$100-$400 each
Hank and Judy Norman Collection

C1920-1935

All of the styles covered so far continued to be produced in various numbers, from few to many, all through this period of time. But there were two more styles that developed almost concurrently. Each is a variation of the preceding style, but with sufficient differences to render them unique. The Arkansas Style is thought to be a modified version of the Illinois River Style. It is quite obvious that the P. S. Olt calls have a strong influence on the construction of the Arkansas Style calls. The calls are constructed of wood for the most part. The one-piece stem has a notch cut out at the beginning of the tone board so that the straight reed could be held in, independent of insertion of the stem into the barrel. It is likely that the Arkansas Style evolved around the late 1910s. Presently, it appears that the earliest makers are probably Clyde Hancock and W. T. Lancaster, both of Stuttgart,

Ark., followed closely by A. M. Bowles of Little Rock in the mid 1920s and Darce Manning "Chick" Major of Stuttgart in the early 1930s.

Louisiana Style duck calls, or Cajun Style as they are sometimes called, have probably been around as long as the Arkansas Style calls. But for now we cannot substantiate any commercial production before the 1930s. The earliest names associated with the Louisiana Style calls are Faulk and Airhart. Clarence "Patin" Faulk of Lake Charles, is known to have made calls much earlier than the 1935 date generally accepted as when he began making calls to be sold in commercial quantities. Although he produced thousands of calls, it was not until 1950, when his son Dudley Faulk went into business, that we recognized the company as it exists doing business today, Faulk Calls. The other famous name in the Louisiana Style of call making is Allen J. Airhart. He started the Cajun Call Company in Lake Charles in 1944. It is still in business today. Although many are made of wood and other materials today, most classic Louisiana Style calls are made of cane. They are generally of the two-piece design much like the F. A. Allen calls.

The Golden Age (1935-1950)

The Early History Era was a terrific growth and development era in call making where everyone was experimenting and perfecting what they thought were the best in effective game calls. But there was not an impetus for large scale manufacturing until 1935. Heretofore using baited field and/or live decoys was common, especially in the Mississippi Flyway. Who needed to produce calls in any quantities when you had the benefit of having a few live English calling ducks, or Suzys as they were affectionately known? Hunters could have the double benefit of live ducks making real live, authentic calls when desired and a few family pets at the same time.

In 1935, two significant things happened that would have a profound and lasting effect on the way wildfowl hunters pursued their prey. First, Ducks Unlimited was formed in the interest of proper wildlife management and conservation. Second, the federal government made baiting fields and the use of live decoys illegal. The previous year had seen the birth of the Federal Waterfowl Stamps and the publication of Joel Barber's classic work on decoys.

All of these events had an impact on the current hobby of collecting calls and decoys.

There was suddenly a very good reason for obtaining and learning to use game calls. Thus was born the Golden Age of duck call making. Many of the older call-making operations expanded to accommodate this sudden demand. Call makers began producing thousands of calls and new companies were born, also producing calls in the thousands to meet this demand. Everybody and his brother seemed to be in the call-making business. This included the P.S. Olt Company, turning out several thousand calls a year. Also, decoy makers got into the business. The big sporting goods firms such as Von Lengerke and Antoine (VL&A) of Chicago, Sears Roebuck, H. D. Folsom Arms Company, and the like began commissioning call makers to manufacture calls for sale through their stores and catalogs, some even with their own logos on them. This was also the time when duck-calling competition came into its own.

Quiet Times (c1950-1970)

By about 1950, the wildfowl population had dwindled again. Good efforts were being made at conservation, but it was slow to get started and gain support. It came almost too late. At this point, general interest in hunting waterfowl was on the wane and the number of hunters was declining. There were a good many commercial call-making companies doing business. The decline of waterfowl population and hunter interest, and the ready availability of inexpensive, manufactured duck calls combined to put quite a damper on the business of hand-production of fine duck calls. This depressed situation remained at a status quo until renewed by growing interest in Americana beginning in the 1970s.

New Golden Age (1970-Present)

The 1970s saw a renewed interest in all things related to American craftsmen and especially those things that were uniquely American. With this came the now famous explosion of interest in old hand-made hunting decoys and all sorts of other Americana. Good game conservation and management had begun to pay off with rapidly increasing waterfowl populations. Along with these conservation efforts, heavily supported by hunters and other outdoor sportsmen, came a new appreciation for what was almost lost. There was a new appreciation for the sheer pleasure of the hunt. It was a heightened awareness of the experience of the hunt, being outdoors, enjoying it with a friend or introducing a child to the magic. It is a great pleasure and satisfaction to introduce a non-outdoorsman friend or a child to this world of outdoors, knowing that you helped bring it back. You and they will continue to practice good game management to assure it will not be lost. With all of that came the renaissance of the fine duck call. It can only get better.

Chapter Six:

Modern Duck, Goose and Game Calls

This chapter is meant to complement my emphasis on modern items for the collector. Just as Chapter Four documented the growth in collecting more recent or modern decoys, the call collector should be aware of modern calls and mass marketed calls while searching for items for his/her collection. Although each of us would love to add any of the calls in the foregoing chapter, it is unlikely for many of us to find or acquire such exceedingly rare calls, at least not more than a few of them.

Mass-produced calls from the 1940s and '50s are still readily available. They can be purchased online, in antique stores, at flea markets and even in some sporting goods

stores if one is diligent in searching. Many of the calls will still be found in their original one- or two-piece cardboard packaging and with package inserts telling how to use the call or little pocket catalogs. These make great additions to a collection and further one's knowledge of a company's products. Even concentrating on just a few of the larger or better known companies can take quite an effort to acquire all calls known to exist. Even some of the calls of more recent 1970s companies, such as Mallardtone, are getting harder and harder to find.

There were likely dozens, if not hundreds, of small mom and pop call companies in the later '40s and early '50s that have yet to be documented. Nearly every small community had a small company operating out of a kitchen or a garage. These small companies were cheap to start, but most did not last due to the inability to market the products widely enough. Most of these little companies lived on local sales, direct marketing to sports shops and word of mouth.

Black Duck Calls

All I know is what is in the photo. This is a newer post-Zip Code box with a duck call made in Whiting, Ind. Call-maker Joe Jaroski paid $25 for the call at a meet some time back and the value is likely double that or more today. I did not see any advertisements for the call company in my literature review. But, it is indeed an example of modern duck hunting products from the Hoosier state. Of course, Indiana also gave us the famous Hoosier Crow Call.

Not much is known about a Black Duck call that was made in Whiting, Ind.
$50+

Burnham Brothers Calls

Burnham Brothers Calls of Marbles, Texas, made a number of calls. They are collectible, not because the plastic calls are unique, but because they came in very nice two-piece cardboard boxes with detailed inserts explaining the use of the calls. Although it did not make as wide a variety as Herter's or Olt, Burnham made any number of predator calls that command up to $60 each if still found in their boxes. I have sold about a half dozen the last few years and always get a good price. I would guess that the calls are worth from $15 without a box up to $100 each for some of the less common models. I am sure we will see these values continue upward as more folks learn about this company.

Duk-Em Duck Calls

The Shooter's Bible for 1947 lists two of these calls for sale: the Pull-Em Crow Call and the Duk-Em Duck Call. Both calls use the phrase "Tone Tested" in their call names as well. I have shown a Duk-Em wooden duck call but do not have a crow call example.

The advertisement read as follows: "…are of hand made quality, each one individually tested for tone by an expert in the art of calling…sounding mechanism…will not fall apart when removed from the receiver." It goes on to say they are very easy to use with little effort and that they are made of hard wood and hand-rubbed satin finishes to show the grain. One thing interesting about the ad is that the Lohman type calls do fall apart when removing the "sounding mechanism," which is frustrating to the uninitiated in calling. It takes a little skill to place a Lohman reed back in the correct position and my guess is that this advertisement was capitalizing on this fact.

This company also advertised a duck decoy in some of the same advertising. It is a nice call and does indeed make a nice sound. Either of these calls would bring about $75, more with the box.

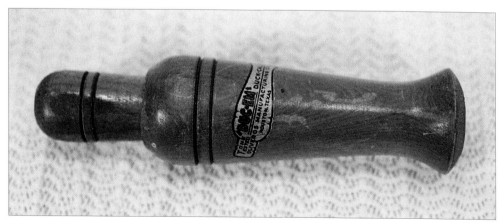

Here is a photo of a Duk-Em Duck Call.
$75
Lewis Collection

Dye-Call Company

Dye-Call Company was located at 1309 N. 77th, Seattle, WA 98103 in 1972. This company is listed as a supplier of both game calls and decoys. Harry Dye of Dye-Call produced a nice looking wooden call named Dye's Mallard Call and a 45-minute L. P. record of calls. He also offered a six-hour class on duck calling in various western states. I have not found a catalog of his items.

The Mallard Call is a rounded shoulder call with a straight stem with two groves in the end and a slight shoulder near the stopper entrance. The call barrel itself is widest at the stem end with a lathe groove about one-quarter of the way down. The call has a straight, not flared, mouthpiece. The call is marked on the side as Dye-Call in one line with Mallard underneath it. It appears the wood is two-toned. It is similar in design to a Faulk's, but more rounded on the stem end.

Faulk's

Already discussed briefly in the previous section, this company began commercial call production in about 1935 in Lake Charles, La. The company made a number of calls in the 1940s, '50s and '60s. Any of these would make nice additions to a call collection, especially the ones still in their original packaging with package inserts. As a general rule, the presence of original packaging tends to at least double the value of an item such as a game or duck call.

One dating technique on Faulk calls is its own use of advertising on the call labels, the boxes and the paper inserts. Faulk Calls won a number of competitions and liked to list the years in which it won on the call labels, boxes and inserts. However, an interesting thing is that the years often did not match, showing that Faulk would use calls on hand, boxes on hand and place updated inserts into the box. One call clearly shows the box as a 1959 model, the call as a 1961 model and a paper insert dated 1963. Thus, the call is really from 1963, likely made in 1961, and placed in a box on hand from 1959. So, when you get a Faulk, look at all the dates to determine the likely date of your item.

Another possible dating technique is the box design and/or color. I have shown three boxes from the '50s and '60s. The earliest one is red, then orange, then yellow. The design on the box stayed the same, but the colors changed. Also, all of the ones shown from this period are the plastic slide top boxes. Earlier boxes would have had plastic lids over cardboard or would have been two-piece cardboard boxes. Later boxes may have a cellophane insert as seen on some later Olt boxes shown in the Olt section. As collector attention is placed more and more on these factory calls, we will learn smaller distinctions in box types to help us date the items.

The 1970 Parker Distributors (New Rochelle, N.Y.) wholesale hunting and fishing catalog offered the following Faulk Calls for sale:

1. WA-33 Deluxe Duck Call with walnut barrel
2. CH-44 Deluxe Goose Call with cherry/walnut barrel
3. C-50 Crow Call, walnut barrel, cherry tip
4. P-60 Predator Call, walnut barrel, metal reed
5. Pat. Pending P-60A Adjustable Predator Call
6. H-10 Hawk Call, walnut barrel, cherry tip
7. EK-8 Elk Call, plastic with cork insert
8. CA-11 Duck Call, bamboo (cane)
9. WA-11 Duck Call, walnut
10. CA-22 Duck Call, bamboo with metal ring
11. WA-22 Duck Call, walnut with metal ring

12. Q-20 Bob White Quail Call, walnut with cork insert
13. S-80 Squirrel Call, rubber bulb with metal device
14. D-50 Deer Call, walnut barrel
15. SG-49 Speckled Belly Goose Call, walnut, metal reed
16. Advertised as "NEW" for 1970, WD-30 Wood Duck Call, walnut with rubber reed
17. SC-77 Supreme Duck Call, extra large, walnut
18. SCJ-66 Supreme Duck Call, smaller, walnut
19. C-100 Duck Call, myrtlewood and walnut
20. WA-33-A Adjustable Duck Call, walnut with adjustable ring
21. RW-14 Professional Duck Call, rosewood, large
22. PL-22 Popular Goose Call, plastic/wood
23. PH-95 Pheasant Call, walnut, metal reed
24. H-100 Honker Call, walnut
25. Q-19 Quail Call, box type for Western Quail
26. D-8 Dove Call, plastic construction
27. Advertised as "NEW" for 1970, the T-40 Turkey Call, a box/striker type call
28. Duck-Goose calling record

The 1981 Point Wholesale catalog still offered the following Faulk products:

1. Faulk's DL (double lanyard to hold two calls)
2. Faulk's Crow Call Model 50
3. Faulk's Regular Duck Call Model WA 11 (Walnut)
4. Faulk's Regular Duck Call Model CA 11 (Bamboo)
5. Faulk's Special Duck Call Model WA 22 (metal band)
6. Faulk's Deluxe Duck Call Model WA 33 (heavy duty)
7. Faulk's Adjustable Duck Call Model WA 33A
8. Faulk's Duck Call Model C 100 (fancy zebra wood)
9. Faulk's Pintail Whistle Model PW 70
10. Faulk's Popular Goose Call Model PL 22 (clear)
11. Faulk's Deluxe Goose Call Model CH 44 (cherry)
12. Faulk's Predator Call Model P 60

13. Faulk's Adjustable Predator Call Model P 60A
14. Faulk's Model S 80 Squirrel Call (rubber bulb)

The 1982 Buckeye Sports Supply from Canton, Ohio, another big wholesaler of sporting goods, listed in addition to the above:

15. Faulk's Professional Duck Call Model RW 14 (large, fancy wood)
16. Faulk's Wood Duck Call Model WD 30
17. Faulk's Honker Call Model H 100
18. Faulk's Elk Call Model EK 8 (rigid plastic/cork insert)
19. Faulk's Bob White Quail Call Model Q 20
20. Faulk's Deer Call Model D 50
21. Faulk's Box/Striker Turkey Call Model T 40
22. Faulk's Presentation Gift Set Model GS 12, contains one each of the lesser models of duck, goose and crow calls in a gift box
23. Also offered were general reeds and goose reeds

Thus, in 1982, Faulk still offered more than 23 products for sale with two major wholesalers. Most of the calls were made from walnut and/or cherry. The clear plastic goose call (PL 22) is plastic and wood. The elk call is also plastic. Faulk used a beautiful cherry wood and the calls are attractive. They are also easy to use and well tuned.

The more unusual calls to find would be the gift set, the turkey call (just beginning to get popular in the northern states in the early '80s), the expensive professional duck call (wholesale was $12.45, retail was $22.95) and the calls for the more unusual species. Most of the calls listed were in the Faulk line for a number of years, allowing the collector to amass examples from different time periods. A most unusual Faulk item was its Faulk's Big Duck Call, Model FGD (Faulk's Giant Duck). In 1970, Cabela's offered this item for $15.95. It was a giant working call measuring 11 3/4" overall, but actually properly tuned to work. It was meant as a gift for the sportsman with everything already, a nice item for the duck blind or bar. One is shown in the Joe Jaroski group photos in this chapter.

On Faulk's CH-44 goose call, the box is marked through 1959 and the call itself is marked through 1961, as explained in the text.

$40+

Lewis Collection

Faulk's WA-33A, adjustable duck call is in mint condition.

$40

Lewis Collection

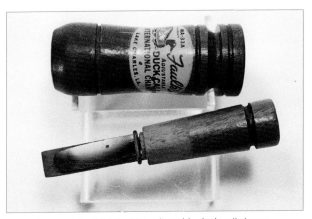

A second Faulk's WA-33A adjustable duck call shows reed details and cork insert.

$30

Lewis Collection

A Faulk's Model PW-70 Pintail whistle/call came in an orange pre-Zip Code slide top box.

$50+

Lewis Collection

Faulk's Model WA-11 (walnut) Duck Call from 1959 came in a red pre-Zip Code slide top box.

$50

Lewis Collection

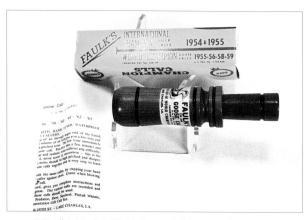

A Faulk's Model CH-44 Goose Call is in a yellow pre-Zip Code slide top box. This one shows a 1959 box, a 1961 call, and a 1963 paper insert.

$60

Lewis Collection

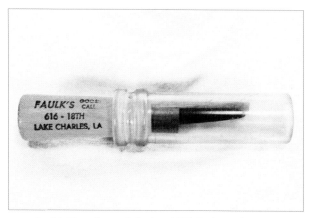

Faulk's Clear Goose Call, circa 1970, is shown in 1970 catalogs.

Lewis Collection

Here are a Faulk's Duck Call and an unmarked Faulk's type adjustable goose call.

$30 each

Lewis Collection

FAULK'S Goose Call

(Canadian Pat., 534,179)   (U.S. Pat., 2,730,836)

WORLD CHAMPIONS — '55 - '56 - '58 - '60 - '61 - '62 - '63

FAULK'S GOOSE CALL is GUARANTEED, HAND TUNED, WATERPROOF, PATENTED and tested by EXPERIENCED CALLERS.

INSTRUCTIONS: Blow a small volume of air through larger end of the barrel, then suddenly increase air pressure. A small volume of air will give you a low tone and the sudden increase of air will give the high pitched tone. The low tone immediately followed by the high pitched tone is the goose call. Practice this a few minutes and note that the goose call will break into a clear and realistic tone without any difficulty. Once this note has been learned, add 2, 3, 4, more notes in succession — this is the call of the snow goose. For blue geese, the notes should be high pitched and sharper. It is effective to use the snow and blue goose calls together and is very easy to learn on FAULK'S PAT. GOOSE CALL.

CANADIAN HONKERS can be called with the same caller, by cupping your hand over end of small barrel and placing end of caller against chest. Grunt when blowing. Learn the goose call first and then the honker call.

FAULK'S DUCK & GOOSE calling record, gives you complete instructions and demonstrations on how to call ducks and geese. The various calls are recorded and if imitated, will teach you how and when these calls should be used.

OTHER FINE CALLS: Duck, Crow, Predator, Deer, Squirrel, Pintail Whistle, Pheasant, Hawk, Quail and Elk Calls, and Presentation Gift Call Set.

FAULK'S GAME CALL CO., INC. — 616-18TH ST. — LAKE CHARLES, LA.

A page of details inserted with Faulk's Goose Calls also has instruction on how to use the call.

Fetch-It

Although not a game call, I thought this was the best place to illustrate a great duck retrieving item and the beautiful advertising graphics that went with it. This nifty little "retrieving lure" attached to the end of your fishing rod. You simply cast out and reeled your dead duck in to you. I am not sure how handy it would be to carry along a rod and reel in a duck blind, but it may have actually been handy for those of us shooting ducks on farm ponds. It is amazing the contraptions that various companies present to us for consumption. I would not want to use this item, but I am glad I have a couple in my collection. Shown are photos of the box and the lure. The item was new about 1947-48, according to advertising.

A Fetch-It duck retrieving lure, with a two-piece cardboard box, is made of wood with a metal loop. It was made in Hayden Lake, Idaho, for duck hunters who would rather carry a fishing pole to the pothole than use a dog.
$65+
Lewis Collection

Herter's Inc.

Herter's, Inc. of Wasceca, Minn., was documented in Chapter Four on modern decoys. However, Herter's also made nearly every imaginable call for game, ducks, and geese and needs to be covered in this section as well. Most of the calls follow the Glodo style and are so called by Herter's. The Herter's specialty catalogs detail the calls nicely. But even the general Herter's catalogs list all calls available from the company: duck, goose, any imaginable flying game bird, crow, deer, elk and predator, to name just a few. Not all calls were available for the entire 40 or so year span, so one needs to study catalogs to precisely date calls. But this is affordable with Herter's catalogs. Maybe just pick up a catalog for every five-year span to check out the model continuity. Of course, since Cabela's purchased Herter's, we will need to see what future collectibles may be in the offing.

The previous owner of Herter's still marketed the famous Glodo Duck Call in an old Herter's two-piece cardboard box. So make sure you can tell the old ones from the newer ones, the package being the best guarantee. I have included a shot of the newer one, showing the packaging to look for. The oldest Herter's calls had brass rings and bring hundreds, if not thousands, of dollars each. However, for the most part, the new collector is more apt to find nice old Herter's calls from the '40s or '50s than one of the very early calls.

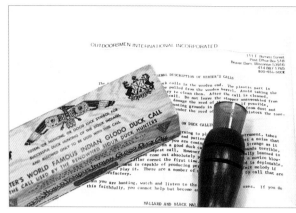

A series of photos shows a modern Herter's Indian Glodo duck call new in its box with papers. This is one of the Herter's calls marketed by the company that bought Herter's in 1977. It was likely made prior to 1977, with the marketing material updated when distributed.

$70

Lewis Collection

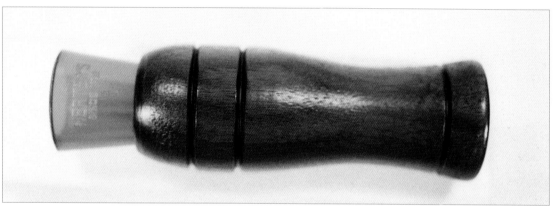

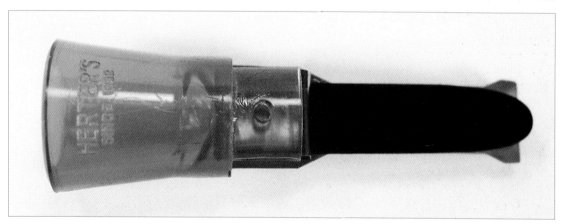

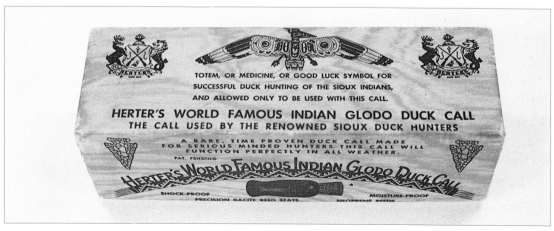

Hoosier Crow Call

This fairly common and successful crow call was made in Delphi, Ind., and advertised nationally in sporting magazines. It sold well. It is an attractive, well-made call that brings $45 loose, and $60 or more in its cardboard box. One early advertisement indicated that the company also made some decoys, but I do not have any examples of them.

Joe Jaroski, Jr. Calls

Joe Jaroski, Jr. made his first call in 1945 and another in 1946. He then started making them in greater numbers and selling them in 1947. Jaroski worked as an underground coal miner in Southern Illinois and found call-making an excellent creative outlet. He now finds it a way to fill the hours since retirement. Joe has been making calls ever since his first year of production for sale and trade. As with many call makers, he trades a lot of calls and has a fine collection of calls made by many modern makers.

Jaroski has made around 2,000 calls. Price range is from $50 to $400. Among his calls are corn cob calls and some beer bottle calls. Since he retired from mining, his creations keep him busy almost every day. He has a love for call-making and for coming up with different and new ideas. All of Joe's beer bottle calls are working calls, both duck and goose.

Jaroski has won a number of awards, including Blue, Purple, Orange and Red Ribbons, for call-making from the Callmakers & Collectors Association of America. These include many ribbons for Fancy Call Contest, Checkered Division Fancy Call, Miniature Fancy Call, Matched Sets and more. He also took the Best Exhibit award plaque in 1994 and the Most Outstanding Exhibitor's Booth in 1995 at Reelfoot Lake Callmakers & Collectors Association.

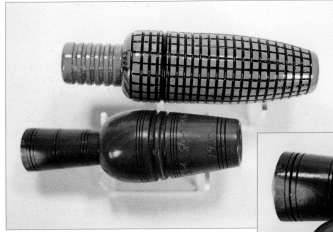

Here are a Joe Jaroski, Jr. corn cob duck call from 2000, and a gold label and signed duck call from 1954. Details show the early metal reed on the 1954 call.

**$75 for corn cob call,
$150 for the early duck call.**
Lewis Collection

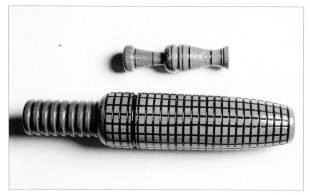

Joe Jaroski, Jr.'s corn cob goose call is shown next to Joe's miniature working call.

Miniature, $25; Goose, $100

Two fancy Jaroski calls, both duck, are signed and have dates with labels.

$75 each

A variety of Joe Jaroski, Jr.'s calls are displayed.

$60-$200+ each

A close up shows some of Jaroski's collection: Top left is a "Champ" duck call, fifth over is a Strut reed Owl Hooter, seventh and eighth are Olt's, tenth over is a Hoosier crow call, then a St. Croix game caller, then a Wildlife with the wood-burned Indian on crow call, and lastly a Hoosier Crow call with label still intact. The second row starting fourth from left is a Weems Wild Call, a Thomas #122 Converts-A-Squirrel Call (squirrel to predator), both from Texas. The third row starts with two Ol' Magic duck calls by Gene Avery of Malan, Ill., the fifth call in is a "Sears" with a band so marked, the seventh is a Broadbill, the ninth is a copy of a Perdew crow call and the tenth is a copy of a Perdew duck call, both made by Tom Swanson.

The seventh call on the top row from right is a giant Earl Dennison call, the call to its right is a Gooden Hoosman call. Next to the Dennison call on the left is a Dale Fleming call from Chillicothe and to its left is a Charlie Bishop goose call. The second row from right is a Faulk's call third in, then sixth is a Busch Beer advertising call, followed by a Sure Shot and to its left a duck call by Jim Blakemore.

On the bottom row from right are four Ken Martin calls. The first one has a label, second is a goose call, the fourth one has a carved duck by Gerald Droege from Anna, Ill., making it very unusual. Ken Martin calls are very collectible. The screwdriver handle is a novelty call made by Joe Jaroski, Jr. The second row from right starts with a signed Jack Wilson call and the four calls in the center with metal rings are all J & K calls made by Jerry and Kelly Weatherford, a father/son team from McKenzie, Tenn. They are still making calls.

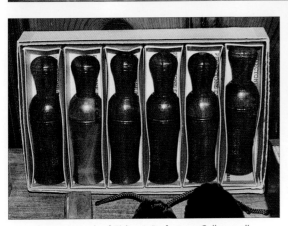

A rare six pack of Bishop's Perfectone Calls are all new in package.

$300+

A store advertising call was made by Charlie Bishop for his Perfectone Call Company. It was given to stores for advertising purposes.

$500+

Kumduck Calls

This green plastic duck call with a plastic reed is manufactured similarly to an Olt in style. It is marked with a patent number of 2,711,614 and location. According to the patent data, the call was made in circa 1955. The patent was applied for on May 5, 1952, and granted on June 28, 1955, to Gordon E. Hallsten of Beaverton, Ore. According to the patent application, the main purpose was to construct a call that took little effort to blow and used a straight reed construction. The call is all plastic, the material of the hour in 1952 when the patent was requested. This is another good example of our modern era calls.

This company was brought back to life recently. The call is now made in black and packed in a great case. Learn about it at www.kum-duck.com.

My thanks to the owners for a call and this update.

A KumDuck call was made in Beaverton, Ore., circa 1955.
$50+ due to rarity
Lewis Collection

Lohman Calls

Lohman Calls was located in Kansas City, Mo. Lohman marketed its calls directly through wholesalers to sporting goods dealers. The calls also were carried in many major publications such as Stoeger's. The photos show some Lohman calls in boxes and some without. If the calls themselves are not marked, usually the reed holder inserts were marked. See the two crow calls for two different examples showing two different dates, with the Kansas City 27 being the earlier of the two.

The *Shooter's Bible* by Stoeger Arms Corporation for 1966 shows the following Lohman calls available:

Lohman Duck Call No. 103
Lohman Crow Call No. 104
Lohman Squirrel Call No. 109
Lohman Chukar Call No. 117
Lohman Turkey Call No. 110
Lohman Predator Call No. 111
Lohman Goose Call No. 112
Lohman Deluxe Crow Call No. 106
Lohman Quail Call No. 115
Lohman Duck Call No. 200
Lohman Goose Call No. 201
Lohman Coon Talker No. 118

The 103, 104, 112, 106, 200, and 201 are not marked on the barrels. All of the other calls are clearly marked on the barrels. The Chukar and Squirrel are nearly identical and if anything like Olt's. Both likely sound a lot like squirrel chatter when one pushes the rubber air bellows on the end of the call. The difference between the two crow calls is the quality of the wood, with the 106 being hardwood. The lower crow call in the photo has nicer wood. In 1966, all of these were plastic reed calls but they work very well and adjust easily. These calls are found often, with the chukar, quail and turkey being hardest to find.

Point Sporting Goods Company, a major wholesaler from Stevens Point, Wis., in its 1981 catalog, still carried the Lohman Crow Call, but claimed the No. 104 was now black walnut with a cherry insert, which would indicate the No. 106 had become the No. 104. The wholesale cost was $4.90 in 1981. Other Lohman Calls carried by Point in 1981 included: No. 103 Duck Call at $4.90; a cherrywood No. 420 Lohman-Bill Harper Deluxe Duck Call with double reeds at $11.60 wholesale; No. 430 Lohman-Bill Harper Marsh Call in walnut/cherrywood at $11.60; No. 440 Lohman-Bill Harper

Wood Duck Call in walnut/cherrywood at $4.90; No. 109 Squirrel Call at $4.90; No. 112 Goose Call at $4.90; advertised as new, a No. 31 Deer Call at $4.90; advertised as new, two new turkey calls, Diaphragm type No. 802 at $3.35 and a box call with hinged lid, No. 870 at $13.40. Point also stocked two Lohman call cassettes, No. 51 Duck Calling and No. 50 Goose Calling for $6.75 and $7.15, respectively.

An examination of the catalog shows a number of calls no longer offered and a number of new ones beginning in the early '80s. Thus, without packaging, it is difficult to precisely date the calls. But this at least gives a range of availability from 1966 until 1981. Lohman Calls predate 1966 by a long time.

Values on Lohman Calls would depend on rarity and condition, boxed or loose. I would rate the boxed calls at $25 minimum, up to $100 for some of the rarer calls in boxes. The loose calls would bring about 50 percent of that value for the most part.

A Lohman Model 103 Duck Call includes the box and pocket catalog. The box is pre-Zip Code.
$50+
Lewis Collection

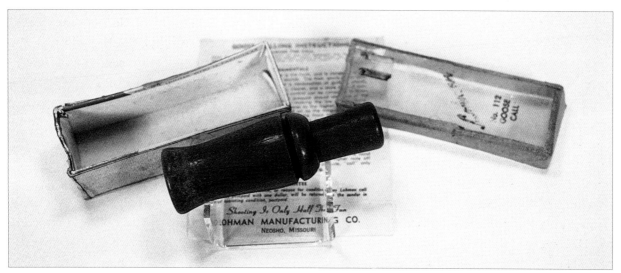

A Lohman Model 112 Goose Call from Neosho, Mo., includes the call, box and instructions.
$35 due to rough shape of call
Lewis Collection

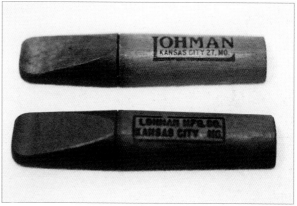

Shown are two Lohman Crow Calls and a Lohman Duck Call, with the oldest Crow Call on top. There are also markings on stem inserts.
$25-$40 each
Lewis Collection

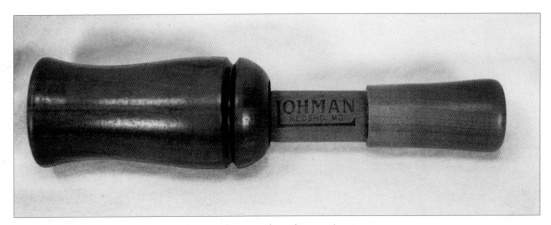

A Lohman Duck Call from Neosho, Mo., has a mark on the stem insert.

$40

Lewis Collection

A Lohman Duck Call (large) and Goose Call are shown together.

A Lohman Calls brochure marked 1957 shows the full range of Lohman's bird and game calls.

Mallardtone Game Calls

Mallardtone Game Calls are some of the most recent calls in this section, officially beginning in 1957. Most of them appear to date from the 1960s or even '70s. I did not start finding advertising for the calls in wholesale catalogs until that time period. One magazine advertisement from 1962 indicates that the company won the National Crow Calling Contest in 1962, both first and second places. One can infer the company had been around a few years as it indicates winning "…numerous other championships with duck and goose calls." The address given in 1962 was 2100 Stadium Drive,

Dept. 962, Rock Island, Ill. The calls were also distributed in Canada by Canadian Sauer Ltd., 103 Church St., Toronto, Canada.

In 1962, the company offered: Crow calls, Predator calls, Squirrel calls, Duck calls, Goose calls, Deer calls and Pheasant calls. In addition, Deluxe model duck and goose calls were available for $10. The other calls were all $2.95 each. An instruction record was also available for $2. All calls came with an unconditional guarantee.

However, like other modern calls, one does not often find these calls in pristine condition in their packages. I have most of the Mallardtone calls and do not have a package. They were marketed in bulk through wholesalers in addition to being individually packaged. I know this was the case with some of our less expensive fishing lure lines.

I like the calls and find them well made with excellent finishes. Also, the engraving gives them a nice distinction from other mass marketed calls. The advertising for them in Buckeye Sports Supply said: "Made of finest materials available. The barrel (or body) of each call is American Black Walnut, assuring beauty and lasting durability. All calls are hand tested by an expert." The wholesaler offered the following calls in 1982:

1. Mallardtone M-5 DC Duck Call
2. Mallardtone M-296 DCJ Duck Call
3. Mallardtone M-5 GC Goose Call
4. Mallardtone M-295 CC Goose Call
5. Mallardtone Close Range Predator Call M-295 CRPC

6. Mallardtone Predator Call M-295 PC
7. Mallardtone Squirrel Call M-295 SC (wood/bellows)
8. Mallardtone Turkey Call M-395 TC (box type)
9. Mallardtone Hawk Call M-295 HC
10. Mallardtone Deer Call M-295 DrC
11. Mallardtone Pheasant Call M-295 PhC
12. Mallardtone Coon Call M-350 CoC

The squirrel call was wood with rubber bellows on the end. The following calls did not have stems: predator calls (either type), deer, and pheasant. A deer call is shown for example. Again, these calls are well made and attractive due to the engraving on them. Each call is clearly marked as to type of call and many have engravings of the animal being pursued, e.g. a duck, a coon, a fox or a squirrel. Collectors must make their own collecting decisions, but for my money I like these calls a lot. Apparently so do other collectors as they have a fairly high value for being so new.

Here is a mint Mallardtone Deer Call.
$50
Lewis Collection

Mallardtone Duck, Goose and Fox calls are shown, along with a Wisconsin miniature Mallard pair.
$50 each call, ducks: $300
Lewis Collection

Ken Martin Calls

Although not as prodigious as some of the larger companies, Ken Martin marketed beautiful duck and goose calls through a number of outlets. The 1970 Cabela's catalog offered his Model KMG (Ken Martin Goose) Call for $10 and his Model KMD (Ken Martin Duck) Call for $5. Both of these calls were clearly marked on the barrel so the collector will have no trouble identifying them. This would be an example of a vintage call maker responding to mass-marketing pressures to sell his calls. The Martin calls are very collectible and would command at least $100 each, likely more. Martin is deceased and his calls will continue to appreciate in value. The unique Droege carved Martin call shown would command at least double the average price due to its uniqueness.

Shown is a Ken Martin Goose Call from my collection and a shot showing three Ken Martin Duck Calls and one Goose Call. The Ken Martin call in the multi-call shot with a carved duck is unique. Gerald Droege from Anna, Ill., carved the duck for Ken. Droege is not a call maker but a collector of calls and is very knowledgeable about calls and their history.

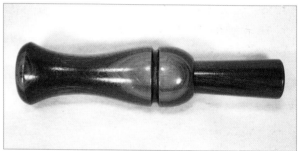

Here is a Ken Martin Goose Call. Note the beautiful burl on the one side of the call. Also shown are the four Martin calls in the Jaroski collection.

$200

Lewis Collection

Natural Duck Call Manufacturing Company

A unique and desirable call from the 1930s was manufactured in St. Paul, Minn. The call has a nice sound and details are shown, with the call in the closed and open bill positions. The call was patented in 1932 by Francis J. Muchlistein. There are early calls that are simply marked "Patent Applied," so be aware of this variation.

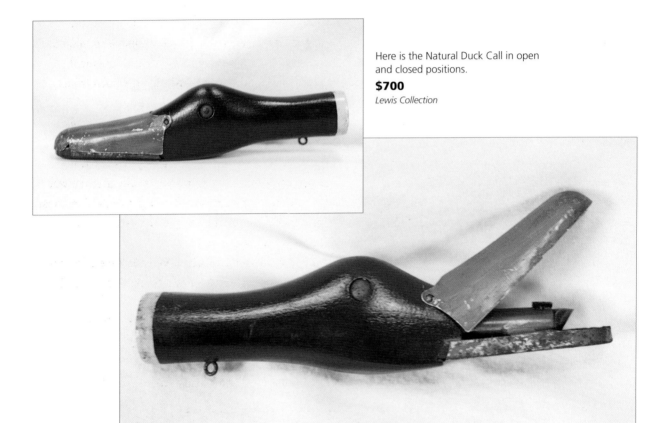

Here is the Natural Duck Call in open and closed positions.
$700
Lewis Collection

Perfectone Calls

Charlie Bishop lived from 1912-2001. He made calls during many of his 89 years, and produced a highly collectible call of fine quality. Some of his calls are shown under the Joe Jaroski Jr. call section. Included is a unique store advertising piece, a large Perfectone call to hang in the sporting goods store as an advertising gimmick. These large calls were often carved by call makers who marketed their wares locally or regionally. I have also shown a rare Perfectone Duck Call six pack in the Jaroski call section. These would sell for $50 each new in the packages due to pristine condition. The six pack would bring a premium over this amount due to rarity.

P.S. Olt

Like Herter's, Inc., P. S. Olt was also mentioned in the section on Vintage Calls. That shows the age of the company located in Pekin, Ill., which recently closed. The biggest challenge to an Olt collector is dating with accuracy any of the hard rubber calls. There are some clues in addresses, model numbers on calls, logos on calls, shape of stoppers, etc. However, even many fairly recent Olt calls command more than $50 if still found in the original packaging. An individual could, and many do, concentrate on just Olt calls and never get bored looking for a new one.

Olt, like Herter's, made every conceivable call. Some of the calls are harder to find than others. They also made "Junior Models," not for kids, just smaller sized calls that are more difficult to find. The Olt calls were plentiful because they were excellent calls and still are. In addition to hunting ducks, I have been an avid squirrel hunter from when my now departed dog Bandit treed his first squirrel in 1983 until his death in 1996. Bandit "loved to hate" those pesky little devils that used to bug him in our back yard. One day, I discovered the Olt Perfect Squirrel Call shown in both black and brown. I picked up the

black one at a farm auction for a song but it turned out to be quite an old model sold from a now defunct Detroit sporting goods store. I used the black one for nearly 20 years with success each time I went to the woods. The calls are shown with the stopper purposely stuck in on the black one to show the operation of the automatic caller. Just push in on the one end and the call sound is made automatically. It provides a little chatter that nosey squirrels just cannot resist due to their territoriality.

According to Stoeger Arms Corporation's *The Shooter's Bible* for 1947, Olt had been making the famous D-2 Duck Call for 40 years (1907). Businesses were just gearing up again after the war years and the offerings were meager in 1947 by most companies. Olt offered only seven calls available through Stoeger Arms:

1. Model D-2 Duck Call, wholesale price of $1.50

2. Model E-1 Crow Call, wholesale price of $1.50

3. Model A-5 Goose Call at $3.50

4. Model B-4 Adjustable Bird Call at $2.75

5. Model C-3 Mallard Call at $2.50

6. Model G-7 Hawk Call at $1.50

7. Model F-6 Turkey cedar box call at $1.50

An ad for Philip S. Olt in the Sporting Goods Dealer catalog announced "Nine great calls for 1950" including another "black hard rubber" call.

The Shooter's Bible for 1966 listed the following Olt Calls:
1. Model E-1 Crow
2. Model M-9 Crow
3. Model B-10 Squirrel
4. Model S-8 Perfect Squirrel
5. Model W-12 Pintail/Widgeon
6. Model D-2 Duck
7. Model G-7 Hawk
8. Model L-22 Goose
9. Model A-5 Perfect Goose
10. Model A-50 Canada Honker
11. Model R-25 Perfect Deer
12. Model T-20 Fox/Coyote
13. Model N-27 Perfect Coon
14. Model F-6 Turkey box call
15. Model Q-30 Quail
16. Model 500 Chukar
17. Model O-32 Pheasant

The 1970 Cabela's catalog offered the following:
1. Mark V wooden Duck Call
2. Model 33 wooden Predator Call
3. Model A-50 Honker Call
4. Model Q-30 Quail Call
5. Model EL-45 Elk Call
6. Model S-8 Perfect Squirrel
7. Model N-27 Coon Call
8. Model R-25 Deer Call
9. Model CP-21 Close Range Predator
10. Model F-6 Two Tone Turkey Call

The 1981 Point wholesale catalog had the following available:
1. Model E-1 Crow Call
2. Model 400 Wood Crow Call
3. Model 32 Pheasant Call
4. Model D-2 Duck Call
5. Model 66 Wooden Duck Call
6. Model 200 Wooden Duck Call
7. Model B-10 Squirrel Call
8. Model S-8 Perfect Squirrel Call
9. Model 300 Wood Goose Call

10. Model A-5 Goose Call
11. Model A-50 Canadian Honker
12. Model 77 Wood Goose Call
13. Model T-20 Fox/Coyote Call
14. Model R-25 Perfect Deer Call
15. #90 Game Call Holder
16. D100 Mallard Records
17. G101 Goose Records

The 1982 Buckeye Sports Supply wholesale catalog listed the following Olt Calls for sale:
1. Model D-2 Duck
2. Model E-1 Crow
3. Model T-20 Predator
4. Model B-10 Squirrel
5. Model L-22 Goose
6. Model 44 Crow (wood)
7. Model 33 Predator (wood)
8. Model 99M Duck (wood/metal reed)
9. Model Mark V Duck (wood)
10. Model DR-115 Duck (wood)
11. Model F-6 Turkey (box type)
12. Model GB-110 Turkey (box/lid)
13. Model N-27 Coon
14. Model EL-45 Elk
15. Model 600 Deer (wood)
16. Model 800 Goose (wood)
17. Also three lanyard types

By 1970, Olt had begun to distribute more and more wooden calls to capitalize on the revived interest in American game calls produced in natural wood. The 1970 Cabela's catalog offered only 10 Olt calls, but three of them were in wood: The Mark V Duck Call, the Model 33 Predator Call and the Two Tone Turkey Call. An examination of the Parker Distributors Catalog from 1970 shows a complete line of 27 Olt calls, and even more wooden duck and goose calls are available. These, along with other wooden Olt calls such as the Model 66 and Model 77, are already quite collectible. A comparison of just these catalog years shows the extensive possibilities of putting together a nice P.S. Olt collection. Even the differences between 1981 and 1982 are immense with many new wooden calls being available in 1982. Most Olt calls are affordable but there are some rarer ones out there commanding more than $100. However, most of the calls will bring between $25-$75 loose, maybe double that with clean, crisp boxes and any inserts that came with the call.

The values given are obviously a general "range." One must remember there are some short production run calls that will command premium prices. There are also color variations, logo variations, presence of lanyard ring variations and many other items to learn about with Olt calls, all of which affect valuation. I am certain that there are some Olt calls that will start commanding some premium prices once we have documented their rarity and once the demand increases even more with additional collectors entering the hobby. A person could concentrate on just Olt calls and keep very busy indeed building an exemplary collection from early call-making through the modern era.

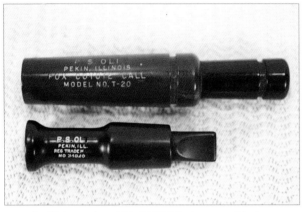

An Olt brown barrel Model T-20 fox/coyote call is shown with a difficult-to-find Junior Duck Call by Olt.
T-20, $40; Junior, $100+
Lewis Collection

This is an Olt Model Perfect No. A-5 Goose Call.
$50-$75
Lewis Collection

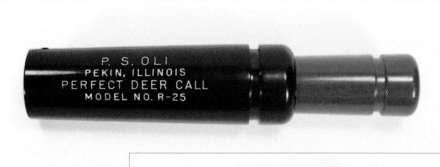

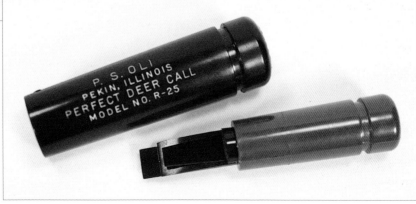

This is an Olt Perfect Deer Call, Model No. R-25, and details of the reed.
$50
Lewis Collection

The Olt M-9 Crow Call is new in package. This packaging was being advertised as early as 1970. Shown are the front and back of the package.

$50 in package

Lewis Collection

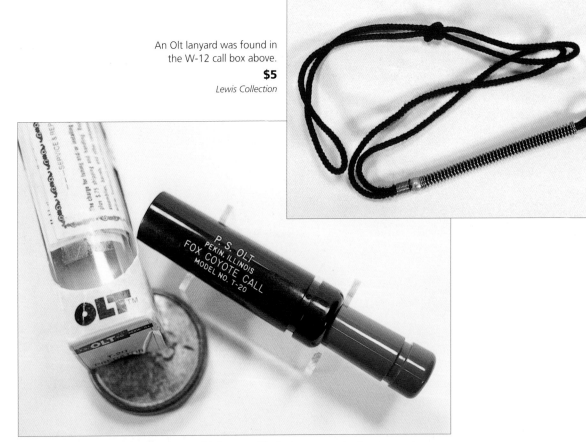

An Olt lanyard was found in the W-12 call box above.

$5

Lewis Collection

An Olt T-20 black barrel Predator Call is in a post-Zip Code green and yellow box with a cellophane insert common in 1960s and early 1970s. This is the box that was just before the yellow hang box shown with the M-9 crow call.

$60+

Lewis Collection

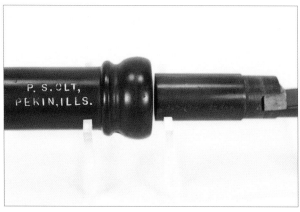

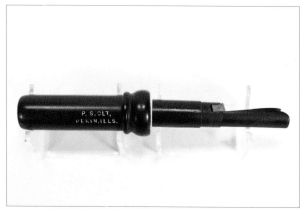

An Olt D-2 Duck Call, keyhole stopper variety, shows the reed construction in several views. This is an earlier call.

Most D-2s, $40-$60; keyhole models are more

Lewis Collection

An Olt Perfect Squirrel Call has a brown barrel.

$100

Lewis Collection

An Olt Perfect Squirrel Call has a black barrel with an early sports shop label. This is the author's personal call.

$125

Lewis Collection

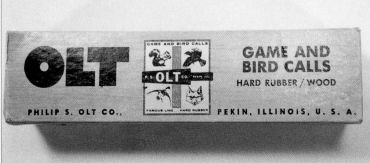

An Olt W-12 Pintail Whistle/Call is in a cardboard box with plastic top, pre-Zip Code. Details of box graphics are shown along with internal parts of call.

$75+ boxed

Lewis Collection

An Olt Chukar Call of wood/rubber has worn lettering.

$40

Lewis Collection

An Olt Model D-2 Duck Call was made in Pekin, Ill.

$40-$60

Lewis Collection

This is a second Olt Model D-2 Duck Call.
$40-$60
Lewis Collection

Here are Olt Model 26 and Model 13 calls.
$75-$100 each
Lewis Collection

A desirable Olt Model D-2 Duck Call has the "world logo," Pekin, Ill. There is also a close-up of the logo.
$75-$100
Lewis Collection

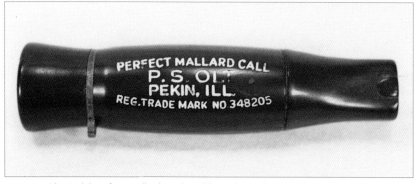

An Olt Model Perfect Mallard Duck Call has a lanyard ring and end shot to show keyhole pattern.
$125+
Lewis Collection

An Olt Model J-15 is a Junior Duck Call.
$125
Lewis Collection

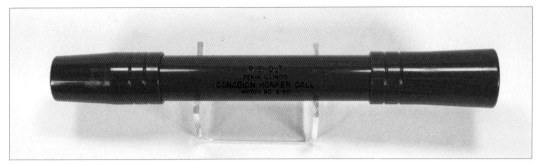

An Olt Canada Honker Call, Tri-County special issue is numbered 142.

$75

Lewis Collection

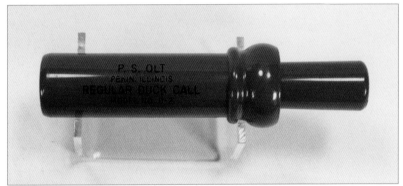

An Olt D-2 Duck Call, Tri-County special issue is numbered 142 to match the goose call.

$75

Lewis Collection

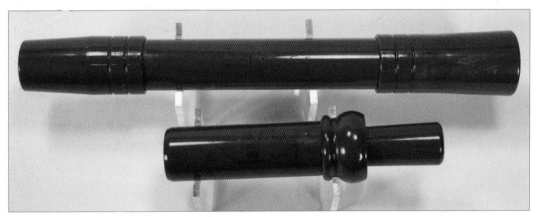

A map diagram is shown on the 1995 special issue calls by Olt.

Scotch Game Calls

These are a neat invention for those of us not wanting to learn to call with our own wind. They are calls constructed in the fashion of a regular wooden call, shaped similar to many Lohman calls, with a rubber bellows then placed over the mouth piece of the call for air inlet. When the bellows move and emit air, the call sound is produced. Yes, they really do work. One issue is that they call anytime one moves

the bellows, including while walking or moving around if not careful. This could be an unwanted noise emitted at just the wrong time in the blind.

However, it is a neat idea that was apparently new in commercial production about 1955. An advertisement for the duck call (Patent Pending) appeared in the October 1955 *Outdoor Life*. The call was available for $7.50 and only duck, goose, and

Here are Scotch duck and goose calls and some details of them. These are both marked Oakfield, N.Y. The goose call is No. 1605 and the Duck is No. 1401. Shown as well is a papier-mâché goose next to the goose call for scale and a close-up of the wooden calls and their inserts.

$40 each

Lewis Collection

crow calls were available at the time. The Detroit address was 173 Victor Avenue, Dept. L10, Detroit 3, Mich. The L10 likely stood for the advertising source (e.g. *Outdoor Life*, October with the code L for *Outdoor Life* and 10 for October) to track sales similar to how Pratt Decoys used different names in advertising.

I have shown a Scotch Predator Call No. 1503 new in its box, a Duck Call No. 1401, and Goose Call No. 1605. It also made a Crow Call No. 1707 and

a Squirrel Call No. 1911. A wholesale catalog also listed a Deer Call No. 1809 advertised in 1968 that must have been short lived indeed. The interesting thing that I noted on the Predator call shown is that the call itself is imprinted with a Detroit address and so was the box originally. However, on the box, Detroit was lined through and the New York address added without a Zip Code. The booklet inside the box had the New York address with the Zip Code. The duck and goose calls shown have the New York imprint on them. The calls were invented in Detroit and produced there briefly. Thus, the Detroit calls are harder ones to find. I have owned all but the Squirrel Call and do not see it listed in as many wholesale catalogs.

If one removes the bellows, the calls function just fine if one knows how to blow them. I have shown the reed construction in the photos. The value on these is between $25 and $60, depending on age, box type, and condition. The 1970 Cabela's catalog offered all five models at $4.75 each. The 1982 Buckeye Sports Supply wholesale catalog still offered the duck, goose, predator and crow calls for $7.55 to $8.95 each wholesale. They also offered a double or single Scotch Lanyard at that time. Retail on these calls was an average of about $12.50 in 1982, so expect to pay double for even one of the early 1980s models. As noted already, the Squirrel Call did not appear in the 1982 wholesale catalog so it is likely more difficult to find.

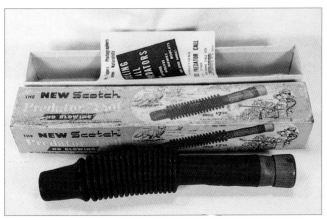
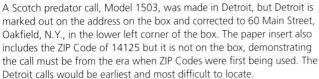

A Scotch predator call, Model 1503, was made in Detroit, but Detroit is marked out on the address on the box and corrected to 60 Main Street, Oakfield, N.Y., in the lower left corner of the box. The paper insert also includes the ZIP Code of 14125 but it is not on the box, demonstrating the call must be from the era when ZIP Codes were first being used. The Detroit calls would be earliest and most difficult to locate.

$50+

Lewis Collection

Thompson Calls

Like Ken Martin, Tom Thompson made vintage calls and then marketed his calls nationally at a later time. He made calls using both wood and plastics, and his plastic goose call is excellent. Most of his earlier calls from Illinois bring from $50-$150 at this time. He was first located in Illinois and later moved to the high country of Idaho.

A Thompson T-550 Goose Call from Boise, Idaho, has a green plastic reed.

$50

Lewis Collection

Trutone Calls ———————————————

Some of the most beautiful modern calls were made by this Oak Park, Ill., call-making company headed by call maker L. G. Larson (1888-1947). Many of these beautiful calls were made with curly maple, special burl walnut, or a combination as shown. The calls were normally marked on the top of the sound barrel in lettering in an arc stating on the top line: "TRUTONE" with "Oak Park, Ill." underneath it.

A beautiful TruTone Call is circa 1930s.
$700
Lewis Collection

Unknown Calls and Newer Calls ——————

I am unsure about a few calls shown. They are all without markings and/or I could not verify them in advertising literature or other texts.

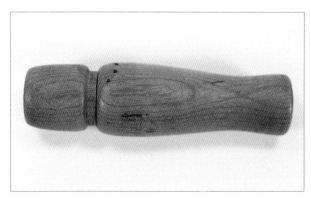

A Predator call with plastic disk insert with four holes works well.

New Ron Benson Game Calls include a deer bleater, Muskegon, Mich., circa 1998, a gift from a good friend.

This wooden goose call with plastic end is similar to many modern calls.

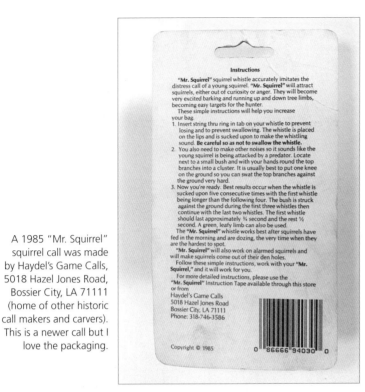

A 1985 "Mr. Squirrel" squirrel call was made by Haydel's Game Calls, 5018 Hazel Jones Road, Bossier City, LA 71111 (home of other historic call makers and carvers). This is a newer call but I love the packaging.

A nice sounding Mallard duck call in camouflage is from Primos Wild Game Calls, Inc. Primos is still available in Cabela's.

The Enticer Doe Bleat call was made by Outdoor Trader.

An unknown duck call is newer but still "take-apart."

This is a modern Ducks Unlimited duck call.
$25
Lewis Collection

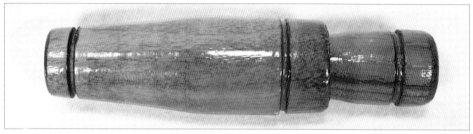

This large plastic reed, very long stem wooden goose call has three grooves in the barrel. It could be an Olt.
$75
Lewis Collection

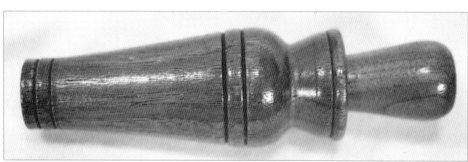

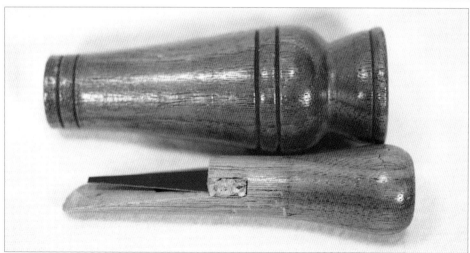

A wooden duck call has five grooves in barrel, a cork holding red plastic reed, and rounded Louisiana/Arkansas stem style. It could be a Faulk's.
$75
Lewis Collection

Weems Wild Call

The Weems All-Call Lot 100 shown is a neat little package from the Weems Wild Call company of P.O. Box 7261, Fort Worth, Texas. This is a pre-Zip two-piece cardboard box and is likely from the mid to early 1950s. It is also a Pat. Pending box, making it more valuable. I have shown the neat details on the little call inserts in the photos. This was basically four calls in one with a squeaker that could be used for squirrel or chukar, a coon call insert, a cottontail insert and a jack rabbit insert. A person could predator-hunt a variety of animals with the squeaker as well. The unusual thing about this call is that it is complete and virtually new in the box. I am sure most of these found in the field are missing most of the inserts.

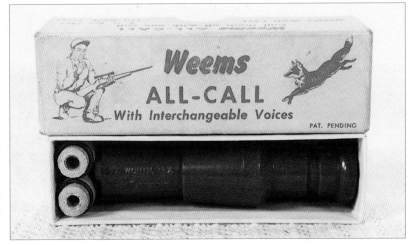

A Weems All-Call Lot 100 is new in box. Details are shown.
$125
Lewis Collection

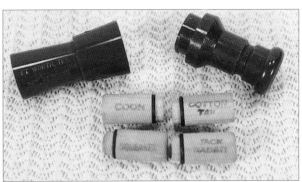

Chapter Seven:

Hunting Collectibles

We have covered classic duck decoys and other traditional decoys, vintage factory decoys, modern factory decoys, vintage and modern game calls, and some miscellaneous decoys. In addition, the decoy collector has many related or ancillary fields of collecting available. It is important to give the beginning-to-intermediate collector a taste of items that eventually will adorn his/her walls and shelves if decoy collecting takes its normal path.

Most of the items being collected today are from distinctly different time periods, with the big break being prior to 1940 and post-1940. This break in history is important due to the many technological changes brought about after World

War II in the manufacturing of decoys and related items. There is also the legal break of an antique being considered 100 years old or more. Thus some concentrate only on items from the 1800s or very early 1900s. Of course, a natural break also occurs in decoy collecting based upon the end of market gunning in 1918 and the related demise of most factory decoy companies.

The year 1940 was definitely the end of the golden age of hunting in America for vintage decoys, vintage guns, vintage boats, vintage shot shell boxes, and the list goes on and on.

Not that interesting things were not made after 1940, but that date signifies the gearing up for war for most factories in the country. They were not really able to get back into full production of items for consumer consumption until 1947. Many, if not most, sporting goods companies did not even produce catalogs from 1941-1946. Then, at the end of the war, we had new synthetic materials developed for gun stocks, Tenite 1 and Tenite 2, many other types of Nylon, Durlon, Styrofoam, use of pulp by-products (papier-mâché), etc., that were being used for the production of decoys and other items.

Items were now cheaper to produce, more small companies had a hand at it for a while, and many familiar items took on new forms. However, the period of 1947-1960 also gave us some collectible items that were produced in mass quantities but used, rather than collected, at the time. This makes the items somewhat scarce today. You may be a purist collecting only "vintage" items from pre-WWII. Or you may be a baby boomer content to find items with which you are familiar from your youth dating from the 1950s. Either way, I am certain there are many items in this chapter to pique your curiosity.

Shot Shell Boxes

The shot shell box is likely the most common hunting collectible related to duck decoys, after the duck call. Shot shell boxes make great collectibles. They are relatively affordable, plentiful for the common models, take up relatively little space to display (they stack on themselves), and are as colorful as one's imagination. They are also clearly an item that was needed in the hunting of ducks and other waterfowl. All duck hunters used shells.

The shot shell box itself has an evolutionary history usually broken in time by the earlier two-piece box and the later one-piece box. The two-piece box had a bottom, over which was placed a top that contained the graphics and the shot particulars. These boxes are more desirable by most collectors, but are getting fairly hard to find. They mainly pre-date 1940, or earlier (most were not in production after 1932). Some of the two-piece boxes are also some of the finest examples of graphic design showing dogs in action, ducks in flight, etc. However, many of the one-piece boxes are equally pleasing on the eyes. They also are getting harder and harder to find. The Hi Power duck boxes are about as beautiful as they come, with their turquoise color schemes and the beautiful flying Mallard on each size of the shot boxes.

Some collectors insist on having shells in the box and some prefer the boxes empty. To preserve the boxes, I recommend removing the shells or gravity will eventually win out and place small tears in the cardboard from pressure exerted on the box sides by the shells. Some collectors cut a piece of Styrofoam to place inside the box to preserve the shape. Others also cover the box with clear plastic wrap to protect the cardboard from dust and elements. Personally, I do not like to cover my display pieces, but it would indeed protect them from deterioration.

In addition to shell boxes, the shells themselves make interesting displays and would add a nice bit of color secured in a shadow box. According to the Remington Arms/UMC Web site, modern shotgun shells have a shelf life of 10 years to use. So, once your collectible shells are found, most of them should not be used for hunting anyway. There are many individuals who spend great amounts of time and money attempting to collect just examples of the end stamping found on the shells.

Most boxes are affordable. The two-piece boxes usually begin at more than $50. Many bring hundreds of dollars. But many of the more common one-piece boxes from the 1950s can be purchased for as little as $5 if empty. However, many of the finer examples of one-piece boxes will garner upwards of $50 if full or if they have nice graphics of flying ducks or rare photo images. Most of the shell boxes I have sold recently bring between $15 and $25 for empty early one-piece boxes by either Remington or Winchester-Western. The more expensive boxes tend to be unusual or rare gauges such as 10 gauge or 28 gauge boxes. The boxes in this price range are without special graphics, just standard earlier one-piece boxes. The addition of a dog/duck/goose would at least double this range for even the more recent boxes.

One more word needs to be said about shot shell box collecting. Be very careful if you become involved in shipping any boxes with shells, even with just primers, as it is likely a violation of federal law. It is perfectly legal to ship empty boxes through the mail but not full ones. UPS will ship boxes but only under special provisions. Most online auctions no longer allow the sale of boxes with shot shells.

Here is a grouping of collectible Federal Hi-Power and Monark boxes.
$35-$60 each

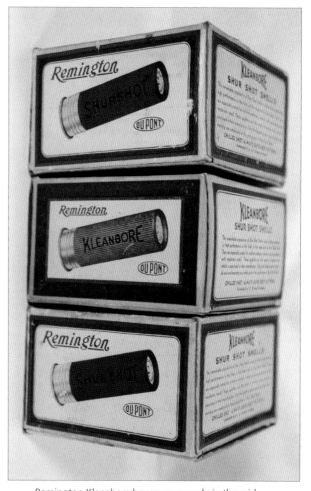

Remington Kleanbore boxes were made in the mid-1930s. One is green shell without red trim, the other two are red shell with red/green/cream boxes.
$25 each empty

A Hunters Red Dog 12 gauge box was made in Colgate, Wis.
$50
Lewis Collection

A Western Super X 12 gauge, #5 shot, is pre-warning label.
$10-$15

A Hoppe's Dealer display includes a Federal .410 box and Monark 20 gauge Mallard box.
$25-$50 each

Value of a Peters High Velocity Mallard drake box, is $50-$100 depending on condition and if full or empty, more for odd gauges.
$10-$15

This is a Winchester Ranger Super Trap Load, pre-warning label, full, 12 gauge, 2 3/4" shells.
$50-plus (paid $20 in 1995)

A Mallard scene decorates this Peters Power Piston plastic shell box, full, with post-warning label.
$50 full
Lewis Collection

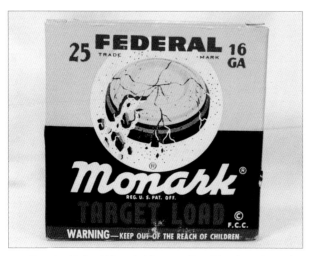

Here is a Federal Monark 16 gauge Target Load, post-warning, and shell details to show a colorful post-warning 1960s box.
$25
Lewis Collection

The Peters High Velocity 16 gauge, drake Mallard box, full, is a very highly desirable box, especially gauges other than 12s.
$100
Lewis Collection

Full boxes of Nitro Express 2 3/4" shells and Shur Shot 2 5/8" shells are shown. Note the color difference on "Wetproof" indicating shell colors.
$100 each full
Lewis Collection

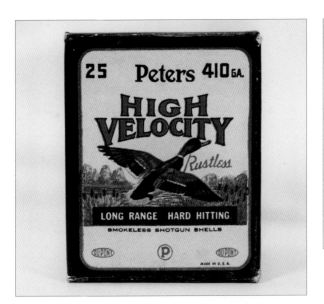

A very rare Peters High Velocity .410 drake Mallard box is full.
$150
Lewis Collection

Four very collectible boxes.
$50 to $200 full
Lewis Collection

Western Xpert and Peters Victor 12 gauge boxes are shown with my favorite miniatures. Both boxes are full and have 2 5/8" shells. The Victor box is harder to find.
$50-$100 each

Western Xpert and Remington Shur Shot 16 gauge boxes are grouped with my favorite Mallards again. Both of these early boxes are for 2 9/16″ shells.

$40-$60 each

A newer Western Auto 16 gauge box and Winchester 12 gauge box show recent "animal" boxes and children's warnings. Even these inexpensive additions add color to a decoy collection.

$10 each

Lewis Collection

Magazines, Catalogs, Etc.

To me this is the most exciting area of collecting. It provides knowledge for collecting. But the paper items are collectible themselves. An original Mason Decoy Factory catalog from 1920 is a wonderful item and has the added bonus of providing information on Mason decoys. The same is true of many early hunting magazines. Artwork by individuals such as Lynn Bogue Hunt adorns the cover of many magazines. And the graphics inside of most magazines from the 1930s and 1940s are worth the purchase price alone. The advertisements inside the magazines are the invaluable sources of information on dating companies, introductions of new items, and new techniques of manufacturing items, addresses of companies no longer in business, reviews of new items, and popularity of certain items. I would suggest that the uninitiated spend a good deal of time reading sporting magazines from 1930 through about 1955. This will give one a sense of the historical changes that took place in sporting goods manufacturing in American society during that time period of changing from vintage to classic.

The wholesale catalog is a commonly overlooked source of information on decoys and related items. These catalogs were produced by wholesale houses and jobbers throughout the country and made certain items of major companies available at reduced prices to retail outlets. For instance, many post-1940 decoys were offered in limited models and colors only, or primarily, through these outlets. Gateway, Belmont Hardware, Point Sporting Goods and others put out catalogs that are veritable histories of sporting goods available at certain periods. The really nice aspect is that these wholesale catalogs are usually only a few dollars each compared with a catalog from a company.

Obviously, we would all like a catalog from Mason Duck Decoys, Herter's from the '30s, '40s, or '50s, an old Pratt and Stevens, a Dodge or two, an Evans brochure, and more. However, many of these are not available at any price and, if available, are the cost of a good duck or two. So, look at wholesale catalogs as an option, study magazines, buy a catalog if you can find one, and use reproductions when available. This is an area where one cannot go wrong because the knowledge alone is usually worth the investment. Also, most paper investments have traditionally gone up in value consistently due to the fact that the supply is very limited and very fragile.

Forest & Stream, September 1929. Shorebird decoys are placed for the hunt.

Hunting & Fishing, September 1930. Green-wing Teal come in to a spread.

Outdoor Life, October 1930. Wings are set and flaring for a decoy spread.

National Sportsman, December 1936. This is every "boy's" Christmas wish list.

Field & Stream, November 1937. Birds land in the spread.

Outdoor Life, February 1938. A goose family is featured.

Field & Stream, October 1951. Mallards come into the spread.

Hunting & Fishing, December 1953. Success!

A nice advertising envelope for L. C. Smith Guns is valued at **$75.**

The cover of a J.C. Higgins gun booklet features two ducks. **$5-$10**

Shot Shell Crates

In addition to shot shell boxes, the wooden crates that shot shell boxes were shipped in up until the last 40 years have become very collectible in their own right. These are collectibles desired by three different groups: the household decorator, the sporting collectibles groups and the gun collector. A group of crates averaged about $25 each at a recent outdoor farm auction. Some of the more unusual Remington and Winchester crates likely have a retail value of $50-$75 each with some nice early Nitro cases and unusual sizes included. The crates make nice decorator items.

Reloading Equipment and Practice Equipment

This is an area with many colorful and unusual additions to a collection of decoys. Many hunters reloaded their own shot shells due to the costs involved in buying factory- produced loads. This reloading effort resulted in a whole industry dedicated to the re-loader. Many tools are available that have beautiful wooden handles, many special shot shell boxes are available for the sale of wads and primers only, and many tools such as primer ejectors are available for collecting. This could itself be a full collection. But just a few nice reloading tools complement any decoy collection nicely.

Also related to this area is the practice shooting equipment available for collecting. One easy item to acquire is the hand trap thrower made by any number of major gun companies and some ammunition companies. Of course, there are also shot shell boxes marked "Trap" and "Skeet" that were meant for practice in duck hunting.

One of the most colorful items related to practice shooting is the "practice ball," or glass target ball, the predecessor of the clay pigeon. These are getting rare and difficult to find but are beautiful examples of hand blown and molded balls meant for a short life until shot. Many antique dealers do not know what they are and thus cannot price them accordingly. I have a nice array of target balls in amber, blue, cobalt, red, yellow, etc. I picked up all of them for a reasonable price in a shop because the owner did not know what they were. So keep your eyes open for such items.

Duck Stamps, Licenses and Artwork

Books have been written on the subject of Duck Stamps. I cannot do the topic justice here other than to mention the importance of duck and other related stamps to our sport. Federal Duck Stamps are required for all waterfowl hunting regardless of the state, and many states also added their own duck or waterfowl stamp. Iowa and some other states also added pheasant or grouse stamps. These game bird stamps are gorgeous and in some cases quite valuable. Some of the most valuable stamps are the artist proofs that were available only from the artist of the stamp. They were mounted in a limited edition of the original painting or print from which the stamp was initially made. Sad to say, many states such as Michigan have gone to computer issuance of stamps and no longer require the beautiful state stamps (but still charge the fee!) that once adorned our state licenses, in addition to the Federal Migratory stamps. This has likely ended the collecting of licenses per se, as there is little beauty left in a sticky piece of paper spit out by a computer printer that one carries on one's person while hunting or fishing.

As to the collecting of licenses prior to the computer-issued versions, however, there is a vast market and rapidly growing interest. Collectors are especially after the following: the rare buttons issued for limited years (in Michigan in the late 1920s to early 1930s); initial issuance of state duck, waterfowl, grouse, pheasant, trout or other species stamps; the first and last year of issuance of a certain license type; game transfer tags that were often issued along with a license; particularly colorful licenses; early licenses in general; game laws of early years; licenses issued during one's birth year; and, so on. In addition, we have identification tags required by some states for live decoys, Federal tags (leg bands) placed on waterfowl for research purposes, and the list expands.

Again, like many items, prewar and postwar licenses are quite different in many states. The old oilcloth licenses eventually gave way to paper licenses and eventually the back tags gave way to a small pocket version not very collectible.

Artwork related to ducks, waterfowl, hunting, and decoys has filled many texts. One can add much color to a collection with some nice original paintings, limited edition prints, or mass-produced prints of hunting scenes. This area also includes the field of advertising art. Many pieces of advertising art combine shot shell boxes and waterfowl hunting scenes or hunters and waterfowl. These make great additions to any collection and one should always be on the lookout for an addition in this genre.

Oilers, Oil Cans and Cleaning Tools

One cannot duck hunt for long in a wet, nasty environment without running into the need to oil and clean a gun. The oil cans make for great collectibles because of their inherently interesting graphics and use of color. Most of the oil cans are worth from $15-$25, but some of the rare and early ones are worth up to $500, such as the green Winchester. One thing to note is whether the can has a lead screw top cap or a nylon cap. Once the nylon or plastic caps show up (early '50s for the most part), the value of the oiler goes down. Also, the common Hoppe's No. 9 bottle had a cork stopper in the 1930s, going to at least two different types of screw caps into the '50s. All of these little details become important to a collector of oil tins.

In addition to the oil tins, small oilers, wrenches, and cleaning tools add interest to a collection. Some of them are a Marble's Arms cleaning kit and some more common Outer's models. Any of these are nice additions to a decoy collection and are valued from $25 to more than $100 in the case of the Marble's Arms set.

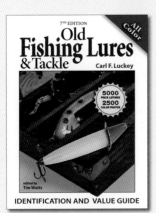

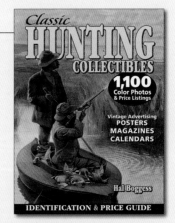

Assess Your Collection
with Up-to-Date Details!

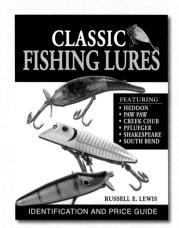

Classic Fishing Lures
Identification and Price Guide
by Russell E. Lewis

Color photos, comprehensive descriptions, and pricing information for 2,000 lures from Heddon, South Bend, Paw Paw, Pflueger, Creek Chub, Shakespeare and more, make this book a must-have!
Softcover • 8-1/4 x 10-7/8 • 368 pages • 2,000 color photos
Item# CFL • $27.99

Collecting Antique Bird Decoys and Duck Calls
An Identification and Price Guide
3rd Edition
by Carl F. Luckey and Russell E. Lewis

Explore the history and discover the worth of the most prominent duck and goose hunting decoys used over the past 100-plus years with this detailed reference.
Softcover • 8-1/2 x 11 • 496 pages
432 b&w photos • 64-page color section
Item# CABD3 • $27.99

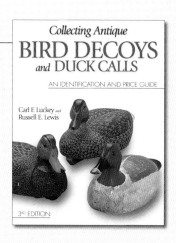

Heddon Catalogs
Over 50 Years of Great Fishing 1902-1953
by Clyde A. Harbin, Sr. "The Bassman" and Russell E. Lewis

This comprehensive volume of the world's most collectible fishing lures covers the famous Heddon catalogs from 1902-1953, with timeless articles on fishing techniques and hundreds of full-color photos.
Softcover • 8-1/4 x 10-7/8 • 256 pages • 150+ color photos
Item# HDLTC • $24.99

Fishing Collectibles
Identification and Price Guide
by Russell E. Lewis

From rods and reels to bait buckets, this must-have reference includes more than 2,000 color photos for easy identification, and descriptions, values, and historic tidbits, to help you be a savvy collector.
Softcover • 8-1/4 x 10-7/8 • 352 pages • 2,000 color photos
Item# FISCL • $29.99

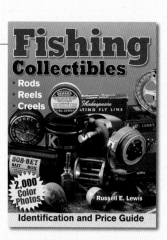

About the Cover

The preening pintail decoy on the cover has set the world record price for wildfowl decoys, selling for $801,500 at a 2003 auction held by Guyette & Schmidt and Christie's. The pintail was carved in 1915 by A. Elmer Crowell of Cape Cod in Massachusetts. The same decoy brought a record price at the time of $319,00 in 1986, purchased by Russ Aitken. The pintail decoy sold in 2003 broke the record price set for another Crowell decoy in 2000 of $684,000.